THE LIBERTY CAP

THE LIBERTY CAP is a venerable symbol of freedom, originally the Phrygian cap worn by freed slaves in ancient times. Before and during the American Revolution it reappeared as an informal badge of patriotism and democracy. Anyone wishing to gather a crowd for an extemporaneous speech could wave the soft cap on a stick or toss it over a lamppost, and passersby would stop to listen. In the French Revolution, the Liberty Cap became the "bonnet rouge", and Liberty herself wears it in Delacroix' stirring painting "Liberty Leading the People." The Liberty Cap in the title of this book symbolizes the revolution in our attitudes towards the characters and capacities of the two sexes — a bloodless revolution, we hope, in which both sexes will be the winners.

THE LIBERTY CAP
A CATALOGUE OF
NON-SEXIST MATERIALS
FOR CHILDREN

ENID DAVIS

 Chicago 1977

Library of Congress Cataloging in Publication Data

Davis, Enid, 1946-
    The liberty cap.

    An updating, revision, and reorganization of the
author's newsletter The Liberty gap which was published
from Nov. 1974 to Dec. 1976.
    Includes indexes.
    1. Children's literature--Bibliography.
2. Children's literature--Book Reviews. 3. Audio-
visual materials--Catalogs. 4. Audio-visual materials--
Reviews. 5. Sexism in literature. I. Title.
Z1035.A1D38   [PN1009.A1]   028.52   77-17208
ISBN 0-915864-15-0

In memory of Violet F. Carty
P.S. 138, Queens
Grades 6-8
(Loved and highly recommended)

LIST OF ABBREVIATIONS USED IN THIS BOOK

ACL   Association of Children's Librarians, California Library Association

BARTOC   Bay Area Radical Teachers Organization

BCCB   *Bulletin* of the Center for Children's Books

CBRS   Children's Book Review Service

CIBC   Council on Interracial Books for Children

ECA   Educational Consortium of America

ERIC/ECE   Educational Resources Information Center/Early Childhood Education

Kirkus   *Kirkus Review Service*

NOW   National Organization for Women

NYT   New York *Times*

SLJ   *School Library Journal*

WAA   Women's Action Alliance

WEAL   Women's Equity Action League

TABLE OF CONTENTS

FURTHER RESOURCES FOR PARENTS
AND PROFESSIONALS

INDEXES

INTRODUCTION

The contents of this book originally appeared in my serial publication, *THE LIBERTY CAP : A Bimonthly Journal of Recently Published Non-Stereotyped Children's Books and Resources.* Many of the reviews and subject bibliographies have been rewritten and updated. The entire contents of the sixteen issues of the newsletter (November, 1974 to November/December, 1976) have been reorganized for this book.

My concern with non-stereotyped literature evolved naturally from my profession and my politics. In 1973, as a children's librarian in a large public library, I began to get more and more requests from parents for non-sexist books. In the same year I became founding president of the Palo Alto Chapter of the National Organization for Women (NOW). I began to study the books in my own library's collection and to give workshops on sexism in children's literature for women's groups, college classes, and library patrons.

In 1974 my second child was born and I resigned from my half-time library position. I cashed in one of Bradley's bonds to subscribe to several professional journals, hoping to keep up with the world of juvenile publishing. By the time my son was four months old, it was clear to me that keeping abreast was not enough for my head. While I was keeping busy, clipping reviews of books that seemed to be about sensitive boys and lively girls (in all colors), the idea grew on me that teachers and parents might be interested in a bibliography highlighting new, non-sexist titles.

The first issue of *The Liberty Cap* came out in November, 1974. This three-page sample newsletter quoted reviews of new children's books from various periodicals, and listed articles, bibliographies, and other resources. The last issue (November/December, 1976) contained sixteen pages of my reviews and comments on more than fifty titles, book and non-book.

The growth of the newsletter in content and circulation took a long time. Because I worked alone, I had to divide my time between clerical and business tasks on the one hand, and reading and writing on the other. My main object was to read as many of the books as I could and to rely on the opinions of others as little as possible. You will note that books published in 1976 are almost all reviewed by the editor.

The people who made it possible for me to read more and more new titles must be acknowledged here. Mary Greeno, employee of the Peninsula Book Shop in Palo Alto, allowed me to borrow all the books I wanted and to return them at my leisure. She made her store into a public library for me and enabled me to examine the books hot off the press. Publishers began to send me review copies soon after the first issues were out. I want to thank the many publishers who supported my efforts by supplying me with their books and other materials. Surely they knew that my circulation could not compare with that of *School Library Journal*! In addition, I want to thank Joanne Leone and Joyce Rubenstein, two librarians who contributed to the newsletter.

In June 1976 the goals which I set myself in publishing *The Liberty Cap* had been met, and I decided to stop publication. I had kept up with the field of children's books and could return to public library service. Editing the newsletter entailed long hours of creative and dull, exciting and lonely, work. I am now an active children's librarian, and I will never be the same again. And neither, I hope, will the world of publishing.

I have seen a substantial improvement in children's literature in the last few years. From a boy's point of view, however, things are changing rather slowly. There are only a handful of books that offer relief from the macho world of comics and television. And there is still not enough good material for Asian and Native American children.

Sexism in children's books is no longer the joke it was in the early 1970's. Rather, concern over sexism has become a threat in some ways. It has caused publishers to take a good look at their own work, and it has influenced the way books are reviewed. But it has begun to alarm people who abhor censorship, whether by liberals, or by the traditional conservative critics. The question of censorship is complex, and alarm is an honest response to the new trend toward attacking "isms" in children's books. It is a question with which I have uncomfortably struggled while writing *The Liberty Cap*.

As a librarian, I oppose political censorship, though I know librarians censor or "select" materials on literary, artistic and other grounds all the time. On the other hand, as a mother and a humanist, I do not like to see books present a narrow range of social and professional options to my children, or to any child. If I did not believe in the power of books to delight, inspire, and excite, and in many cases to prejudice, I would probably try to get a job in my cousin's advertising company.

What I want for children are books of high quality and unlimited horizons. In my reviews and articles I have tried to inform and to question things which need to be questioned. *The Liberty Cap*'s purpose is to educate rather than to dictate choices. It is a selection tool for people who want both literary merit and imaginative humanism reflected in their collections. It is not *the* selection tool for all needs and purposes. No one book can be.

PART ONE

Discussions
and Special Lists

CHAPTER I

MODERN CLASSICS AND OLD FAVORITES

1. Eve Merriam: Brava!

Eve Merriam was born in Philadelphia, Pennsylvania on July 19, 1916 and has been publishing poetry and prose since 1946. She is a prolific author, and I regret that I have been able to read only eleven of her works. (Libraries and bookstores stock only a small selection of them.) Because she is as versatile as she is prolific, my diverse sampling has given me a familiarity with her style, and makes me feel secure in highly recommending her work.

Although over 40% of the U.S. labor force is composed of women, Eve Merriam's *Mommies At Work* (1961) was, until two years or so ago, the only picture book I had seen on the subject of employed mothers. It is still, I might add, the most successful one. In 1972 she published *Boy and Girls, Girls and Boys,* a picture book about friendships between girls and boys of different races, who discuss their plans for varied careers, not dictated by biology.

Besides picture books, Ms. Merriam has written several books about women's history. *After Nora Slammed the Door: American Women In the Sixties, the Unfinished Revolution* is a unique feminist work. Through an interesting mixture of history, personal opinion, satire, and poetry, Eve Merriam constructs her argument against the myths concerning, for example, motherhood, men, and nature, which have stifled and oppressed American women. *Growing Up Female In America* is a collection of the diaries, letters, and journals of ten American women who have led courageous and outstanding lives. Not merely a passive editor, Merriam provides interesting introductions to these women, lively narration between selections, and a final section, "The Attic," a miscellaneous bouquet of essays, speeches, and glimpses into the lives and feelings of our foremothers.

Eve Merriam's great literary love is poetry. She has written both adult and children's poetry and has received various awards. Her adult poetry tends to be more political than her children's work, which is generally about nature or language. *The Nixon Poems* is a collection of poetry concerned with our mass-produced, war oriented, prejudice-ridden society under Richard Nixon. It's terrific! And her brief but powerful, *Inner City Mother Goose* is not to be missed.

Ms. Merriam's poetry for children is concerned with two major themes: the sensuousness of things around us — whether it be an autumn leaf or a new housing project, and the endless possibilities for fun that words and poetic structure have when happily combined. Merriam is clearly a teacher of poetry and language, as well as a poet. Her collections are recommended for children in grades three to eight.

If you look at the copyright dates on Eve Merriam's works, you realize what an early voice of feminist humanism she has been. Her feminism, combined with high quality writing, makes her books an important part of a non-stereotyped collection.

I look forward to future Merriam books on the order of Evaline Ness's *Amelia Mixed the Mustard and Other Poems* (Scribner's, 1975), but in her own wonderful style, of course. I know we are ready for some strong political poetry for all the young Noras still trapped in their Barbie and Ken dollhouses all over America.

Books Referred To In This Article

After Nora Slammed the Door. World, 1958.
Boys and Girls, Girls and Boys. Illustrated by Harriet Sherman. Harcourt Brace, 1972. $4.59.
Growing Up Female In America. Doubleday, 1971. $7.95.
Inner City Mother Goose. Simon & Schuster 1969. $5.95.
It Doesn't Always Have To Rhyme. Atheneum, 1964. $4.25.
Mommies At Work. Illustrated by Beni Montresor. Knopf, 1961. $3.00.
The Nixon Poems. Illustrated by John Gerbino. Atheneum, 1970. $4.95.
Out Loud. Illustrated by Harriet Sherman. Atheneum, 1973. $4.95.
Rainbow Writing. See No. 495.

2. Ionesco: Have You Met Josette?

Many picture books are like the Woody Allen movie I saw last Saturday night: colorful, enjoyable, and forgettable. Not so with the surrealistic fantasies Ionesco weaves around simple domestic tales. Beautifully illustrated to match the startling text, Ionesco's work may confuse or mildly shock the reader, but it will hold the audience — who knows what they'll find on the next page? It is a rare pleasure for a grown-up to turn pages breathlessly, not knowing what to expect, but certain that it will be something delightfully out-of-the-ordinary: chicken heads sprouting from finger tips, airplanes zooming down the hall, and so forth. My daughter especially enjoys the unexpected twists and turns.

Harlan Quist publishes these handsome books on oversize glossy paper, with very large print and generous full page drawings, at $5.95. All this, and non-sexist too. Could you ask for more?

It is interesting to note the rather small role mother plays in these four stories. She is either busy, sleeping, or out of the house, leaving papa to care for and entertain Josette. Although mama complains that papa's stories will drive Josette crazy, this is obviously a close and loving family. It is nice to meet a fictional father who is loving, patient, and full of lunatic imagination.

Story Number 1. Illustrated by Etienne Delessert. 1967. Josette is 33 months old and is told a preposterous tale by her exhausted papa one morning. (Poor father celebrated much too long and late the night before. So did mother; she can't move.) Papa's tale of how Josette meets an entire society of people with the same first name gets her into trouble later at the local market when the story seems to be coming true.

Story Number 2. Illustrated by Etienne Delessert. 1970. Josette's father takes her to his office and teaches Josette "the real meaning of words," e.g. "A chair is a window. A behind is a head." It is not difficult to imagine the heyday a surrealistic artist can have with this plot — and a successful heyday it is. This story led to a terrific discussion of how language can limit our perspective if we let it, and that there is no inherent characteristic in a "chair" that gives it the particular sound the English language provides. After ten minutes a six-year-old, a fifteen-year-old, and your aging editor (29) were all talking like Ionesco. It was fun.

Story Number 3. Illustrated by Philippe Corentin. 1971. One lazy winter Sunday morning Josette's papa tells her a story about their pretend trip on an airplane. Included in their adventure are a trip to the moon (made of melon and delicious) and a visit to the sun, from which they had to walk home because it melted their plane. Ionesco has successfully captured the dialogue of an adult telling a child a simple story and the child's response.

Story Number 4. Illustrated by Jean-Michel Nicollett. 1975. Father has once again gone too far in his restaurant-and-puppet-show-hopping the night before, and when Josette enters her parent's bedroom, she finds mother already gone and papa too exhausted to meet the demands of his 33-month-old child. Sneaking into the bathroom to hide from the sun and his daughter, papa tells Josette that she must find him. He tells her he is in places he is not and can obviously never hope to be. Suddenly mother comes home and we surprisingly begin all over again with Josette entering her parents' bedroom. This is the only tale with an inexplicable ending.

3. Bernard Waber's Changing World

Bernard Waber, who illustrates his own work, has fifteen children's books credited to him in the 1975 edition of *Books In Print*. What attracted me to Waber's work was his 1972 title, *Ira Sleeps Over*. Ashamed to bring his teddy bear on an overnight visit to his friend's house, Ira is astonished and relieved when his pal surreptitiously slips his own toy bear into bed. Aside from allowing boys to reveal needs, the entire family is portrayed as having a non-sexist style; for example, household chores are not divided according to sex. The book is very well written, most humorous, and attractively illustrated.

After reading as many Waber titles as I could find, I came to the conclusion, that, like mine and perhaps yours, too, Bernard Waber's consciousness has been but recently raised. No one would pin a non-stereotyped medal on such books as *A Rose For Mr. Bloom, An Anteater Named Arthur,* or any of the Lyle books previous to *Lyle Finds His Mother.*

Waber is probably best known for his picture books about a friendly crocodile named Lyle, who lives happily with the Primm family (Father, Mother, and Son) in a comfortable New York City brownstone: *The House On East Eighty-Eighth Street, Lyle, Lyle Crocodile, Lyle and the Birthday Party* and *Lovable Lyle.*

Waber begins *Lyle Finds His Mother* with these words: "The world was changing. But if changes were taking place, Lyle the crocodile scarcely noticed." But I noticed the changes, and maybe the publisher noticed the need for change. In the previous stories, Mrs. Primm is the stereotype of the middle-class woman: aproned, worrisome, fretful, serviceable, and having no interests outside the family. Nothing more than mildly irritating, Mrs. Primm was the mass-produced fantasy mother. Previous titles depicted women and girls in dresses only, with the latter in ribbons and curls. In addition, only white people were shown in scenes and other gatherings.

The 1974 Lyle depicts Mrs. Primm out of apron and "very active" in politics; she is working for a woman candidate. Females are now physically active and dressed in pants, and Waber's classroom and playgrounds are integrated. The elementary math teacher is male, another is Black, and the kitchen chores are performed by Mr. and Mrs. Primm.

Lyle is, of course, the star of these tales. He is kind, generous, and gentle and has the very same fears and joys as the human child. Lyle does not have to flex his muscles (or in this case, teeth) to gain attention and admiration, and the children like his innocent antics. In the latest story Lyle is in search of his mother, whom he imagines to be an ever present love and food dispenser, dressed in hat and pearls, too. When he finds her — an undomestic trick-performing ham, like himself, Lyle sighs. Or is it Bernard Waber who is actually sighing, lamenting the changing world?

Other highly enjoyable Waber titles are:

But Names Will Never Hurt Me. Dr. Alison Wonderland, now a veterinarian, tells the amusing and touching story of how it was to grow up with her unique name. Ages 5-8.

You Look Ridiculous Said the Rhinoceros To the Hippopotamus. A hippo becomes dissatisfied with her looks when the jungle animals point to her lack of their best features. Ages 4-8.

Books Mentioned in This Article: (all published by Houghton Mifflin)

The House on East Eighty-Eighth Street. 1962. $5.95.
Lyle, Lyle Crocodile. 1965. $4.95.
Lyle and the Birthday Party. 1966. $4.95.
You Look Ridiculous Said the Rhinoceros To the Hippopotamus. 1966. $5.95.
An Anteater Named Arthur. 1967.

A Rose For Mr. Bloom. 1968.
Lovable Lyle. 1969. $5.95.
Ira Sleeps Over. 1972. $5.95.
Lyle Finds His Mother. 1974. $5.95.
I Was All Thumbs. 1975. $6.95. See No. 164.
But Names Will Never Hurt Me. 1976. $6.95.

The Lively Fiction of Patricia Beatty

Patricia Beatty, where were you and John when I was de-
vouring Rosamond Du Jardin books along with my after school
snack of milk and chocolate cookies?* Instead of adventuring with
Beatty's sharp and gutsy heroines in the rough Southwest of the
1880's, I waded through Du Jardin's *A Man For Mary* (Lippincott, 1954), in which, as the jacket copy says, "Marcy is left high
and dry in high school when her steady date, Steve, departs for
his freshman year at college."

My regrets at being born too early for the Beattys are not just
ideological. Literary critics of children's books have only the
highest regard for Ms. Beatty and her late husband's books. A
Critical History of Children's Literature (Macmillan, 1969) tells
us that "John and Patricia Beatty [are] very competent writers
and collaborators on historic fiction . . ." In *Children and Books*
(Scott, Foresman, 1972), we read that "John and Patricia Beatty's
historical novels are based on sound research and their aim is to
entertain rather than to instruct readers." (p. 514). And that:
"There is never a dearth of action in the books by the Beattys or
in the books that Patricia Beatty writes alone." (p. 514).

Along with sound research, constant action, and an unpedantic
style, the Beattys offer rare portraits of girls and women as real
people — alert, alive, and to be reckoned with.

Patricia Robbins Beatty was born in Portland, Oregon on
August 26, 1922. Wife of the late John Luis Beatty (d. 1975) and
mother of Ann Alexander, she has worked as a high school
teacher of English and social studies and as a business and
science librarian. *Books In Print* (1975 edition) credits Patricia
with twenty-five titles, ten co-authored with John Beatty. Her
publisher is William Morrow & Co. The copyright dates range
from 1962 (*Bonanza Girl*) to her newest 1976 title, *Something To
Shout About.*

Beatty's historic novels usually take place in 18th and 19th-century America and England. I am most familiar with her books written since 1970, which are concerned with the 19th-century Western/Southwestern United States. In 1970 she wrote *Hail Columbia!*, the humorous story of how suffragist Columbia Baines returns to her sedate Oregon home town to shake some humanist sense into its inhabitants. In 1971 we met the unsinkable Beeler Quiney and her younger brother, Nat, who lived in the lawless 19th-century Southwest (*Long Way To Whiskey Creek*). Happily, we will meet Beeler again in 1974 in (my favorite) *How Many Miles To Sundown*.

Dauntless characters, such as Hattie Lou Mercer, a half-Prima Indian from the Arizona Territory (*Red Rock Over the River*), Rosalind Broomes, alias Robin, who dressed in boys' clothes in order to find adventure in Shakespearian England (*Master Rosalind*), and Damaris Boyd, competent businessgirl during the California Gold Rush (*By Crumbs, It's Mine!*) stride through the Beatty titles accompanied by excellent writing and humor.

Most of us are familiar with another memorable heroine, Karana, the young Indian woman in Scott O'Dell's *Island Of the Blue Dolphins*. Legend has it that an undisclosed publisher, previous to Houghton Mifflin, requested that the self-sufficient protagonist undergo a sex change before publication. Since his tale is based on historic truth, Scott O'Dell was wise not to acquiesce. While both boys and girls will read books about boys, only girls will read books about other girls, the publisher reasoned.

I have long believed that this polarization of "boy's" and "girl's" books is caused in part by the standard formula used in creating male and female protagonists: the self-reliant, adventurous boy and the sniveling, dependent girl. (Note how quickly Marcy became "high and dry.") Books like *Island Of the Blue Dolphins*, *Harriet the Spy*, and Marjorie Sharmat's "Maggie Marmelstein" titles are filled with people, not pink and blue robots, and so are enjoyed by children of both sexes. So with the females (and nonstereotyped males, as in *Who Comes To King's Mountain?*) created by the Beattys. Patricia is quoted in *Something About the Author* (Annie Comire, editor. Gale, 1971. Vol. 1, p. 22) as saying: "My books are not intended for people of any particular age. I am most delighted to learn that they are appreciated by people over sixty-five. I am even more delighted to learn that men like the books written in my mind's forsaken fancy for teenage girls."

I might have been born too late to incorporate the likes of Beeler Quiney into my self-image, but I certainly intend that Patricia and John Beatty's titles will be placed alongside the milk and cookies when my daughter and son come home from school.

Books Mentioned in This Article:

Beatty, John and Patricia. *Master Rosalind*. Morrow, 1974. $5.95.
Who Comes To King's Mountain. Morrow, 1975. $5.95.
Beatty, Patricia. *Bonanza Girl*. Morrow, 1962. $5.95.
By Crumbs, It's Mine! Morrow, 1976. $6.95.
Hail Columbia! Morrow, 1970. $5.95.
How Many Miles To Sundown. Morrow, 1974. $5.95.
Long Way To Whiskey Creek. Morrow, 1971. $5.95.
Red Rock Over the River. Morrow, 1973. $5.95.
Something To Shout About. Morrow, 1976. $6.95.
Fitzhugh, Louise. *Harriet the Spy*. Harper & Row, 1964. $5.95.
O'Dell, Scott. *Island of the Blue Dolphins*. Houghton Mifflin, 1960. $4.95.
Sharmat, Marjorie. *Getting Something On Maggie Marmelstein*. Harper & Row, 1971. $3.95.
Maggie Marmelstein For President. Harper & Row, 1975. $4.11.

* Miss Beatty's Reply To My Question:

May 9, 1976

Dear Ms. Davis,
Where was I in the 1950's when you were reading Rosamund du Jardin? I was writing my first book here in Riverside.
Thank you for your editorial devoted to my heroines in *The Liberty Cap*. The girls come "naturally" to me. I've always been a feminist. The women's movement came along and suddenly, lo and behold, I was there on the spot with the "strong girl character!" I have a great time when I'm writing about a Beeler or Hattie Lou or Columbia Baines.
There have been some changes in my life since the article on me appeared in *Something About The Author*. I have remarried — once more a university professor. Carl Uhr is an economist, a Swede, and like myself a graduate of Reed College. He's now in the wild world of children's literature and finding himself, to his amazement, a "critic." He's good, too.

Again, thank you for your kind words about my novels. Best
wishes to you and good luck with *Liberty Cap.*

Yours,

Patricia Beatty Uhr

5. The Authentic Heroines
Of Vera and Bill Cleaver

The Cleavers are a married couple who have been writing
books for children since 1967. They are unusually gifted authors,
and have the distinction of creating heroines of true individuality
and fortitude.

Their books, which contain both humor and pathos, are often
concerned with the suffering caused by prejudice. Characters are
shunned by their small society because of mental or physical
handicaps, a family suicide, illegitimacy, or poverty. Many heroines are from poor families and are determined to support their
kin with economic and moral strength.

Out of eleven published novels, nine have female protagonists.
Even *Grover,* although the title is a boy's name, presents Ellen
Grae as the most important character.

Unlike many movement inspired heroines, the Cleavers' girls
and young women are not consciously determined to be treated
equally. Rather, they are often left alone in a cold, hostile world to
fend for themselves and their relatives. And they always make it,
as individual, successful human beings, who just happen
(happily) to be of the female sex. Because characters are not
stereotypic, the books should appeal to both boys and girls. The
following is a list of their works:

(All hardcover editions are published by Lippincott except
when otherwise noted.)

Delpha Green and Company. 1972. $4.19. Delpha turns the small
  town of Chinquapin Cove upside down when she and dad establish an unconventional church. Grades 6+.
Dust Of the Earth. See No. 264.
Ellen Grae. 1967. $4.75. Ellen bears the responsibility of a ter-
  rible secret. Grades 4-6.
Grover. 1970. $4.50. A boy recovers from the effects of his
  mother's suicide. Grades 4-6.

I Would Rather Be a Turnip. 1971. $4.50. An illegitimate ne-
phew makes Annie an outcast. Grades 4-6.

Lady Ellen Grae. 1968. $3.95. Ellen resists being made into a
"lady." Grades 4-6.

Me Too. See No. 265.

Mimosa Tree. 1970. $3.95. Marvalla's poor family finds hard-
ship in both the city and country. Grades 5-7.

Mock Revolt. 1971. $3.95. The story of Ussy Mock and his ado-
lescence in the 1940's. Grades 6+

Where the Lillies Bloom. 1969. $4.95. An Ozark girl is left to sup-
port aging grandparents. Grades 4-8.

The Whys and Wherefores Of Littabelle Lee. Atheneum, 1973.
$5.95. An Appalachian girl is the head of her family.

6. Maidens With Spunk: Books By Jay Williams

Delighted with the non-sexist (and attractive) world of Jay
Williams's *The Practical Princess,* I decided to investigate his
other picture books. I wanted to know if humanism was inherent
in his imagination or merely suggested by his publishers.

Jay Williams is the author of some seventeen picture books and
early readers, as well as numerous other fiction and non-fiction
titles on other reading levels. In his picture books he almost
always creates a modern fairy tale, using contemporary language
and attitudes to supply much of the humor.

In my review of eleven of these titles I have discovered heroines
as liberated as Bedelia the Practical and some disappointi..g re-
lapses into stereotyped characters and attitudes. Except for
Prudence in *The Silver Whistle,* all of Williams's heroines are
beautiful, in addition to being wise and kind. In fact, one of his
princes says this about his love: "And if she is brave, sensible,
energetic, and wise, she is also very beautiful." (*The Good For
Nothing Prince.*) Is she all right in spite of the former qualities
because she is also pretty? Williams also has the irritating habit
of calling his adult heroines "girls," but his heroes "young men."
On the whole, however, Williams should be knighted for his attempts to individualize his young women and still keep to a traditional fairy tale structure — trouble, rescue, marriage.

A word of admiration should be given for Friso Henstra who
illustrates Jay Williams's picture books with sophistication and
humor.

The Silver Whistle. Illustrated by Friso Henstra. Parents Magazine Press, 1971. $4.95. The Wise Woman of the West has a daughter named Prudence who is cheerful, wise, and homely (although she is pictured as being quite pretty). Upon mother's death Prudence inherits a magic whistle which is to help her make her way in the world. Prudence becomes employed by a witch who instructs her to seek and gain a magic mirror. Returning with the treasure, which turns the gazer into a beauty, Prudence is rushed to the castle with the witch, who wants to be chosen as the prince's bride. At the audience with the prince, however, Prudence realizes what a dreadful queen the seemingly lovely witch would make. She uses the whistle for the final time in order to break the witch's magic. The witch, ugly again, disappears in a fit of anger and the prince chooses Prudence because she suits him best. Never a gushy heroine, Prudence answers his proposal with an "Oh, I don't mind. It will make a nice change." The book certainly does. Picture Book. Ages 4-10.

The Question Box. Illustrated by Margot Zemach. Norton, 1965. Because of Maria's insatiable curiosity, she learns the mechanics of the town's Great Clock, thus striking the warning bell and saving the people from an enemy attack. Maria is portrayed as adventurous, liking and analyzing machinery, not wilting without parental approval, resourceful, brave, and logical. It is a very nice read-aloud tale and Zemach's drawings of an old world village are very pleasant. Picture Book. Ages 4-10.

Petronella. Illustrated by Friso Henstra. Parents Magazine Press. 1973. $4.95. Princess Petronella, who should have been born Prince Peter according to family tradition, goes off to seek her fortune, despite protests from the royal parents. She sets out to find a prince to rescue. She discovers one — a lazy oaf who does crossword puzzles and sun bathes all day. The prince seems to be a captive in the home of a young enchanter. The enchanter sets three tasks for Petronella to do to rescue her prince; these tasks are accomplished easily by her. During the rescue of the reluctant prince, whom she has to drag out of bed and throw on his horse, Petronella learns that the enchanter is hotly pursuing her and not his tiresome guest. The two fall in love and set off to Petronella's kingdom where she must explain her failure to come home with a prince. The book's humor and sophisticated illustrations have no age limits. Ages 5+.

The Practical Princess. Illustrated by Friso Henstra. Parents Magazine Press, 1969. $4.95. Upon her birth, Bedelia is blessed with common sense, and this gift saves her life and earns her a captured prince. When Lord Garp, an ancient, greedy man, hears that Bedelia once slew a dragon and saved her own life, he decides to marry her. Bedelia tries to trick him out of the marriage but the wicked Garp won't take no for an answer. He banishes Bedelia to a deserted tower, vowing to keep her there until she agrees to marry. Bedelia soon realizes that she must rescue herself, and on her exploration of the tower discovers an enchanted prince put under a sleeping spell by Lord Garp. Bedelia breaks the spell, and she and the prince destroy Garp and return home to wed. A very humorous and enjoyable story. Picture Book. Ages 5+.

Stupid Marco. Illustrated by Friso Henstra. Parents Magazine Press, 1970. The intelligent, but easily bored Sylvia helps the likeable but incompetent Prince Marco find the tower where the princess is awaiting rescue. (The king wrote down the instructions but Marco lost them.) Together, using Sylvia's brains and Marco's charm, they find the tower, only to be told that someone else had found the instructions and had already rescued the princess. Sylvia reminds Marco that she is also a rescued princess, never having known a dull moment since joining him. A humorous and well illustrated tale. Picture Book. Ages 5+.

The Youngest Captain. Illustrated by Friso Henstra. Parents Magazine Press. 1972. $4.95. Williams diverges from his fairy tale setting in this modern story about a boy who wants to be captain of the family boat. Although his parents take turns navigating, it is not until the boy has a make-believe adventure with his lazy playmate, Prim, that his parents give him a turn as captain. The parents are depicted as equally competent sportspeople and there are several striking illustrations by Mr. Henstra. A simpler Williams tale, recommended for children aged 3-7.

Forgetful Fred. Illustrated by Friso Henstra. Parents Magazine Press. 1974. $4.50. Fred, the loyal but absent-minded servant of the wealthy Bumberdumble, sets off on a mission to find the heavily guarded Bitter Fruit of Satisfaction. On his travels he meets Mellisa who is employed by a miserly witch. With three magical gifts which have been left to her by her father, Mellisa helps Fred approach the fruit, only to be foiled by, the witch and his own stupidity. With further help from Mellisa, Fred destroys the witch (although losing the fruit) and the two marry. The final picture shows Fred merrily playing the flute and Mellisa cooking the dinner. Picture Book. Ages 5-10.

The Good For Nothing Prince. Illustrated by Imero Gobato. Norton, 1969. A lazy, illiterate Prince finds himself transported into a tower where Princess Ola is held captive. He is reluctantly convinced by the determined princess to rescue her. Once in the forest, the witch Sordilla steals the sleeping Ola during the prince's turn to keep guard. (He fell asleep.) Becoming less lazy and more determined to save Ola, the prince manages to find the tower where Sordilla is awaiting him. Ola is free, claims the witch, and now you must choose your fate. She points to various doors hung with signs which spell his future. Unable to read, the shamed prince sees a short word beginning with "O" and hopes that Ola is behind it. She is. And soon after she laughs at his first reading lesson. The word is OUT.

Ola is prepared for rescue; ropes, food, etc. are in her suitcase. Yet she waits for the prince before making her move. You cannot portray a person as energetic and resourceful and then keep her waiting for a poor excuse of a man to help her get out of her prison. Easy to read book. Grades 2-4.

Books of Lead

The King With Six Friends. Illustrated by Imero Gobato. Parents Magazine Press, 1968. $4.95. Easy to read book. Grades 2-4.

School For Sillies. Illustrated by Friso Henstra. Parents Magazine Press, 1969. $4.95. Picture Book. Ages 5-10.

A Box Full of Infinity. Illustrated by Robin Lawrie. Grosset & Dunlap, 1970. Easy to read book. Grades 2-4.

In these three books the hero overcomes all obstacles without the help of the princess. In the first book the princess never speaks. "The princess is yours," says the king, as the "princess was brought" to meet her mate. The female servant in the inn visited by the king and his six white male friends was "a pretty girl who served them." And for her help and service the king "paid the girl, and gave her a kiss of thanks."

In the second title, Kit, a cheerful and kind scholar, finds a princess weeping from loneliness in the palace garden. He makes it all better by promising her a wedding and proceeds to teach her arrogant father a lesson. She then disappears from the plot and the only other woman mentioned has just finished mopping a floor.

In the third book, Ben, a poor prince, rescues a princess from a wizard who stole her because "he likes to be able to tell his friends that he has a princess doing his housework." "I don't mind the work," reveals the princess, "but I am so sick and tired of this wizard." Ben tells her not to worry and he goes on to accomplish three tasks set by the wizard. In the illustrations the women are in paler colors than the men and have downcast eyes. (Downcast eyes are a dead giveaway. Check the cover of Rosamond Du Jardin's *A Man For Marcy* (Lippincott 1954). Marcy has a bowed head as well.)

The scales tip in Jay Williams's favor, of course. His golden books outweigh those of lead. His 1974 title, *People Of the Ax* (Walck, $5.95), is written for grades 5 and up. It is a fantasy about how our civilization will be looked upon in horror someday by creatures far better than ourselves and is a fine example of anti-sexist writing. (And a fairly exciting tale.) See No. 391.

I believe Jay Williams is sincere and comfortable creating brave and intelligent heroines. No publisher could force such an apparent lack of prejudice. I'm with Sylvia. Jay does rescue princesses from boredom!

7. Cinderella Meets Mollie Whuppie: A New Look At Fairy Tales

John Fowles, author of *The French Lieutenant's Woman*, has recently translated Perrault's *Cinderella*. Little, Brown and Company announce in the Spring 1976 catalog: "The story of the young girl who is mistreated by her stepmother and stepsisters but who never loses her sweet disposition, and who is rewarded by having a prince fall in love with her."

While it is considered fair play to criticize new titles which are stereotyped and poorly written, e.g. Cavanna's *Ruffles and Drums* (Morrow, 1975) or Lattimore's *The Taming of Tiger* (Morrow, 1975) books which are new, well done and sexist are a little harder to put down. For example, while receiving a strong "no!" vote from *School Library Journal* (1/75), Greenfield's *She*

Come Bringing Me That Little Baby Girl (Lippincott, 1974) was included on the "ACL Distinguished Book List, 1976" as well as on many others.

The older the book and the more beautifully written, the more reluctant we are to attack it for such "political" reasons as anti-feminism and racism. Imagine then, the gasps of shock and disbelief when one criticizes the most sacred cow in all of children's literature: the fairy tale.

But fairy tales were not made in heaven. They incorporate the customs, myths, superstitions, and mores of the primitive societies from which they have sprung. They did not appear from any more mystical or enchanted a source than did Lois Lenski's *Let's Play House* (Walck, 1944) or Phyllis Krasilovsky's *The Very Little Girl* (Doubleday, 1953). (They just have a lot more charisma.) And when it comes to the roles of men and women, the society which produced Phyllis's girl wearing pink hearts on her cheeks is not very different from the earlier culture which created the girl who wore ashes on her pretty nose.

Not all of us, however, revere the Cinderellas of the literary world. Not when we see the effects of the passive princess syndrome on our daughters. But to throw out the past (which is also our present) would leave literature-loving feminists and librarians with almost nothing to read. Therefore, it is imperative that we seek out and provide fairy tales with less passive heroines, for to deprive youngsters of the enchanting world of make believe is not acceptable either. Because fairy tales are not only relics of the past but prescriptions for the future, let us make certain that we celebrate the daring of Mollie Whuppie as well as the sweetness of Cinderella. By doing this, we shall create individual heroines. Cinderella, Snow White, and Little Red Riding Hood would be looked upon as individual characters and not as symbols of the "weaker sex," in need of a male defender.

What follows is 1) a list of alternative folk and fairy tales, some adapted, some new; 2) a list of popular fairy tale collections; and 3) a list of books and articles relevant to this topic.

Books

Single Stories

The Little Giant Girl and the Elf Boy. By Else Minarik. Illustrated by author. Harper & Row, 1963. $5.89. When a giant girl catches a boy elf, she very reluctantly lets him go. The tiny boy, however, is not so sorry to end the relationship. Ages 3-7.

The Milkmaid. By Randolph Caldecott. Illustrated by author. Warne, 1882. $2.95. In this adaptation of an old folk song, a poor young man in search of a wealthy wife happens upon an independent young woman. Ages 4+.

Molly and the Giant. By Kurt Werth and Mabel Watts. Illustrated by Kurt Werth. Parents Magazine Press, 1973. $4.95. In this adaptation from the Molly Whuppie tale, a daring young woman slays a giant and manages to win a prince for herself and one for each of her two sisters. Ages 4-9.

The Princess and the Admiral. By Charlotte Pomerantz. Illustrated by Tony Chen. Addison Wesley, 1974. $5.50. Based on Kubla Khan's invasion of Vietnam hundreds of years ago, this story is about a princess who brings peace to a small kingdom about to be attacked. Grades 3-6.

The Princess and the Lion. By Elizabeth Coatsworth. Illustrated by Evaline Ness. Pantheon, 1963. $4.79. A brave princess does the rescuing in this story by a well-known writer of children's books. Grades 3-6.

Three Strong Women. By Claus Stamm. Illustrated by Kazue Misumura. Viking, 1974. (1964) 95¢. A tall tale from Japan about three women who teach the art of wrestling to a man. Grades 2-5.

Two Beastly Tales: Kids and Dragon. By J.B. Grant. Illustrated by Joan Pachen. *The Wizard's Daughter.* By Katherine Houghton. Illustrated by author. Lamplighters Roadway Press: Freestone Box 1 500 Bohemian Highway, Firestone, CA 95472. $3.50. Two modern fairy tales about resourceful heroines. In the first, a sister and brother overcome an evil dragon, and in the second story a terrible wizard creates a flawless daughter who rises above her nasty environment. Grades 3+.

The following books, discussed elsewhere, are also relevant to the topic:

Mollie Mullet. By Patricia Coombs. See No. 35.
Pampalche Of the Silver Teeth. By Mirra Ginsburg. See No. 53.
Petronella. By Jay Williams. See "Maidens With Spunk: Books By Jay Williams."

The Practical Princess. By Jay Williams. Same as above.
The Princess Book. Ida Chittum, editor. See No. 261.
The Queen Who Couldn't Bake Gingerbread. See No. 159.
The Forest Princess. By Harriet Herman. See No. 299.
The Squire's Bride. By Peter Asbjornsen. See No. 241.
Well Done! By Barbara Morrow. See No. 123.
The Wizard In the Tree. By Lloyd Alexander. See No. 236.
The Wizard's Tears. By Ann Sexton and Maxine Kumin. See No. 145.
Womenfolk and Fairy Tales. Rosemary Minard, editor. See No. 338.

Collections

Arnott, Kathleen. *African Myths and Legends.* Walck, 1963. $6.00.
"Urbana and the Elephant." An African mother makes a long journey to find the two-tusked elephant who has eaten her beautiful children.

Asbjornsen, Peter. *Norwegian Folk Tales.* Viking Press, 1961. $5.00.
"The Squire's Bride." A young peasant woman tricks an aging squire out of forced wedlock.
"Not Driving, Not Riding." A short tale in which a young woman solves a riddle and wins a prince.

Baker, Augusta. *The Talking Tree.* Lippincott, 1955. $3.39.
"The Horned Woman." A spooky Irish tale with an all woman cast.
"The Green Sergeant." A Brazilian tale in which a woman becomes a soldier when father orders her death.
"The Parrot of Limo Verde." A tale from Brazil in which a young woman accomplishes a difficult task to recover her lost lover.
"Krencipal and Krencipalka." A Polish story in which a woman and man seek their fortunes and outwit the devil.

Chase, Richard. *Grandfather Tales.* Houghton Mifflin, 1948. $5.95.
"The Two Old Women's Bet." Two old women hold a contest to see who can make the biggest fool of her husband.

Fenner, Phyllis. *Princesses and Peasant Boys*. Knopf, 1944. "Timo and the Princess Vendla." A well educated princess weds a learned lad who speaks the languages of all the animals. "Queen O' the Tinkers." A princess refuses to wed her father's choice and runs off with an alleged tinker.

Fillmore, Parker. *Czechoslovak Fairy Tales*. Harcourt Brace, 1919. "The Wood Maiden." A peasant girl has an adventure in the forest with an enchanted wood maiden.

Filmore, Parker. *The Shepherd's Nosegay*. Harcourt Brace, 1958. "Clever Manka." A clever daughter marries a young judge and becomes his legal adviser.

Gag, Wanda. *Tales From Grimm*. Coward McCann, 1943. $6.95. "The Fisherman and His Wife." At last, a woman with political aspirations!

Grimm Brothers. *Household Stories*. Dover, 1886. $2.50.
"Clever Grethel." A hungry cook outwits Master and enjoys a fine dinner all by herself.
"The Twelve Brothers." The 13th child born, a girl, rescues her twelve brothers, who were forced to flee at her birth. (This is a variation of "The Seven Ravens" by Grimm.)

Haviland, Virginia. *Favorite Tales Told In England*. Little Brown, 1959.
"Mollie Whuppie." She tricks a giant and wins three princes!
"Cap O' Rushes." A tale with a Cinderella-King Lear theme.

Jacobs, Joseph. *English Folk Tales and Fairy Tales*. Putnam, 1904. $5.00.
"Tenny Tiny." A little woman stands her ground in this scary tale.
"The Golden Arm." A short but powerful ghost story.

Manning-Sanders, Ruth. *A Book Of Ghosts And Goblins*. Dutton, 1969. $5.95.
"The Skull." A Halloween tale about a brave girl and the frightening skull she befriends.

Thomas, Marlo and others. *Free To Be . . . You And Me*. McGraw, Hill, 1974. $7.95.
"Atalanta." by Betty Miles. A princess manages to determine her own fate using wit and physical strength.

Ure, Jean. *Rumanian Folk Tales.* Watts, 1960.
"Cleverer Than the Devil." A somewhat amusing tale about an elderly woman who outwits the devil.
"Luck and Wit." There is a contest between (masculine) Luck and (feminine) Wit, and she wins.
"The Poor Man's Clever Daughter." A wise young woman solves three riddles, marries a young lawyer, and becomes his legal adviser.

Wiggin, Kate Douglas and Nora Archibald. *The Fairy Ring.* Doubleday, 1967.
"The Young Head of the Family." A Chinese tale in which a young married woman becomes head of the house and manages very well.

Although several of the books listed are out of print, the individual stories can be found in other story collections. See *Index To Fairy Tales, 1949-1972, Including Folklore, Legends and Myths In Collections.* Norma O. Ireland, editor. Faxon, 1973.

Writing About Fairy Tales

Brownmiller, Susan. *Against Our Will: Men, Women, and Rape.* Simon and Shuster, 1975. $10.95. Ms. Brownmiller makes some interesting remarks about the effects of the passive princess on our society. Check index for pages.

Donlan, Dan. "The Negative Image of Women In Children's Literature." *Elementary English,* 4/72. Includes a discussion of women in fairy tales.

Ephron, Nora. *Crazy Salad: Some Things About Women.* Knopf, 1975. $7.95. Ms. Ephron discusses the fairy tale in her chapter on sexual fantasies.

Gersoni-Stavn, Diane, ed. *Sexism and Youth.* Bowker, 1974. $9.95. Includes a section on children's literature which reprints the Donlan and Lieberman articles.

Lieberman, Marcia R. "Some Day My Prince Will Come: Female Acculturation Through the Fairy Tale." *College English,* 12/72. A detailed and very well written article on the unfortunate effects many popular fairy tales have had on generations of girls.

Lurie, Alison. "Fairy Tale Liberation." *New York Review of Books,* 12/17/70. Ms. Lurie sees the fairy/folk tale as creating many positive and assertive female characters.

"Witches and Fairies: Fitzgerald to Updike." *New York Review of Books,* 12/2/71.

Moore, Robert. "From Rags To Riches: Stereotypes, Distortions and Anti-Humanism in Fairy Tales." Council on Interracial Books for Children. *Bulletin.* Vol. 6, no. 7, 1975. A very interesting article which goes beyond sexism and questions class values as well.

McCulloch, John A. *The Childhood of Fiction.* 1905. Used constantly as a source by Mr. Yearsley (see below), McCulloch traces the origins of fairy tales in order to strip them of their mystery and explain their themes and mores.

Yearsley, Macleod. *The Folklore of Fairy Tale.* Watts, 1924. Reissued by Singing Tree Press, 1968. A very readable account of the origin and meaning of fairy tales which quite often uses sex roles and sexual customs to explain repetitive trends and themes.

I Am A Woman

It is unfortunately the custom among writers, translators, and adapters of fairy tales and fantasies to call mature young women "girls", as though that made them more romantic and interesting. This practice is not very logical. A child of ten is a "girl", but a woman of twenty is a "young girl." To me, a young girl is a little girl, just as a young boy is a little boy — littler, anyway, than just-plain-"boy."

In fairy tales, marriageable princesses are "girls," but the princes they marry are, even at seventeen or eighteen, "men," or at the very least, "young men." A good example of this questionable usage can be found in *Little Sister and the Month Brothers* as retold by Beatrice De Regniers (Seabury, 1976). Here the bride really *is* a "young girl," a flat-chested, babyfaced child no older than ten. Her husband, on the other hand, is a man, not at all boyish-looking.

Let us protest this sexist habit and call a woman a woman. Certainly we are past the stage when women of fifty consider it a compliment to be called "girls." It is about as flattering and welcome for a mature woman as it is for Black men of any age to be called "boys."

CHAPTER II

ROLES PEOPLE PLAY

1. Boys and Girls Together

The following is the first part of a list of books which offers children relief from rigid sex role stereotypes. Teachers and parents can use these books to encourage their children to consider youngsters of both sexes as potential friends. The books, however, are not limited to purposes of bibliotherapy. They stand on their own merits and can be enjoyed at any time. The following books make a direct contrast to the boy-girl friendship in Edward Ardizzone's *Tim In Danger* (Walck, 1953). Don't you agree?

Boys and Girls, Girls and Boys. By Eve Merriam. Holt, 1972. $4.59. Pals of both sexes and all races reveal their wishes and dreams in this action-packed picture book. Ages 4-8.

Christina Katerina and the Box. By Patricia Gauch. Coward, 1971. $4.99. Christina and her male friend make great things out of a tremendous box. Ages 4-8.

Gladys Told Me To Meet Her Here. By Marjorie Sharmat. Harper & Row, 1970. $4.79. Worried Irving has a date to meet his good friend, Gladys, at the zoo. But where is she?

A Hole Is To Dig. By Ruth Krauss. Harper & Row, 1952. $2.95. Boys and girls illustrate a multitude of childhood activities.

Nancy's Backyard. By Eros Keith. Harper & Row, 1973. $4.95. In a peaceful, pastel-colored country scene, Nancy and her friends share their night's dreams and their feelings. Ages 4-7.

Noisy Nancy and Nick. By Lou Ann Gaeddert. Doubleday, 1970. $4.50. Nancy shows her new neighbor, a country boy, how to have fun in the big city. Ages 4-8.

The Story Of The Four Little Children Who Went Around The World. By Edward Lear. Macmillan, 1967. An entertaining fantasy about two girls and two boys who share the action. Ages 4-8.

Tommy and Sarah Dress Up. By Gunilla Wolde. Houghton Mifflin, 1972. $1.25. Preschool friends dress up in old clothes in this brightly illustrated, role-free story. Ages 2-5. (See the complete works of this Swedish writer.)

The following books, discussed elsewhere, are also relevant to the topic:

Best Friends For Frances. By Russell Hoban. See No. 66.
He Bear. She Bear. By Stan Berenstain. See No. 186.
Jackie. By Luevester Lewis. See "Alternative Presses," page 45 .
Let's Play Desert. By Inger Sandberg. See No. 143.
The Magic Hat. By Kim Chapman. See "Alternative Presses," page 999.
Rosie and Michael. By Judith Viorst. See No. 163.
So What If It's Raining. By Miriam Young. See No. 178.
Won't Somebody Play With Me? By Steve Kellog. See No. 84.
Yolanda's Hike. La Aventura de Yolanda. By Tomas Gaspar. See "Alternative Presses," page 45 .

Books for older readers:

Free To Be . . . You and Me. Compiled by Margo Thomas. Ms. Foundation, 1974. $8.95; $5.95. A gay and lively anthology of songs, stories, and poetry for the whole family to enjoy. The record of the same title should be in every child's collection, and everyone should see the 16mm film at least once. Ages 5-12.
Peter and Veronica. By Marilyn Sachs. Doubleday, 1969. $4.94. Peter finds himself defending his friendship with Veronica, the class bully. Grades 3-5.
The Pigman. By Paul Zindel. Harper & Row, 1968. $4.95. A teen-age girl and her male friend share the guilt of taking advantantage of the elderly, unconventional Mr. Pignati. Grades 6-9.
Snow Bound. By Harry Mazer. Delacorte, 1973. $5.95. Tony and Cindy form a close, realistically portrayed relationsip, when they are trapped in a major storm together. Grades 5-9.

The following books, discussed elsewhere, are also relevant to the topic.

Grover. By Vera and Bill Clever. See subject article, "Vera and Bill Cleaver — Creators of Authentic Heroines."
Me Too. By Vera and Bill Cleaver. See No. 265.
People of the Ax. By Jay Williams. See No. 391.

2. Freeing the Boys

If the characters from American children's storybooks and texts were fed into a computer and we programmed the word "MAN," the machine would read out a white, dark-haired, well-built man of about thirty-five. Profession: community helper (e.g. police officer or businessman.) Personality: financially and morally responsible; protective (but not nurturing); dauntless, and strong (even stiff) in mind and body.

The word "BOY" would produce an image of a twelve-year-old, fair-haired male. A responsible but curious, dependable but adventurous, sportsminded, nonexpressive, sexist ("Girls are dumb!") Junior Patriarch.

The following titles offer alternative role models: a boy who wants a doll to cuddle; a father who spends his day caring for a small son; and a mighty king who learns to bake for himself. Let's start feeding some new and true experiences into the minds of our children. Perhaps, unlike the computer, they won't think only in pat images and stereotypes.

Alternatives To The Bionic Man

Cesar Chavez. By Ruth Franchere. Crowell, 1970. $4.50. An easy introduction to the life of a great social reformer. Grades 2-5.

The Daddy Book. By R. Steward and D. Madden. McGraw Hill, 1972. $4.95. An adequate look at the way different daddies play and love their children. Ages 4-7.

Langston Hughes: American Poet. By Alice Walker. Crowell, 1974. $4.50. Grades 2-5. This biography, part of the Crowell series, emphasizes the childhood of the famed Black poet.

The Night Daddy. By Maria Gripe. Delacorte, 1971. $4.95. A working mother leaves her daughter in the care of a special young man. Grades 3-6.

Picture Life of Martin Luther King, Jr. By Margaret B. Young. Watts, 1968. $3.90. A simple introduction with many photographs, this book is one of a series which includes such people as Malcolm X, Jesse Jackson, and Thurgood Marshall. Grades K-4.

The Sunshine Family and the Pony. By Sharron Loree. Seabury, 1972. $5.95. An appealing portrayal of a communal family with no sex-role stereotypes. Ages 4-8.

This Is My Father and Me. By Dorka Raynor. Albert Whitman,
1973. $4.25. Children and fathers are depicted in many briefly
captioned photographs. The scope is international. Ages 3+.

What Is A Man? By Fernando Krahn. Delacorte, 1972. $4.95. A
small animal, Orestes, goes on a journey to discover what man
is like. Many animals differ in their opinions, but Orestes finally happens on a gentle, blind man who teaches him about love.
Ages 4-8.

The following books, discussed elsewhere, are also relevant to
the topic.

Arthur Mitchell. By Tobi Tobias. See No. 232.
Charlie Needs a Cloak. By Tomie De Paola. See No. 38.
John Muir. By Glen Dines. See No. 197.
Make A Circle Keep Us In. By Arnold Adoff. See No. 3.
Martin's Father. By Magrit Eichler. See "Alternative Presses"
page 45.
Mr. Whittier. By Elizabeth Vining. See No. 525.
My Special Best Words. By John Steptoe. See No. 152.
The Queen Who Couldn't Bake Gingerbread. See No. 159.
Ralph Bunche: A Most Reluctant Hero. By James Haskins. See
No. 458.
Roger Williams. By William Jacobs. See No. 469.
The Story of BIP. By Marcel Marceau. See No. 115.
Ira Sleeps Over. By Bernard Waber. See subject article, "Bernard
Waber's Changing World."
Max. By Rachael Isadora. See No. 74.
Peter Learns To Crochet. By Irene Levinson. See No. 226.
Walter the Wolf. By Marjorie Sharmat. See No. 148.

Alternatives For Boys and Beasts

Arthur's Christmas Cookies. By Lillian Hoban. Harper & Row,
1972. $2.95. A boy chimp plays havoc with a cookie recipe. Easy
to read and digest. Grades K-2.

The Boy Who Didn't Believe In Spring. By Lucille Clifton. Dutton,
1973. $5.95. A young Black child and his Puerto Rican friend
are very excited when spring comes to their urban neighborhood. Ages 4-7.

Blood In the Snow. By Marlene F. Shyer. Houghton Mifflin, 1975.
$5.95. A sensitive boy must stand up to his father's macho ways
in this gentle animal story. Grades 3-5.

Go and Hush the Baby. By Betsy Byars. Viking, 1971. $4.95. Big
brother is asked to amuse the baby while mother paints. Ages
4-6.

Grownups Cry Too. By Nancy Hazer, Lollipop Power, 1973.
$1.75. A young boy learns that people (male and female, young
and old) cry for many reasons, and that's all right. Ages 3-9. See
No. 63.

Izzard. By Lonzo Anderson. Scribners, 1973. $5.95. A young boy
finds himself the "mother of a lizard. Ages 4-7.

Repair Of Uncle Toe. By Kay Chorao. Farrar Straus & Giroux,
1972. $3.95. A young orphan expresses his need for love in this
well-told story, nicely illustrated by the author. Ages 4-8.·

The Story of Ferdinand. By Munro Leaf. Viking, $4.50. Ferdi-
nand is a young bull who would rather sniff flowers than spill
blood. Ages 4-8.

William's Doll. By Charlotte Zolotow. Harper & Row, 1972.
$4.95. William wants a baby doll to cuddle and love, but father
cannot understand. Ages 4-7.

3. My Mother The Mop

In September of 1975 I gave a talk to women taking an adult
education course entitled "Creative Homemaking." I thought the
students would be interested in the image of mothers in children's literature, especially in picture books (preschool-3rd grade).

The instructor expressed the concern many women feel that
the feminist movement looks down on mothers who do not hold
outside jobs. Feminists, they said, make us feel guilty for not pursuing "glamorous" careers. "What many people don't realize," I
told them, "is that feminists are the persons responsible for
pushing legislation raising the status of homemakers; e.g.
equalized community property laws, banning credit discrimination, and acts funding counselling and job training for newly divorced housewives. Indeed, feminists have been demanding
social security benefits, pension plans, and salary scales for
women employed in the home."

Females have been apologizing long before the resurrected
women's movement (c. 1966) for being "just a housewife." Why is
this career held in such low esteem? How is it portrayed in the
books young children have been reading for the last twenty-five
years? Are mothers shown as interesting, responsible, independent, resourceful, creative, encouraging, diverse individuals?
Quite the contrary.

Images of Mom

What does Mom do all day? Mother wears an apron
and bakes and cleans. When she sits, she knits. She is often
waiting at home to welcome her sons back from adventures. Can

you think of one book where dad is waiting to serve a hot meal to an heroic daughter? Mother does not read, have outside interests, do chores relating to carpentry or mechanics. She does not work outside the home, often not even to mow the lawn. Animal or human — mama is a pure domestic. Several new titles are allowing mother a greater range of indoor activities. *Little Rabbit's Loose Tooth* provides Mother Rabbit with a flute, a music stand, and Mozart's music. Other new titles stay with the old and familiar. One such book shows Mama Alligator, dressed only in a mini-apron, baking pies for her daughter's Halloween party. The apron is mom's symbol. At least 90% of adult females (human/animal) appear aproned in picture books.

Does she work outside the home? In real life she does. Forty percent of the U.S. labor force is composed of women. Yet fictional mothers, with few and new exceptions, work only in the home. When we are shown as professionals (and not as mommies), we are nurses, teachers, librarians, saleswomen and secretaries to Mr. Jones. Happily, these things are changing.

What is Mom's personality like? Most women have almost total responsibility for their children. They need to make important decisions. About 10% of our families are headed by single mothers. And yet, the picture book mama (human or animal) is often worrisome, nagging, dependent on papa for advice and moral support, emotional, and tearful. In one 1974 title a mother goat depends on papa to rescue their stolen kid. While he gives the other children further instructions, she is quietly weeping in her hankie. If she is not crying, she is fainting or "yesing" papa. In an October 1975 book, a duchess loses her thirteen daughters at a Halloween outing. Bursting into tears (at least twice), she pleads with the duke to come out of a sick bed to rescue the girls. In another new title for grades 2-3, Mother is such a dingbat that father and son must lock her up for her own safety. In the Caldecott winner *Sylvester and the Magic Pebble* by William Steig (Windmill, 1969), Mrs. Donkey cries when her son disappears. Mr. Donkey does not cry, but he comforts the weeping mother. And to make her feel better he "takes her" on a picnic and lets her do all the work.

Ask Mr. Bear by Marjorie Flack(Macmillan, 1932) is a masterpiece of story-telling for two-year-olds. Danny is searching for a birthday gift for mother. The farm animals, Mrs. Hen, Mrs. Goose, Mrs. Sheep, Mrs. Goat, and Mrs. Cow suggest presents they produce, e.g. milk, feathers, etc. Danny turns them down and ventures alone to hear a suggestion from Mr. Bear. (The animals are afraid to accompany him.) Mr. Bear recommends a bear hug and solves the problem. Why not Mrs. Bear?

I am sure that authors do not start out with a fierce determination to make mom look like a fool. Many books use stock characters, familiar formulae for behavior, and the dependent, silly female is as common as 2+2=4.

What does Mom look like? Real mothers come in a variety of sizes, colors, and dress preferences. The book mama — to sum it up — is neat. Average in weight, height, and hair length, she usually wears flowered dresses, pearls, and an apron. The newer books are dressing human mothers in slacks (even jeans) and making the greatest strides in appearances. But the only heavy young mother I remember seeing is the Black woman in *Snowy Day.* I wonder why.

In the new and successful *Little Rabbit's Loose Tooth,* something looked different about mother rabbit's face, making her appear "feminine". It was not her flowered dress. I was baffled. Then I noticed that mother had very heavy eyelashes and father had none.

Books Mentioned In This Article:

Many of these titles and countless others have excellent writing and art work. But together they form a false picture of mothers that does not provide the best role model for a small girl learning to identify with grown women. I am not asking for their removal from shelves or from consideration for purchase. The article is to make you aware of how mothers are often portrayed to young children.

An Anteater Named Arthur. Bernard Waber. Houghton Mifflin, 1967.
The Birthday Goat. Nancy Watson. Crowell, 1974.
Can I Keep Him? Steven Kellog. Dial, 1971. See No. 82.
Gunhilde and the Halloween Spell. Virginia Kahl. Scribner's, 1975. See No. 79.
Henry Explores the Jungle. Mark Taylor. Atheneum, 1968.
Hester. Byron Barton. Morrow, 1975. See No. 7.
The House That Sailed Away. Pat Hutchins. Greenwillow/Morrow, 1975. See No. 306.
Is Susan Here? Janice Udry. Abelard, 1962.
Little Rabbit's Loose Tooth. Lucy Bate. Crown, 1975. See No. 8.
Snowy Day. Ezra Jack Keats. Viking, 1962.
Where The Wild Things Are. Maurice Sendak. Harper & Row, 1963.

Mothers Are Real People

Many mothers do get down on the floor and play with their kids. Many read books and play sports. Many work outside the home, are in politics, and in love with their husbands. (You'd be surprised how little contact there is in children's books between mother and father.) Many do not care about occasional dirt, lapse of perfect manners, and not having a male around as a security guard. And many, I know you won't believe me, children, — don't wear aprons!

Just as the women's movement has demanded and obtained legislative change, most of the following books would never have seen the light of day if today's feminists had not helped to raise the public consciousness — by about 1,000 feet.

Abby. By Jeanette Caines. Illustrated by Steven Kellog. Harper & Row, 1973. $4.95. A loving Black mother with one eye on her kids and her nose in the books. Ages 4-7.

All Kinds Of Mothers. By Cecily Brownstone. McKay, 1969. $2.95 A multi-ethnic title depicting mothers who work at home and outside the house. Grades 4-7.

Black Is Brown Is Tan. By Arnold Adoff. Illustrated by Emily McCully. Harper & Row, 1973. $4.95. A multi-racial family enjoying one another's company. Ages 4-10.

City In the Winter. By Eleanor Schick. Macmillan, 1973. $5.95. Mother works and grandma takes care of her young son. Ages 4-7.

Getting Smarter. By Julia First. Prentice Hall, 1974. $4.95. A twelve-year-old girl must adjust to her mother's recent outside employment. Grades 4-6.

Joshua's Day. By Sandra Puroweicki. Lollipop Power, 1972. $1.75. Mother is single and works as a photographer, and Joshua attends a childcare center. At the end of the day they exchange experiences. Ages 3-6.

Mom, the Wolfman, and Me. By Norma Klein. Pantheon, 1972. $5.49. Mom is a photographer who loves her single life, her job, and her daughter. (See other titles by Ms. Klein.) Grades 5+.

Mommies At Work. By Eve Merriam. Illustrated by Beni Montresor. Knopf, 1961. $3.00. All kinds of mothers at all kinds of employment, who love seeing their children at the end of the day "best of all." Ages 3-7.

Mothers Can Do Anything. By Joe Lasker. Whitman, 1972. $4.25. Mothers do a great variety of jobs and are still mothers. Ages 3-8.

On Mother's Lap. By Ann H. Scott. Illustrated by Glo Coalson. McGraw-Hill, 1972. $4.95. A loving Eskimo mother nurtures her young son and his little whims. Ages 2-7.

Turnabout. By William Wiesner. Illustrated by author. Seabury Press, 1972. $5.95. From the old fairy tale, "The Husband Who Was To Mind the House," comes this story about the difficulties of women's traditional work. Ages 4-8.

The following books, discussed elsewhere, are also relevant to the topic.

The Adventures of B.J. the Amateur Detective. By Toni Sortor. See No. 371.

Amanda the Panda and the Redhead. By Susan Terris. See No. 154.

A Bedtime Story. By Joan Levine. See No. 99.

Frankie and the Fawn. By Marcia Polese. See No. 357.

Fresh Fish and Chips. By Jan Andrews. See "Alternative Presses," page 45.

Go and Hush The Baby. By Betsy Byers. See "Alternatives for Boys and Beasts," page 28.

Ira Sleeps Over. By Bernard Waber. See "The Changing World of Bernard Waber."

Kevin's Grandma. By Barbara Williams. See No. 168.

King of the Dollhouse. By Patricia Clapp. See No. 262.

Lyle Finds His Mother. By Bernard Waber. See No. 165.

The Magic Three of Solatia. By Jane Yolen. See No. 393.

Mother Is a Pitcher. By Maxine Kahn. See "Alternative Presses," page 45.

My Mother the Mail Carrier. By Inez Maury. See No. 118.

Nice Little Girls. By Elizabeth Levy. See No. 100.

Of Time and Seasons. By Norma Johnston. See No. 307.

The Real Me. By Betty Miles. See No. 337.

The Sunshine Family and the Pony. See "Freeing the Boys," page 27.

The Terrible Thing That Happened At Our House. By Marge Blaines. See No. 12.

That Crazy April. By Lila Perl. See "Two Novels About the Women's Movement," page 45.

Too Hot For Ice-cream. By Jean Van Leeuwen. See No. 158.

CHAPTER III

YESTERDAY AND TOMORROW

1. Biographies of Equality

Now that state and federal laws are beginning to require schools to include the study of women's cultural contributions into the social studies curriculum, teachers are avidly searching for suitable materials. Parents, too, are seeking non-stereotyped books to counter-balance society's message to their daughters, that women of yesterday were nurses, flag-sewers, or wives of United States Presidents.

There are many new dimensions in the field of biography for children. A well written biography can be an entertaining and inspiring experience for a youngster. Biographies come in many forms: photographic essays with little text; collected biographies interwoven with chapters of historic background and events; biographies which read like novels; and books which include examples of the subject's creativity. No child has to make do with the 1936 edition of *Threader Of Knots: The True Story of Betsy Ross*.

The following is a selective guide to the juvenile biographies in print today: the publisher's series; and individual titles of above average intelligence and style. Sources for further information are also listed, and over seventy biographies appear in Part Two: The Reviews that are not repeated here. Most of the titles mentioned here were published prior to 1974.

The Series

Thomas Y. Crowell, Co. is the leading publisher of non-sexist juvenile biographies. Both of the Crowell series contain titles of consistently high literary quality and an impressive selection of subjects.

A Crowell Biography. Series editor, Susan Bartlett Weber. $4.50 each. Grades 2-5.
There are about twenty-eight titles in this series of biographies, among them many minority and female subjects. Written by such distinguished authors as Sharon Bell Mathis,

Eloise Greenfield, and June Jordan, each book is an excellent introduction to its subject. The biographers often stress the formative person's childhood years. Large print and profuse illustrations permit this series to be read to children as young as four years old. For the purpose of this article, the following subjects are worth noting: Jane Addams, Marion Anderson, Martha Berry, Fannie Lou Hamer, Rosa Parks, Eleanor Roosevelt, and Maria Tallchief.

Women of America. Series editor, Milton Meltzer. $5.95 each. Grades 5+.
Excellent biographies of American women of great courage, perseverance, and genius: Emma Goldman, Dr. Florence Sabin, Bessie Smith, Gertrude Stein, and Lillian Wald, to name a few. Approximately twenty-one women are included. Most are social reformers, and several are artists. Each book has a bibliography, an index, and black and white photographs. One of the best juvenile biographies available today is in this series: Margaret Hope Bacon's, *I Speak For My Slave Sister: The Life Of Abby Kelley Foster*. See No. 402.

Individual Biographies

Many of the following authors have written several biographies.

Brownmiller, Susan. *Shirley Chisholm: A Biography*. Doubleday, 1970. $3.95. The story of the first Black congresswoman and the first Black female presidential candidate. Grades 4-8.

Buckmaster, Henrietta. *Women Who Shaped History*. Macmillan, 1966. $4.95. A collective biography about Prudence Crandall, Dorothea Dix, Mary Baker Eddy, Elizabeth Cady Stanton, and Harriet Tubman. Grades 6+.

Bulla, Clyde Robert. *Pocahontas and the Strangers*. Crowell, 1971. $4.50. Grades 3-5.

Clarke, Mary Stetson. *Bloomers and Ballots: Elizabeth Cady Stanton and Women's Rights*. Viking, 1972. $6.50. Mrs. Stanton was the brains behind the American suffrage movement. Grades 5+.

Crane, Louise. *Ms. Africa*. Lippincott, 1973. $4.95. A collective biography of twelve modern African women. Grades 6+.

Crary, Margaret. *Susette La Flesche: Voice Of the Omaha Indians*. Hawthorne, 1973. $5.95. The story of a woman (1854-1903) active in the Native American civil rights cause. Grades 6+.

Crawford, Deborah. *Four Women In a Violent Time.* Crown, 1970. $4.50. An unusual interweaving of history and the fates of four courageous pioneers. Grades 5+.

D'Aulaire, Ingri and Edgar P. *Pocahontas.* Doubleday, 1949. $4.95. The colorful, large illustrations in this older title help make this biography of the Native American princess a perennial favorite. Grades 3-5. Read to younger children.

Other Publisher's Series

There are several other publishers of biographical series, but they are not consistently of high quality, as Crowell's are, and each title must be judged individually. In many cases the books may succeed as functional, rather than inspirational reading material, satisfying the homework assignment and some curiosity.

There are a healthy number of female and minority subjects in the following series:

Children's Press, Inc. Publishes simultaneously with:

Creative Educational Society, Inc. 123. S. Broad Street, Mankato, MN 56001. $4.95 to $6.60 each. These two firms co-publish many biographies. They have a *Super Star* series with many titles written by Ann and Charles Morse and James Olsen. Some female athletes are included. The Morses and Olsen have written about popular female singers, such as Carly Simon, Aretha Franklin, and Roberta Flack. (For grades 3-6.)

Garrard Publishing Co. *Garrard Discovery Books.* The titles may be appealing to some reluctant readers.

G.P. Putnam, Sons. *See-and-Read Books.* For the early elementary grades. *Sports Hero,* by Sue and Marshall Burchard. $4.69 each. Grades 3-5. Adequately written, with large print and many black and white photographs, this series includes a few female athletes. See No. 413.

Davidson, Margaret. *The Story Of Eleanor Roosevelt.* Four Winds, 1969. $3.95. One of the better books about this remarkable humanitarian. Grades 4-6.

Faber, Doris. *Oh, Lizzie! The Life Of Elizabeth Cady Stanton.* Lothrop, 1972. $5.95. A lively, fictionalized account of Susan Anthony's closest colleague. Grades 4-8.

Felton, Harold. *Mumbet: The Story Of Elizabeth Freeman.* Dodd, Mead, 1970. $4.50. In 1781 a Black slave won her freedom in a Massachusetts courthouse; this is the story of her struggle. Grades 3-6.

Gurko, Miriam. *Restless Spirit: The Life Of Edna St. Vincent Millay.* Crowell, 1972. $4.50. A highly readable biography about this gifted poet. Grades 6+.

Jones, Hettie. *Big Star Fallin' Mama: Five Women In Black Music.* Viking, 1974. $5.95. A look at music through the lives of Aretha Franklin, Billie Holiday, Mahalia Jackson, Ma Rainey, and Bessy Smith. Grades 6+.

Katz, Bernard and Jonathan. *Black Woman: A Fictionalized Biography of Lucy Terry Prince.* Pantheon, 1973. $5.97. A moving and detailed account of an intelligent and courageous Black woman struggling to make a life for herself and her family in eighteenth-century Massachusetts. Grades 6+.

Lawrence, Jacob. *Harriet and the Promised Land.* Simon & Schuster, 1968. $6.73. A stunning picture book; poetic and moving account of the travels of Harriet Tubman and the Underground Railroad. Grades K-6.

Leighton, Margaret. *Cleopatra: Sister Of the Moon.* Farrar Straus, 1969. $3.95. An unromanticized look at the woman and her times. Grades 6+.

Levenson, Dorothy. *Women Of the West.* Watts, 1973. $3.90. Realistic and readable accounts of the hardships of American women of many races and backgrounds. Grades 4-7.

Longsworth, Polly. *Emily Dickinson: Her Letter To the World.* Crowell, 1965. $3.95. *I, Charlotte Forten, Black and Free.* Crowell, 1970. $4.95. Two lively biographies of very different, but equally fascinating, subjects. Grades 5+.

Mann, Peggy. *Golda: The Life Of Israel's Prime Minister.* Coward, McCann, 1971. $6.95. This biography of a great contemporary woman was recommended by *MS* 10/73. Grades 5-8.

Meigs, Corneila. *Invincible Louisa.* Little, Brown, 1968. A Newbery Award winner and still a "good read," this is the story of nineteenth-century American writer, Louisa May Alcott. Grades 5+.

Mossiker, Frances. *More Than a Queen: The Story Of Josephine Bonaparte.* Knopf, 1971. $5.99. A sympathetic and entertaining account of Napoleon's first love. Grades 6+.

Neilson, Frances and Winthrop. *Seven Women: Great Painters.* Chilton, 1969. $8.50. One of the few juvenile biographies (or art history books) about great women artists. Grades 5+.

Petry, Ann. *Harriet Tubman: Conductor On the Underground Railroad.* Crowell, 1955. $3.95. Grades 6+.

Ross, Nancy. *Heroines Of the Early West.* Random House, 1960. $4.39. Biographies of several Native American and white women. Grades 6+.

Sabin, Francene. *Women Who Win.* Random House, 1975. $3.95. One of the several recent adequate biographies of female athletes, this includes both professional and amateur players. Illustrated with photographs. Grades 5+.

Stoddard, Hope. *Famous American Women.* Crowell, 1970. $7.50. This collective biography may serve as a reference aid to students and teachers. Grades 5+.

Taylor, Kathryn. *Generations Of Denial.* Times Change Press: 62 W. 14th Street, New York, NY 10011, 1971. $1.35. Seventy-five brief biographical sketches of women in many times and places. A handy little book. Grades 5+.

Yates, Elizabeth. *Prudence Crandall: Woman Of Courage.* Dutton, 1955. $4.50. The story of a white woman who was persecuted for opening a school for Black children in the 18th Century. Grades 6+.

2. Aspirations Unlimited!

Very early in life children decide that men are doctors, women are nurses; men are pilots, women are stewardesses; men are principals, women are teachers, and so on. Not only do they incorporate these observations, they steadfastly defend and preserve them. Woe to the boy who wants to be a ballet dancer and to the girl who announces that she will be a "fire lady" when she grows up! Even the land of make believe cannot allow such strange ambitions.

The following is a bibliography in two parts. The first Part is a list of career guidance books which do not limit career choices according to sex. These non-fiction titles span all age levels and can be used for discussion, display, and reference. Additional books on men and women in untraditional careers can be found in the subject bibliography, "Biographies Of Equality." Other materials on this subject can be found in Part Two, Chapter X under pamphlets, films, records, and toys. The second part is a list of fiction titles featuring girls who aspire to untraditional careers. (Women in traditionally male occupations can be found in the section, "My Mother the Mop.")

Non-Fiction Career Titles

Children's Dictionary Of Occupations. By William E. Hopke. Illustrated by Len Epstein. Available through Learn Me: 642 Grand Ave., St. Paul, Minnesota 55105. $5.00. Women and men of various races are shown in over 300 untraditional jobs. Ages 3-7.

An Early Career Book. Series. Lerner Publications. Minneapolis, Minnesota. $3.95 each. Approximately 24 books describing various jobs in different services and industries make up this easy-to-read series. The uniform format for each title is as follows: 1) a one-page introduction; 2) about 15 one-page job descriptions on the left hand side with an accompanying full-page color photograph of a person working at that job on the right side; 3) a list of the jobs covered in that title; 4) a form letter, e.g. from a banker, inviting children to consider banking. The areas of employment include education, Postal Service, conservation, agriculture, etc. The job descriptions are non-sexist. "He" and "she" are both used throughout and titles such as "salesperson" and "mail carrier," replace "salesman" and "postman." The photographs depict a fair number of women and minority men at work, but there are still too few minority women shown in well paying jobs. The titles are geared for readers in grades 2-3 but can easily be used by younger children. More than describing a job, the books give an overview of an industry or service. Functional rather than inspirational, the books are a realistic picture of the job market today. Grades 2-4.

Finding Out about Jobs: TV Reporting. By Jeanne and Robert Bendick. Parents Magazine Press, 1976. $4.96.
A good introduction to TV news. Various types of reporters are discussed, e.g. "anchorperson," "weather person," investigative reporters. Exercises allow the child to play-act the role. At the end of the book instructions are given on how to put on your own news show. Recommended for its clarity and vitality. The illustrations are non-sexist but a bit crude with Blacks having colored-in faces. On the whole, the title makes for an excellent class project. Grades 4-6.

The Making Of a Woman Cop. By Mary Ellen Abrecht. Morrow, 1976. $8.95. Serving as a history of women officers in the Washington, D.C. police force, as well as containing informative career information, this is one officer's perspective on the improved status of female cops. Young Adult/Adult.

Enterprising Women: Their Contributions To the American Economy, 1776-1976. By Caroline Bird. Norton, 1976. $8.95. Sponsored by the Business and Professional Women's Foundation, this title describes the lives of a variety of successful businesswomen (some better known than others) and their historical effect on sex role attitudes and society. Young Adult/Adult.

A Man Is and *A Woman Is.* By Elizabeth Pellett and others. Aardvark Media: 1200 Mt. Diablo, Walnut Creek, CA 94596. $3.33 each. Two books which show men and women from many cultural backgrounds in the same occupations, e.g. a jockey, a dancer. Told simply and with color photographs. Grades 2-4.

Ms. Attorney and *Ms. M.D.* By D.X. Fenton. Westminster Press, 1974. $5.50 each. Two career titles which give detailed information about these professions as well as relevant academic and professional addresses. Grades 7-12.

Saturday's Child. By Suzanne Seed. J. Philip O'Hara, 1973. $6.95. A variety of trade and professional jobs in nontraditional careers are informally discussed by women active in those jobs. Accompanied by full-page black and white photographs of each woman interviewed. Grades 4+.

Vocations In Trades Series. By Arthur Liebers. Lothrop, 1970. $5.50 each. *You Can Be a Carpenter; You Can Be a Plumber; You Can Be a Machinist; You Can Be an Electrician; You Can Be a Mechanic; You Can Be a Professional Driver.* Lots of well organized information, written in an easy, readable style and with many clear black and white photographs. Information in each title includes: job descriptions; duties; salaries; training needed; relevant agencies for more information; and even some sample civil service test questions. Excellently done and purposely non-sexist/non-racist. (It is too bad that in Liebers's title, *You Can Be a Plumber,* he included without comment a woman plumber's statement that she saw an especially good place for women in the kitchen and bathroom speciality.) Grades 5-10.

What Can She Be? Series. By Esther and Gloria Goldreich. Lothrop, 1970. $4.75 each. Eight titles so far in this fine series, which uses clear black and white photographs of women working in untraditional careers: Architect, Lawyer, Musician, Geologist, Dairy Farmer, Veterinarian, Newscaster, and Police Officer. Good photographs and straightforward texts makes this a leading career series for today's elementary school student. Grades 1-5. (See Nos. 442-446 for more information.)

Why Would a Girl Go Into Medicine? By Margaret Campbell, M.D. Feminist Press, 1973. $3.50. A guide to medical schools and to the problems of sexism and health care prevalent in the profession. The author has since revealed her real name, Dr. Mary Howell, and the book's political consciousness is high despite the title. Adult.

Women At Work: A Photographic Documentary. By Betty Meds-
ger. Sheed and Ward, 1975. $7.95. Many large and excellent
photographs of women in almost every imaginable kind of
craft, trade, and profession. Young Adult/Adult.

Women At Work Series. By Beverly Allinson and Judith Lawrence. c/o D.C. Heath: 100 Adelaide St. W., Toronto, Ontario,
Canada. $1.50. Third Graders: *Myra Builds a House; Ellie
Sells Fish; Mary Makes Shapes* (sculptor); *Doctor Mary's Animals* (vet.) Fourth Graders: *Ready For Take-off* (pilot); *Open
Wide* (dentist); *Take One* (TV producer); *Let's Take A Vote*
(school board member). Half the titles have color photos and all
show children interacting with the women workers. Recommended in *Booklegger* 11/75.

Working Women and Their Organizations: 150 Years Of Struggle
By Joyce Maupin. Union WAGE Educational Committee: P.O.
Box 462 Berkeley, CA 94701. Written by a trade unionist, this
history of organizations includes a good bibliography. Adult.

The following books, discussed elsewhere, are also relevant to
the topic:

I Want To Be. By Dexter and Patricia Oliver. See No. 503.
Law and the New Woman. By Mary McHugh. See No. 489.
Other Choices For Becoming a Woman. By Joyce Mitchell. See
No. 498.
Women In Television. By Anita Klever. See No. 475.

Fiction: When I Grow Up

The Dragon and the Doctor. By Barbara Danish. Illustrated by
author. Feminist Press, 1971. $1.25. A little girl doctor heals
the tail of an ailing dragon. Ages 4-8.

Dreams Of Victory. By Ellen Conford. Little Brown, 1973. $5.95.
A girl named Victory imagines herself as all sorts of fascinating people, among them astronaut, spy, and President. Grades
4-8.

Girls Can Be Anything. By Norma Klein. Illustrated by Roy Doty.
Dutton, 1973. $5.50. The young protagonist in this story
refuses to take the back seat in any make-believe career play.
She ends up job-sharing the Presidency with her young male
friend. Grades K-3.

Jellybeans For Breakfast. By Miriam Young. Illustrated by Beverly Komoda. Parents Magazine Press, 1968. $4.95. Two
adventurous little girls have a ball imagining themselves as
explorers and astronauts. Ages 4-7.

Matilda Investigates. By Mary Anderson. Atheneum, 1973. $5.50. Young Mattie aspires to become the greatest woman detective. Grades 4-6.

Quiet On Account Of Dinosaur. Illustrated by Seymour Fleishman. Morrow, 1964. $4.59. A childhood love for dinosaurs and a humorous experience with a most sensitive one, leads a little girl to a smashing career as a top scientist. Ages 4-8.

Two Piano Tuners. By M.B. Goffstein. Illustrated by author. Farrar Straus, 1970. $3.50. Debbie wants to be a piano tuner, like grandfather, but he wants grander things for her. Ages 5-9.

What I Want To Be When I Grow Up. By Carol Burnett and George Mendoza. Photographs by Sheldon Seeuvda. Simon and Schuster, 1975. $3.95. In her own comic fashion, Carol Burnett poses in a multitude of occupational settings. Full-paged color photographs and a bare text make this a poster collection in book form.

Zanballer. By R.R. Knudson. Delacorte, 1972. $5.95. How hard can it be for a girl to have football practice substituted for home economics at her local school? (It's not easy.) Grades 5-9.

The following books, discussed elsewhere, are also relevant to the topic:

Boys and Girls, Girls and Boys. By Eve Merriam. See "Eve Merriam-Bravo!"

Firegirl. By Gibson Rich. See "Alternative Presses" page 45.

Shoeshine Girl. By Clyde Robert Bulla. See No. 257.

Touchmark. By Mildren Lawrence. See No. 325.

CHAPTER IV

MATERIALS INSPIRED BY THE WOMEN'S MOVEMENT

1. Two Novels About The Women's Movement: A Feminist's Critique

The Manifesto and Me — Meg. By Bobbi Katz. Watts, 1974. "Sixth-grader Meg is unprepared for the events that follow her decision to organize a consciousness-raising group to learn more about the principles of women's liberation." Poor: Kirkus 8/1/74; Good: SLJ 11/74. Grades 4+.

That Crazy April. By Lila Perl. Seabury Press, 1974. "A month of crazy and often upsetting events, including a hapless fashion show, causes an eleven-year-old to question her own outlook and role as a girl." Fair: Kirkus 4/1/74; Starred: SLJ 5/74. Grades 4-8.

Books are being written, at last, about the effects of active feminism on girls and women and the people close to them. Just as no one can speak for every reader, no one feminist can represent the women's movement. *But* there are a few basic attentions to history and psychology most of us expect in a novel lauding women's liberation.

You will not find them in Bobbi Katz's book, which begins "Mostly Its A Better deal if you get to be born a boy. That's why I'm a Women's Libber." (p. 1). Shudder. I don't know a feminist who does not cringe upon hearing herself described as a "libber." Many of us spend hours in high school social studies classes explaining why the term is so derogatory. Katz constantly calls the movement "Women's Lib," a term only second in disfavor with serious feminists.

We also spend needless time convincing people that the bra burning story which caused a greater shock than the burning of Joan of Arc was created out of whole nylon-spandex by a male reporter at a Miss America contest. Ms. Katz simply states that "what the real Women's Libbers did was burn their bras," (p. 50) and her characters accept that as truth.

One of her major characters, Abigail Witherspoon, is so unbelievable, she's loony. Miss Witherspoon, presented at first as a cantankerous, ancient county school superintendent, joins Meg's consciousness-raising group uninvited as an "adult advisor." This shows as much sensitivity as a male joining a women's group as an executive director. "Abby" seems to flip her lid soon after the meeting is called to order. Abby suggests, plans, and officiates at the public demonstration to burn (a good idea) the girls' Taffey Teen (shades of Barbie) dolls. She later ends up in jail as a martyr for the cause. Really! Wouldn't she have been more effective in her role as superintendent, directing the schools under her to provide an equal education? Many of the girls complain of the terrible lack of athletic facilities for them in school. Certainly Miss Witherspoon could have effected a change! Instant feminism does not happen in books or in real life. I'm afraid this book was written by someone as unconcerned about the real women's movement as she was about her own plotline.

On the other hand, *That Crazy April* by Lila Perl is a pleasant surprise. It concerns a mother who is an active feminist, an easy going father, and 11-year-old Cress, a bit too short and chubby for her own taste. I recommend this book to all mothers (and their kids, of course) active in the daily organization struggle for women's rights.

This work asks questions we all need to think about: how our beliefs in flexible roles can suddenly turn rigid when it comes to our daughters' traditional interests in baking and dressing up; how our daughters feel when we want to use them as subjects for school discrimination cases; how a decision to take back our original last name can make our offspring a laughing matter.

Perl's language matches her mood. Feminists are "feminists." There are no far out exaggerations of types, such as Katz's Sam (Samantha) who loves sports but hates boys so much her announcement poster reads "Do you want to murder boys?"

The two books provide an interesting contrast. Perl's writing is a bit superior, though both stories have amusing scenes and bright moments. Buy the book by Perl for yourself or someone's youngster. ($5.95). If your library does not purchase Katz's work ($4.95) — maybe it's just as well.

January, 1975

2. Alternative Presses

In the past few years many small alternative presses have appeared. Several of these are run by women, for the purpose of producing non-sexist, non-racist reading material for children and adults. Vast profits are not their major concern; they are more interested in providing inexpensive titles, and publishing experience and leadership roles for women.

The books sometimes look amateurish when compared to the writing, illustrating, and production techniques of the major trade companies. Operating on a shoestring, these small publishers cannot attract highly paid writers and artists. And yet, many of the books are wonderful. Their stories build feminine egos (which come in all colors) and tell a good tale at the same time.

Libraries will benefit from balancing their collections with the best books from small, developing publishing houses. These books make great gifts, teaching aids, and fine examples of what dedicated and talented women can do — even with few funds.

I had expected to list only those books, published in the last year, that I liked best. Unfortunately, hardly *any* of these small press books are available at libraries or bookstores. I decided to select the best of the past *three* years, which I found at A Women's Bookshop in Palo Alto. If you want to order, you will find publishers' and distributors' addresses beginning in Part Four.

Bubbles. Eloise Greenfield. Illustrated by E. Marlow. Drum & Spear Press, 1972. $2.50. A young Black boy is overjoyed with the knowledge that he knows how to read. Beautifully illustrated and well written. Highly recommended. Ages 5-8.

Carlotta and the Scientist. Patricia Lenthall. Lollipop Power, 1973. $2.00. The story of how Carlotta, the adventurous and curious penguin, saves an injured woman scientist trapped on the ice. A good discussion starter on the themes of motherhood and females in science. Ages 4-8.

Children of the Dragon: A Story of the People of Vietnam. People's Press, 1974. $1.75. A North Vietnamese boy from the city is evacuated to his country cousin's home in order to escape the bombings. Full-page color illustrations and a simple, straightforward text make this a good supplement to social studies lessons. Ages 6-10.

Children of Vietnam. Indochina Resource Center. 75¢. A collection of writings by Vietnamese children about daily life in a war torn land. Doubles as a coloring book and a lesson in humanitarianism. This title is a natural partner for Jacob Zim's *My Shalom, My Peace.* See No. 533. Ages 6+.

Exactly Like Me. Lynn Phillips. Lollipop Power, 1972. $1.75. This brief poem, told with humorous sketches, finds a girl declaring her individuality and demanding freedom from traditional sex roles. Exhilarating bibliotherapy if you dare use at your preschool storytime. Ages 4-7.

A Family Grows In Different Ways. Canadian Women's Educational Press, 1974. $1.25. The story of adoption is told simply in this brief problem-solving story. Ages 4-7.

Firegirl. Gibson Rich. Illustrated by Charlotte P. Farley. Feminist Press, 1972. $3.00. Brenda's ambition is to be a fire fighter, and in this super-girl tale she gets her chance. The book also includes multi-racial officers. Although the text is too long and the plot pretty implausible, it will certainly expand the dreams of lots of little Brendas. Ages 5-8.

Fresh Fish and Chips. Jan Andrews and Linda Donnelly. Canadian Women's Educational Press, 1973. $3.25. $1.75. A mother goes fishing for her family's dinner and returns with an octopus, snail, hermit crab, whale, and much more. The humorous verse is accompanied by appealing illustrations, and the book (in paperback) doubles nicely as a unique, non-sexist coloring book. Ages 4-10.

I'm Like Me. Siv Widerberg. Illustrated by Claes Backstrom. Feminist Press, 1973. $1.95. "For people who want to grow up equal" is the collection of brief, poignant poems translated from the Swedish. Ages 9-12.

Jackie. Luevester Lewis. Illustrated by Cheryl Jolly. Third World Press, 1970. $1.00. Jackie is the new kid on the block and if her male pals want to assume she's a boy because she wears pants and plays ball, that's O.K. with her. When she appears in a dress for the first day of school, her friends won't be the only ones surprised. Brief, funny, and a good discussion starter Ages 5-9.

Jo, Flo, and Yolanda. Carol De Poix. Lollipop Power, 1973. $1.75. Triplet girls tell how they are alike and how they are individuals in this brief tale which also features a nurturing older brother. A good filler for pre-school storytime. Ages 4-8.

The Magic Hat. Kim Chapman. Lollipop Power, 1973. $2.00. A humorous fantasy about how toys came to be divided into "girls' toys" and "boys' toys." Although the drawings are crude, the story will hold the interest and amuse children old enough to appreciate the irony. Ages 5-10.

Martin's Father. Margrit Eichler. Lollipop Power, 1971. $1.75. A simple tale showing a father and young son spending a typical day together. Add this to your short list of books appreciated by three-year-old children. Ages 3-6.

Minoo's Family. Canadian Women's Education Press, 1974. $1.24. A brief and understated story about a divorce in a family with young children. This tale is excellent bibliotherapy. Ages 4-8.

Mother is a Pitcher. Maxine Kahn. Illustrated by Gwynne Slade. All of Us, Inc., 1974. $1.25. A book that always raises cheers from the girls in my storytelling audiences. A ten-year-old describes an exciting ball game between the team her mother (Fast Fanny the Pitcher) plays on and the other women's team. Illustrations are not as good as text but worth the purchase price and pleasure it creates. Ages 6-10.

Nothing But a Dog. Bobbi Katz. Illustrated by Esther Gilman. Feminist Press, 1972. $2.25. A quiet and poetic tale about a girl's longing for a dog. The lovely black and grey line drawings enhance the text and make it a very special book indeed. Ages 5-8.

The Travels of Ms. Beaver. Rosemary Allison and Ann Powell. Canadian Women's Educational Press, 1973. $1.25. An adventurous beaver out to seek her fortune builds a lake in the middle of a city park and brings joy to city children. Although the book smacks of feminism, take away the Ms., the female sex of the beaver, wrap it in a major trade book package, and you have a typical animal story. Ages 4-8.

Yolanda's Hike/ La Aventura de Lolanda. Tomas Gaspar. Illustrated by Sue Brown. New Seed Press, 1974. 75¢. A bilingual text in Spanish and English about a young Mexican-American girl and her friends' exciting hike to a neighborhood hill. One could count the anti-sexist, bilingual picture books combining a girl character, interesting story, and attractive illustrations on the first finger of one hand. This is it, and at 75¢ it's the best bargain in town. Ages 5-8.

Youth Liberation: News, Politics, and Survival Information Put Together By Youth Liberation of Ann Arbor. Times Change Press, 1972. $1.35. Written by teenagers who have run away from home, the book describes their disgust with society's oppressve, racist attitudes. Other adolescents will enjoy reading the opinions of their peers in this brutally honest book. Ages 12+.

3. Fun With Books . . .
Or Turning Fisher-Price People
Into Living Feminists

The day I registered my daughter, Jennifer, for public kindergarten, was the day she began her first Women Studies lesson. Figures like George Washington and Abraham Lincoln loomed large on her horizon, and I decided to put giants like Harriet Tubman and Jane Addams into similar dimensions in the same landscape. Here are two of my tried and true ideas.

All children love to build things with blocks. After I read Jennifer a book about Harriet Tubman, we built an Underground Railroad with blocks and toy furniture. We transformed a white Fisher-Price Play Person into a Black woman and led Ms. Tubman and her friends from one house to another. This is a great way to help the young child to grasp the concept of the Underground Railroad, and to understand what must have been the feelings of the escaping slaves. Several books about Harriet Tubman have been written for the kindergarten-to-third grade child. We read *Harriet and the Promised Land* by Jacob Lawrence (Windmill, 1968), a poetic and stunningly illustrated book, and *Runaway Slave* by Ann McGovern (Scholastic, 1965), which is factual and well-written.

Another of my ideas was for us to build Jane Addams's Hull House together. Jennifer pretended she was Jane and invited the whole neighborhood to come in for a good hot meal on a cold, snowy day. (A few pieces of cotton provide enough of a snowstorm to satisfy any child!) By the time we finished that day, Jennifer adored Jane Addams, and Hull House was created and recreated for many an afternoon afterward. Before we started to build, we read *Jane Addams* by Gail Keller (Crowell, 1971) an easy-to read or easy-listen-to biography. NOTE: For more information on the Crowell biography series, see p. 34.

Some fruits of our labor:

Jane Addams
(Founder of Hull House)

Once there was a woman named Jane,
That Jane - her last name was Jane Addams,
That Jane Addams was nice,
She helped the poor people.
When her father died,
And her mother died,
She grew up.
Then she really helped the poor people.
Then she died.

Fanny Lou Hamer
(Civil Rights Activist)

Fany Lou Hamer was very nice,
She voted for other people,
She liked all the people,
She helped everyone, of course;
Not one person did not vote,
All the people love Fanny Lou Hamer.

— Jennifer Davis, age 4

PART TWO

REVIEWS

CHAPTER V

PICTURE BOOKS

PICTURE BOOKS

1. Aardema, Verna. *Why Mosquitoes Buzz in People's Ears.* Il. Leo and Diane Dillon. Dial, 1975. $6.95. A very beautiful picture book based on an African folk tale. Mosquito causes a chain of disastrous events leading to endless night when Iguana refuses to hear her silly stories. Of the eight animals in this gloriously illustrated story, the three females are the mosquito, a scared rabbit, and a mother owl. As usual the more active, powerful creatures are male. Winner of the 1976 Caldecott Award. Recommended. Ages 4 and up.

2. Adoff, Arnold. *Big Sister Tells Me That I'm Black.* Il. Lorenzo Lynch. Holt, 1976. $4.95. Big sister is an inspiration to her young Black brother who learns from her that he and she are Black and beautiful, bright, strong, proud, and equal - in sex and color. The book has more political merit than literary charm. The illustrations do not enhance the work. They have a 1950's textbook appearance. Not one of Mr. Adoff's usual gems. Ages 5-10.

3. Adoff, Arnold. *Make a Circle Keep Us In.* Il. Ronald Himler. Delacorte, 1975. $4.95. Brief poems and pleasant line drawings reflect the daily life of a young family. Especially pleasing are the pudgy, nurturing father and the spunky little girl. A sample verse: "toes da da stuffs them into socks like keys in locks they turn they turn." Ages 4-8.

4. Allen, Jeffrey. *Mary Alice, Operator Number Nine.* Il. James Marshall. Little Brown, 1975. $5.95. Mary Alice does her job of telling the time at the telephone company so well that when she becomes ill none of her acquaintances can take her place. Very clever and humorously drawn. Recommended for ages 4-8.

5. Baldwin, Anne. *Jenny's Revenge*. Il. Emily McCully. Four Winds, 1974. $4.95. Jenny gives her sitter a difficult time because she resents her divorced mother's employment. Warning: reviews note that mother is working only for economic reasons. Fair: Kirkus 2/1/74; Poor: *SLJ* 4/74.

6. Bang, Betsy. *The Old Woman and the Red Pumpkin: a Bengali Folk Tale*. Il. Molly Bang. Macmillan, 1975. $6.95. A skinny old woman on her way to her daughter's house tricks three hungry animals out of eating her. Later, fat as can be and on her way home, she fools them again. A simple, appealing tale with stunning, detailed illustrations. Ages 4-8.

7. Barton, Byron. *Hester*. Il. by author. Greenwillow/Morrow, 1975. $6.95. Simple tale of Hester (an alligator) who goes trick-or-treating to a witch's house and has an unexpected ride on a broom. The childlike pictures are bright, simple, and humorous. Although the setting is urban, mother alligator, wearing only a brief apron, is still in the kitchen baking pies. I'm wondering who hung up all the party decorations for Hester's Halloween feast. Ages 2-6.

8. Bate, Lucy. *Little Rabbit's Loose Tooth*. Il. Diane De Groat. Crown, 1975. $5.95. Rabbit loses her first tooth and discovers "a window in my mouth," and a suspicion that there really is no Tooth Fairy. Charming illustrations full of such details as a book on the shelf titled "Raising Little Rabbits" and a throw rug bearing the design of a huge carrot. Mother practices a Mozart rune on her flute, while Little Rabbit, in overalls and tennis shoes, finds endless uses for her tooth. Warm and cozy. Ages 4-7.

9. Baylor, Byrd. *Everybody Needs a Rock*. Il. Peter Parnall. Scribner's, 1974. $5.95. Black, brown, and gold line drawings reveal more with each new glance, in this story of a girl's pleasant search for her own special rock. A very special nature book. Ages 4-9.

10. Bernstein, Margery and Janet Kobrin. *The First Morning: An African Myth*. Il. Enid Warner Romanek. Scribner's, 1976. $5.95. Spider, Mouse, and Fly agree to convince the Sky King to give the dismal earth some light. Through wit and cunning they trick the evil King into

granting their desire. An appealing story with dramatic black and white illustrations, a humorous surprise ending, and a non-sexist tone (two of the animal protagonists are females). Recommended for ages 4-10.

11. Berson, Harold. *I'm Bored, Ma!* Il. by author. Crown, 1976. $4.95. One difficult day Steve Rabbit hates his friends and toys, and throws a favorite yellow airplane into the trash. Later, when buddy Rat Pack salvages the toy (finders keepers), an angry Steve revitalizes his imagination and runs home for his fire engine. (Rat's house is in flames.) Mother Rabbit's picture book image is improving. She is understanding, yet plays it cool with her bunny. Shown reading the paper and dressed in a caftan and head scarf, she is a positive character. Steve is reminiscent of Sendak's stubborn Pierre. Ages 4-7.

12. Blaine, Marge. *The Terrible Thing That Happened At Our House.* Il. John Wallner. Parents, 1975. $4.95. When "a real" mother returns to work, the neat and secure world of a girl and her younger brother collapses. The book is written from a child's viewpoint, and life certainly *does* become more hectic when both parents leave for the office at 8 a.m. I believe the object (among other things) was to show that compromise and changing lifestyles are necessary - perhaps unfortunately so to the kids, but the book made my five year old say, "Gee, I hope you *never* go back to the library!" The surrealistic illustrations, showing the house and children falling apart, reinforce the scary image of an employed mom and dad. Ages 5-8.

13. Blood, Charles L. and Martin Link. *The Goat In the Rug: By Geraldine.* Il. Nancy Winslow Parker. Parents', 1976. $5.50. Glenmae and her friend, Geraldine, work hard to make an authentic Navajo rug. The wool ("It's called mohair, really") is provided by Geraldine, a goat; the skill provided by the strong and talented hands of Glenmae, a real Navajo weaver who lived in the Navajo Nation at Window-Rock, Arizona. Geraldine explains the rug making process with humor, and Ms. Parker provides colorful, clear illustrations. I would have liked, however, to see more character in Glenmae's cartoonish face. The authors are experts in Navajo culture; an appealing, useful work. Ages 5-8.

14. Boccaccio, Shirley. *Penelope and the Earth.* Il. by author. Joyful World, 1975. $2.95. When the raccoon sisters come to the city seeking Penelope's help to stop a disastrous dam project, the super-girl and her younger brother fly their plane into the wilderness and convince the chief engineer to halt his project. The longish poem is written in rhyming couplets, becoming a little tiring to read. The illustrations are a huge improvement over Boccaccio's earlier "Penelope" titles. Photographs of the real, and very appealing, Penelope and Peter, are pasted onto the black and white drawn background. It's nice to read a tale with a conservation plea and a super-girl heroine! Recommended. Ages 6-10.

15. Bonzon, Paul Jacques. *The Runaway Flying Horse.* Il. William Pene Du Bois. Parents, 1976. $5.50. A pretty little carousel horse becomes bored with his easy, routine life and decided to live with real horses. His adventures are much less rewarding than expected, and the end of the tale finds him contented, back on the job. The illustrations are beautiful and fanciful. Ages 4-8.

16. Bornstein, Ruth. *Little Gorilla.* Il. by author. Seabury, 1976. $6.95. Little Gorilla quite literally has the spotlight in this picture book which glows with beautiful iridescent jungle scenes in reds and greens. The baby gorilla is someone special to all the other animals and remains so even when he grows older and bigger. A nice title for all youngsters, but especially good for 3 to 5-year-olds with new baby siblings who tend to steal spotlights.

17. Bram, Elizabeth. *The Door In the Tree.* Il. by author. Greenwillow/Morrow, 1976. $4.95. A pretty and stylized fantasy about a girl named Lisa who has an adventure. Bright gold, black, and white drawings with bold outline and childlike charm steal the show from the uninspiring story line. A pleasant pastime for the younger picture book set. Ages 2-6.

18. Brandenberg, Franz. *No School Today!* Il. Aliki. Macmillan, 1975. $6.95. Edward and Elizabeth, brother and sister cats, arrive early at school one day and mistakenly assume they've been given a holiday. The book's main attraction are the colorful and clever cat illustrations. Youngsters can read by themselves this simple, rather mediocre tale, which is saved by the attractive drawings. Ages 4-7.

19. Breinburg, Petronella. *Shawn's Red Bike.* Il. Errol Lloyd. Crowell, 1975. $6.95. A young Black boy earns money for a shiny red bike by helping relatives and friends with chores. Told in simple sentences and brightly colored childlike illustrations. Certainly not great literature, but a happy slice of life for young listeners. Ages 4-6.

20. Brown, Margaret W. *The Steamroller.* Il. Evaline Ness. Walker, 1974. $5.95. Get off the road everyone! Here comes Daisy in her great big Christmas gift, a real steamroller. Brava! Well told, well drawn, and just the kind of "Girl Loves Machine" book we have been waiting for. A fantasy for all seasons. Ages 4-8.

21. Byars, Betsy. *The Lace Snail.* Il. by author. Viking, 1975. $4.95. A beautiful book about a snail who suddenly begins to leave a trail of delicate lace behind her. There are great demands for her services and she is very busy creating lace garments for the river animals. The interaction between the snail and her customers is lively and clever. The forest-green and black animals and delicate white lace, are unique and lovely. Even the print, in script and italic, is just right for this special story. The snail, is an extraordinary creature, and when her powers cease as suddenly as they began, she nonchalantly slips onto the river bank to rest. Ages 4-8.

22. Calhoun, Mary. *Euphonia and the Flood.* Il. Simms Taback. Parents, 1976. $5.50. "If a thing is worth doing, it's worth doing well," Euphonia, a spunky old woman in old-fashioned garb, always says. And she successfully saves a variety of animals from a flood with the help of a pig, a broom, and a boat named Mary Anne. Fun to read and fun to look at with everything *and* the kitchen sink floating down the rushing creek with Mary Anne. Ages 4-8.

23. Carle, Eric. *The Mixed-Up Chameleon.* Il. by author. Crowell, 1976. $6.95. A chameleon, tired of merely changing colors, happens upon a zoo and decides to alter its *shape* as well. The chameleon takes on the characteristics and colors of nine animals before it realizes that it is no longer adept at catching a fly dinner. But before our friend returns to its original condition, we witness some funny, large, colorful crayon drawings sowing the metamorphoses of the amazing creature. Recommended. Ages 3-8.

24. Charlip, Remy and Lillian Moore. *Hooray For Me!* Il. Vera Williams. Parents, 1975. $4.95. A bright, happy book illustrated in water colors about relationships of all kinds: "I'm my cousin's cousin; I'm my shadow's body." A simple celebration of self for ages 2-6.

25. Charlip, Remy and Jerry Joyner. *Thirteen.* Il. by authors. Parents, 1975. $4.95. Thirteen pictures, each on a double page, evolve so that, for example, as we turn the pages we watch the fate of a ship in a bottle of green sea water. Unique and entertaining, this book can be shared by adult and child together. Children will enjoy fantasizing about the wordless development of each scene. People 5+.

26. Chorao, Kay. *Ida Makes a Movie.* Il. by author. Seabury, 1974. $5.95. Ida, a spunky girl-cat, decides to make a home movie and enter it in the Children's Film-Making Contest. After the judges misinterpret her winning film as an anti-war protest, she tells the truth at the ceremony, and risks losing her prize - an ugly statue. Well drawn, of course, by the talented artist. The plot rambles a bit but should hold the attention of children. Ages 5-9.

27. — *A Magic Eye For Ida.* Il. by author. Seabury, 1973. $5.50. Ida is feeling rejected by her artist-mother, movie-crazed brother, and snobish doll-loving friends. (Dad has left years ago.) Feeling she has no special purpose in life, she runs away from home and meets a fortuneteller who convinces Ida that her gift of rhyming makes her very special indeed. A good story with humorous black and white line drawings. Ages 4-8.

28. — *Ralph and the Queen's Bathtub.* Il. by author. Farrar Straus, 1974. $4.95. Poor Ralph! He hates playing football with the boys, older brother won't let him join his club, and dad insists he stop hanging around mom and baby brother. So Ralph ventures into the house of an ex-horror film star who is as nutty as Frankenstein's fruit cake. He finally escapes her clutches (and reels of her old movies) and becomes a hero to himself, one who still dislikes football. Ages 5-9.

29. Clifton, Lucille. *Everett Anderson's Friend.* Il. Ann Grifalconi. Holt, 1976. $5.95. A poem for young children with more plot than previous Everett stories. Everett, a young

Black boy, is disappointed that the new tenants in 13A are "a family of shes." One of the shes is Maria "who can win at ball" but nonetheless "girls who can run are just no fun/thinks Everett Anderson." Why not, thinks the reviewer? I can understand why the stereotyped, prim little female would be no pal for an active boy, but not even a winner like Maria? Winner - ah . . . ha! There's the rub. Perhaps it is not tolerable for a boy to be defeated by a girl. Everett decides that Maria is o.k. after spending an afternoon in her apartment, and suddenly there is room for her in the male gang. Nicely written and attractively illustrated, the book's flaw is the assumption that a girl must prove herself to be exceptional before she can be friends with the boys. Ages 4-8.

30. — *Everett Anderson's Year.* Il. Anne Grifalconi. Holt, 1974. $4.95. A calendar of events in the life of a seven-year-old Black child. A gentle book of poems with attractive illustrations. Ages 4-7.

31. — *Good, Says Jerome.* Il. Stephanie Douglas. Dutton, 1973. $5.95. Stunning collage illustrations and a lyrical text tell how a young Black boy worries about a new move and new teachers, but his older sister calms his fears. A good choice for preschool story hour. Ages 4-7.

32. — *My Brother Fine With Me.* Il. Moneta Barnett. Holt, 1976. $5.50. Clifton's words about 8-year-old Johnetta's younger brother, Baggy, who decides to run away from home and become a warrior, feel smooth on the tongue and fall soft on the ear. At first, Johnetta is glad to see him go, but soon she starts to worry about his sleeping alone, and not having anyone to play with. And then Baggy changes his mind, too: "Seem to me, a warrior better stay home and take care of his family." Seem to me that Clifton is building up the ego of little brother at some cost to big sister. Very nicely illustrated with soft pencil sketches which enhance the gentleness of the text. Ages 4-8.

33. Conford, Ellen. *Just the Thing For Geraldine.* Il. John Larrecq. Little Brown, 1974. $4.95. A girl-possum with great juggling skill refuses to be coerced into more "ladylike" activities such as dancing and weaving. Well written and humorous, although the illustrations reflect human sex-role stereotypes in the possum family. Ages 4-7.

34. Coombs, Patricia. *Dorrie and the Amazing Elixir*. Il. by author. Lothrop, 1974. $4.50. Dorrie, the star of this girl-witch series, is undaunted in her attempt to guard her mother's magic receipe even when the evil Green Wizard turns her into a toad. Plenty of action and humor. Ages 4-8.

35. Coombs, Patricia. *Molly Mullet*. Il. by author. Lothrop, 1975. $4.75. Molly, daughter of unpleasant Mr. Mullet, destroys the town ogre and earns a knighthood. The rhyming in this prose tale becomes repetitious ("sniveling and driveling and bawling and squalling"), but the story of an adventurous child, who can't satisfy her father's longing for a son, moves well and reads well out loud. In the end, Mr. Mullet tries to teach his new son bravery by waving the defeated ogre's sword over the baby's head. "I do not think you'll ever learn," says Molly. The soft gray and brown droll illustrations match the unpretentious personality of the heroine. Ages 5+.

36. Craft, Ruth. *The Winter Bear*. Il. by Erik Blegvad. Atheneum, 1975. $5.95. Two boys and a girl walk near their country home and discover a toy bear caught in the branches of a tree. Told in simple verse and illustrated with beautiful pictures of the winter landscape in late afternoon. Once home, the delighted children repair and dress their new treasure. A nice winter tale for ages 3-7.

37. Cutler, Ivor. *Elephant Girl*. Il. Helen Oxenbury. Morrow, 1976. $4.95. After Balooky Klujpop finds Pansy in her garden, she carries him to the kitchen sink and scrubs the large creature with water, milk, orange juice and finally, "washing-up liquid." The two friends play around the house and garden, until Pansy requests that Balooky hide him again so he can finish his nap. An unpretentious, tongue-in-cheek tale with humorous white, black, and brown drawings. The 5x7½-inch size is just right for this little fantasy. Ages 3-7.

38. De Paola, Tomie. *Charlie Needs A Cloak*. Il. by author. Prentice Hall, 1974. $4.95. We watch Charlie the shepherd shear, wash, card, skin, dye, weave, cut, pin, and sew his new cloak. A humorous, brightly illustrated, and simple introduction to the techniques of cloak-making, showing a pink smocked Charlie unself-consciously

working with needle and thread. For the same theme and
a female farmer, *The Sheep Book* by C. Goodyear (Lollipop
Press, 1972). Ages 4-7.

39. De Paola, Tomie. *Michael Bird-Boy*. Il. by author. Prentice
Hall, 1975. $5.95. Michael discovers a factory where "boss
lady" is making sugar and polluting the atmosphere. A
fantasy-lesson on how bees make honey, with charm and
no sex role stereotyping. Ages 4-7.

40. De Paola, Tomie. *Strega Nona: An Old Tale Retold and Illustrated by Tomie de Paola*. Prentice Hall, 1975. $6.95.
An excellent combination of writing and illustrations.
Strega Nona, "Grandmother Witch," is the Italian village's wise woman. She has a magic pot for boiling
noodles. When a simple apprentice misuses the appli-
ance, the whole town almost drowns in pasta. Strega
Nona returns just in time and rules that the apprentice
must eat the results of his misdeed. Ages 3-10.

41. De Regniers, Beatrice Schenk (retold by). *Little Sister and
the Month Brothers*. Il. Margot Tomes, Seabury, 1976.
$8.00.
    Long ago when stepmothers and stepsisters were a
wicked lot, there was a girl named Little Sister, who hum-
med while she labored and grew prettier every day. Fear-
ing the pleasant child will attract a prince, the stepmother sends her on two impossible missions - to gather
first violets, then strawberries, in the wintry forest. The
Month Brothers come to her aid. When stepsister, trying
to find more fresh fruit, is rude to the Brothers, both she
and her mother are lost in a snowstorm. Little Sister,
free at last, marries a gentle farmer who shares life's
chores with her.
    I am a fan of Ms. Tomes, but I found her illustrations
of Little Sister disturbing. Drawn to look about 10 years
old, she hardly seems a rival to her more mature sister.
To call the flat-chested girl going off to bed with her husband a "child bride" is putting it mildly. The clever story,
however, reads smoothly and marriage to a farmer, not
a prince, is a nice touch. Grades K-4.

42. Dragonwagon, Crescent. *Strawberry Dress Escape*. Il. Lillian Hoban. Scribner's, 1975. $6.95. A hot spring day
finds Emily, a young Black girl, slowly slipping out of the

classroom for an adventurous daydream. Excellent: Kirkus 2/1/75; Fair: *SLJ* 4/75; Poor: Children's Book Review Service 3/75. Ages 5-8.

43. Dragonwagon, Crescent. *When Light Turns Into Night.* Il. Robert Parker. Harper & Row, 1975. $4.95. Ellen is a country girl who enjoys running alone, free and thoughtful, for a little while before supper time. Illustrated in muted water colors, the story of a girl comfortable in her own world makes a homey, twilight summer tale. Ages 4-8.

44. Duncan, Jane. *Brave Janet Reachfar.* Il. Mairi Hedderwick. Seabury, 1975. $6.95. The cover shows a girl standing in a country snow storm surrounded by three farm animals. And then there's the title "Brave . . . Reachfar." Don't judge a book by its cover. When Janet ventures out alone in a sudden storm, to rescue a newborn lamb, she needs rescuing herself by two farm hands. Alas, how unlike Mark Taylor's Henry, explorer of jungles and oceans, who always does the rescuing himself. Janet does not look quite so brave or reach as far in this *dull* story with attractive illustrations.

45. Ehrlich, Amy. *Zeek Silver Moon.* Il. Robert Parker. Dial, 1972. $1.75. The first five years of a little boy named Silver Moon are told in ten brief chapters accompanied by full-page paintings in Parker's fine style. Warmth, love and joy radiate from the pages and from the everyday pleasures of a nurturing young family. Ages 4-8.

46. Feelings, Muriel. *Moja Means One: Swahili Counting Book.* Il. Tom Feelings. Dial, 1971. $1.75. A lovely book introducing children to Swahili, the African language spoken by 45 million people. Each of the 10 new words is illustrated on a double page in soft charcoal tones. Presenting words and scenes of everyday country activities, the book is fine for children of all heritages. Ages 4-8.

47. Fisher, Aileen. *Once We Went on a Picnic.* Il. Tony Chen. Crowell, 1975. $6.95. A lovely book for nature lovers. In verse and bold, beautiful pictures, four children (integrated by sex and race) go on a picnic and exult in each other's company, nature's creatures, and their delicious lunch. A chart identifies the creatures and plants the four see on their walk. Ages 4-8.

48. Flory, Jane. *We'll Have a Friend For Lunch*. Il. Carolyn Croll. Houghton Mifflin, 1975. $4.95. Peaches is President of the Bird Watchers Club, a feline group that spies on two robins as they hatch and care for their young. The cat club, however, finally rejects their proposed bird dish because you "can't eat a family you know." Cat lovers will enjoy this simple tale with attractive illustrations. Ages 4-7.

49. Freeman, Lucy. *The Eleven Steps*. Il. Julie Brinckloe. Doubleday, 1975. $4.95. Illustrated in blue, black, and white drawings, this is the story of a boy who dreams he destroyed his older sister's stamp collection and wakes up the next morning bewildered and nervous about the possible reality of the dream. Mary, who is an active, energetic girl, is sorry she was rude to Jimmy, finds her collection after a dramatic search and invites her brother to a stamp club meeting. It is unusual to find a boy idolizing his older sister in picture books, and the theme of a child's confusion over the vividness of dreams is handled well. No great literary or artistic achievement but nice anyway. Ages 5-8.

50. Gackenbach, Dick. *Do You Love Me?* Il. by author. Seabury, 1976. $5.95. A lonely young farm boy wants to capture many pets - from turtles to ants - to keep him company. Upon the accidental death of a hummingbird, his older sister helps him understand "Not all creatures want you to love them." To Walter's delight, however, the puppy she brings him is obviously not one of those creatures. Traditional sex roles do not detract from this homey tale; the relationship between sister and brother is a joy to read. Ages 4-9; an easy reader for G 1-3.

51. Garrison, Christian. *Little Pieces of the West Wind*. Il. Diane Goode. Bradbury, 1975. $6.95. When a clever old farmer locks the West Wind in his cabin and tricks him into searching for his lost socks, a chain of events reduces the giant wind to "a tiny puff of breeze." How Wind manages to become his old self again makes an entertaining tale. Similar in plot to many books in which characters won't help unless they get something in return, the book is distinguished by beautiful four-color illustrations. The West Wind has a personality of his own, and children will enjoy searching the expanse of blue gossamer for his bearded face. Highly recommended. Ages 3-8.

52. Gibeault, Kathi. *Susan In the Driver's Seat*. Il. J. Ike. Western, 1974. $2.45. Mother takes her daughter, Susan, and son, Robby, to visit women holding nontraditional jobs: doctor, police officer, pilot. A good discussion starter. Ages 4-8.

53. Ginsburg, Mirra, editor and translator. *Pampalche of the Silver Teeth*. Il. Rocco Negri. Crown, 1976. $6.95. A Russian folk tale about a young woman who flees from forced marriage to an evil spirit and manages to escape the clutches of a wicked witch. She is aided by a male bear and a female fox, and is assured of safety when her sister weaves a magic ladder which falls into Pampalche's eager hands. The tale is well told, the plot is unusual, and the colorful woodcuts are very lovely. The rescuer in this tale is the sister. Highly recommended. Ages 5 and up.

54. Goffstein, M.B. *Fish For Supper*. Il. by author. Dial, 1976. $4.95. A book with the conciseness and charm of the Japanese haiku. Briefly and succinctly, the author-artist illustrates a typical day in the life of Grandmother, who goes fishing wearing a wide brim hat, baggy pants, glasses, and button earrings. Grandmother is as refreshing as an ocean breeze.Ages 3-7.

55. Greenfield, Eloise. *Me and Nessie*. Il. Moneta Barnett. Crowell, 1975. $5.50. Janell has a pretend friend, a lively super-ego named Nessie, who gives mama headaches. Nessie gives Janell's elderly aunt a chance to battle a ghost when she almost sits on Janell's invisible buddy. Janell starts school, her need for Nessie disappears and so does Nessie. The illustrator makes the two girls equally real, but since the lively story is told by Janell, this is only right. Ages 4-8.

56. — *She Come Bringing Me That Little Baby Girl*. Il. John Steptoe. Lippincott, 1974. $5.95. A Black boy learns to accept his new sister when he is given the role of protector. The book's literary and artistic quality is sound, but the social message is sexist and unacceptable. Some quotes: "I don't want to be a brother to no girl"; "It was a girl, all right,'cause her fingers were way too small"; "You know, when my sister's fingers grow some, maybe I can show her how to throw a football. If she uses both hands." Star review: *Kirkus* 9/15/74; Poor: *SLJ* 1975. Ages 4-8.

57. Haas, Irene. *The Maggie B*. Il. by author. Atheneum, 1975.
$7.95. Maggie wishes for a ship named after herself and
a pleasant crew. The next day finds her sailing the high
seas on a lovely ship with her brother James, "who was a
dear baby." A versatile child, Maggie manages to clean,
cook, paint a portrait, nurture James, tighten up the
ship during a storm, and rock the baby to sleep to the
tunes of her fiddle. The story line is simple, and the illustrations are lovely, though just bordering on Hallmark
prettiness. A cozy tale for children 3-5.

58. Hanlon, Emily. *What If a Lion Eats Me and I Fall Into a
Mudhole?* Il. Leigh Grant. Delacorte, 1975. $4.95. While
trying to convince friend Stuart that the zoo animals will
not hurt him ("The sea lion might want to bounce me in
the air like a ball!"), the little boy grows as apprehensive
as his pal. Then he remembers hot dogs, popcorn and ice-
cream. The trip is on! Delicate and humorous black and
white drawing accompanied by bright green print.
Ages 3-5.

59. Hardendorff, Jeanne B. *The Bed Just So*. Il. Lisa Weil. Four
Winds/Scholastic, 1975. $4.95. A humorously written
and illustrated little book about a tailor who is not able
to sleep at night thanks to a mysterious, bothersome, visi-
tor. The Wise Woman assures him that he is not
"witched" for neither are his feet on backwards nor his
hair growing upside down. It's a "hudgin" she declares
and recommends that the tailor provide it with its own
bed. No matter what he tries, the hudgin complains and
protests until by chance the tailor makes the right choice.

60. Hartelius, Margaret. *The Chicken's Child*. Il. by author.
Doubleday, 1975. $4.95. After Chicken keeps an alligator
egg warm and hatches the youngster, the child's insatiable appetite causes it to be banned from the farm until
it rescues Mother from the fox. An amusing, wordless
picture book about a little "girl" growing mischievous
and powerful.

61. Hayes, Geoffrey. *Bear By Himself*. Il. by author. Harper &
Row, 1976. $4.95. Charmingly illustrated in soft green,
brown, and white this is a simple but wise tale about a
small bear and his need sometimes to be by himself to
think, play, enjoy nature, "or to do nothing at all!" A de-
lightful little exercise á la Thoreau which should have a
calming effect on other little bears. Ages 4-7.

62. Hazen, Barbara. *The Gorilla Did It.* Il. Ray Cruz. Atheneum, 1974. $5.95. Gorilla, a pretend playmate, gets "his" little boy into all kinds of trouble with mother when he just won't settle down and behave. Amusing drawings enhance the entertaining tale. Ages 3-7.

63. Hazer, Nancy. *Grownups Cry Too.* Il. by author. Lollipop Power, 1973. $1.75. Stanley is a young boy who learns that people of all ages cry for many reasons: fear, happiness, pain. He learns that crying is all right, a natural release for both men and women. Soft green paper, crude but nice illustrations and the gentle text make an attractive book. Especially useful as a discussion starter. Ages 3-8.

64. Himler, Ronald. *The Girl On the Yellow Giraffe.* Il. by author. Harper & Row, 1976. $4.95. In this brief tale of a small girl's day in and around New York City, Himler compares her real world to an enchanted fairyland. She rides a yellow giraffe, the famous Fisher-Price toy. She lives in a castle (apartment house), rides in a magic box (elevator), and spends her day exploring with mother until even this adventurous princess finds the city's river "too wide to cross on a yellow giraffe." An attractive, if not memorable, package with soft black and white line drawings and simple text. Ages 3-6.

65. Hoban, Russell. *A Baby Sister For Frances.* Il. Garth Williams. Harper & Row, 1964. $1.95. When Frances finds herself with a new sibling, our little badger discovers that her songwriting talent gets her through some tough times. Ages 4-7.

66. — *Bedtime For Frances.* Il. Garth Williams. Harper & Row, 1960. $1.95. Any child who needs ideas for putting off bedtime will thrill to Frances's expertise. Ages 3-7.

67. — *Best Friends For Frances.* Il. Garth Williams. Harper & Row, 1969. $1.95. Frances sets out to show her ex-pal Albert that "No Girls Baseball" means no fun for anyone. Ages 4-8.

68. — *A Birthday For Frances.* Il. Garth Williams. Harper & Row, 1968. $1.95. Being the sister of the birthday girl is not much fun and Frances vacillates between envy and generosity. Ages 4-8.

69. — *Dinner At Alberta's*. Il. James Marshall. Crowell, 1975. $5.50. The natural combination of two talents has created a very funny and easy to read tale about Arthur Crocodile, boy of repugnant table manners, invited to dinner by sweet Alberta Saurian. Some parents might be turned off by the fight between Arthur and Alberta's rude little brother, initiated to teach Sidney manners and approved of by dad Saurian. Boys will be boys, even if they are crocodiles? G K-3.

70. Hoffman, Rosekrans. *Anna Banana*. Il. by author. Knopf, 1975. $4.95. Berthola and Charlie, two apes, have been in love since childhood. They marry, and when their first child is born, Charlie is rooting for (guess) a boy. When a girl arrives, Berthola is afraid, at first, to tell Charlie. Daughter herself lets Charlie know what she is, and dad is enchanted. The story has humorous brown and white sketches and tells a very human (although monkey) tale. Recommended for ages 4 and up.

71. Holmes, Efner Tudor. *The Christmas Cat*. Il. Tasha Tudor. Crowell, 1976. $5.95. My idea of a successful Christmas story is one that can stand up in July. This one can. It is a gentle animal story about a cat, alone and frightened in a forest with more experienced wild animals, who finds a home in a cozy farmhouse with two boys. The author's famous mother did a fine job illustrating sensuous contrast between the cool blue snowy forest and the yellow-lit farmhouse. Ages 4-8.

72. Hopkins, Lee Bennett. *Kim's Place*. Il. Lawrence Di Fioni. Holt Rinehart, 1974. $4.95. Thirteen short unmemorable rhymes and mediocre illustrations tell about a young girl's daily experiences. Kim relates her desires to be an astronaut: "But they won't laught at me/ When they finally see/ My feet up on Mars/ And my face on T.V." (That's the one I liked best.) Ages 4-7.

73. Horwitz, Elinor L. *When the Sky is Like Lace*. Il. Barbara Cooney. Lippincott, 1975. $6.95. An enchanting tale, with a little too much verse, but with very beautiful illustrations. Three sisters prepare for and enjoy a marvelous night in the forest with gift-giving and feasting animals. Ages 4-9.

74. Isadora, Rachael. *Max.* Il. by author. Macmillan, 1976. $4.95. A whimsical tale about young Max who became interested in his sister's Saturday ballet lessons when he had time to spare before his baseball practice. Max joins the exercises with more enthusiasm than grace, and decides that dancing lessons offer a great warm up for baseball. In order for Max to be really accepted by six-year-old listeners, he has to prove his masculinity in other areas. Excellent, humorous pencil drawings and a light text. Ages 4-8.

75. Jeffers, Susan. *All the Pretty Horses.* Il. by author. Macmillan, 1974. $6.95. Judy's flowered bed quilt becomes a meadow as she dreams of riding wild and free on beautiful horses while small meadow animals shyly peek at her from under the lush foliage. A beautiful experience for those insatiable horse fans. Ages 2-7.

76. Jeschke, Susan. *The Devil Did It.* Il. by author. Holt Rinehart, 1975. $5.95. Children who enjoyed the idea behind *The Gorilla Did It* by Barbara Hazen (Atheneum, 1974) might like to graduate to this tale of misplaced blame. Nana, a young girl who lives with her parents and a wise, sympathetic grandmother, gets stuck with an ugly little demon who delights in annoying her and getting her in trouble. When she finally learns to like the bothersome imp, he leaves in a huff. Imaginative and entertaining black and white illustrations. Ages 4-8.

77. Johnston, Johanna. *Speak Up, Edie.* Il. Paul Galdone. Putnam, 1974. $4.86. Talkative, spirited Edie is struck dumb during a school play, but she bounces back with style. An entertaining title with which children can easily identify. Ages 5-8.

78. Jones, Hettie, ed. *The Trees Stand Shining. Poetry of the North American Indians.* Il. Robert Parker. 1971. Thirty-one brief song-poems of various North American Indian nations and thirteen appealing full-page paintings by Mr. Parker offer a magical glimpse into the world of Native Americans. The anthology's main themes are the miracle of nature and the sadness of war. Ages 6+.

79. Kahl, Virginia. *Gunhilde and the Halloween Spell*. Il. by author. Scribner's, 1975. $5.95. One could hope that a Halloween tale featuring a medieval duchess, her thirteen daughters, and a wicked witch would offer some female assertiveness or wit. But the daughters follow the wrong woman home, and find themselves in a witch's hut. She turns them into toads, and the duke (brought out of a sick bed with a cold) must save them by sneezing and saying the magic word "kerchoo." The thirteen girls learn: (1) They must be grateful to daddy; (2) Little girl children who wander end up in great trouble. The plot is mediocre, the sing-song rhyme tiresome, and the illustrations neat but unimaginative. Ages 4-7.

80. Kantrowitz, Mildred. *Willy Bear*. Il. Nancy Winslow Parker. Parents, 1976. $5.50. A successful tale about a small boy who plays out his fear about his first day in school by pretending his toy, Willy, is the nervous one. Tenderly and patiently he kisses Willy and treats him to all sorts of goodies. The next morning finds the boy a little less anxious. A unique treatment for the school jitters. Ages 4-6.

81. Keats, Ezra Jack. *Louie*. Il. by author. Greenwillow, 1975. $6.95. When Susie and Roberto give a neighborhood puppet show, a child who is too shy to talk relates happily to a puppet. The sensitive and generous puppeteers offer the puppet to their joyful friend. A magical performance by Keats, illustrated in bold colors. Ages 3-6.

82. Kellog, Steven. *Can I Keep Him?* Il. by author. Dial, 1971. $1.75. A little boy imagines how much fun a variety of pets would be, only to have his hopes dashed by an overworked, unimaginative mother. While her son fantasizes about adventures and animals, mother is shown as a complete domestic drudge. (In one scene she is being eaten by a tiger - only her feet stick out of its mouth - while dad sits reading the newspaper.) NOT RECOMMENDED.

83. — *The Mystery of the Missing Red Mitten*. Il. by author. Dial, 1974. $3.95. Annie is missing her fifth red mitten this winter and the search makes for a heartwarming tale. Ages 3-7.

84. — *Won't Somebody Play With Me?* Il. by author. Dial, 1972. $4.95. Kim does not know that Timmy, Annie, and Philip won't play today because they are planning her birthday surprise. Detailed illustrations show the imaginative (non-stereotyped) games Kim was hoping to play. Not recently published but a good find; there are not many books where girls and boys are friends. Ages 4-7.

85. Kent, Jack. *The Christmas Pinata.* Il. by author. Parents, 1975. $4.95. A cracked pot made by Senor Gomez laments its fate as a useless item, until Maria suggests using the pot for a pinata. (" 'I'm needed!' the broken pot said happily to itself.") The sombrero, poncho, and sandal clad Mexicans all look alike, even though drawn in a colorful, appealing style. Young children interested in Mexican customs deserve something better than the sentimental pot and the stereotyped characters. Certainly Mexican children do. Ages 3-8.

86. Kesselman, Wendy. *Time For Jody.* Il. Gerald Dumas. Harper & Row, 1975. $5.50. Jody, a young groundhog, is asked by the animals of Distant Field to be their official groundhog. Jody is a little frightened, but terribly nervous and proud. She takes leave of her parents to begin a successful career, wearing overalls and minus hair ribbons. She is nonplussed by the police rabbit who says, "We were expecting someone bigger. Besides, you're a girl. We were expecting a boy." I look forward to the day when this unnecessary kind of remark wll no longer be printed in picture books. Cozily illustrated. Ages 3-6.

Kids Can Press. Four recommended titles from this women's publishing collective:

87. Allison, Rosemary. *Yak/Le Yak.* Il. Ann Weatherby. 1974. $1.95. A French/English story about a yak who lives in a large cage at the edge of the forest and is happy until Idea, personified as a high-spirited girl, whispers "You can be free!" into his hairy ear. G K-4.

88. Powell, Ann. *Strange Street*. Il. by author. 1975. $1.95. Sam lives on Strange Street, where characters of all sorts dwell happily. His best friend, Patti, lives on Bright Street where boys do not cook, wash dishes, play with dolls or cry, and a neighbor with a sinister face spies from behind his curtain. Sam decides that Strange Street is best. Nicely illustrated. Ages 4-10.

89. Singer, Yvonne. *Sara and the Apartment Building*. Il. Ann Powell. 1975. $1.95. Two active girls experience exciting sights and sounds around and in a tall Toronto apartment house. Ages 4-8.

90. Wallace, Jan and Angela Wood. *The Sandwich*. Il. by authors. 1975. $2.25. A young Italian schoolboy lives in Toronto with his widowed father and learns about being different. When Vincenzo unwraps his mortadella and provolone sandwich at the school lunch table, his friends shout "Peeeew!" and "Dead socks!" How Vincenzo copes with this, taking a stand and refusing to conform with peanut-butter-and-jelly, is told in simple words and line drawings. G 2-4; Read aloud K+.

91. Kindred, Wendy. *Lucky Wilma*. Il. by author. Dial, 1973. Wilma and her Dad, who is divorced from her Mom, learn how to overcome the strange feelings of their Saturday outings and to enjoy these days together. A unique book with attractive woodcuts and brief text. Strong artistic merit. Ages 4-8.

92. Klein, Norma. *Dinosaur's Housewarming Party*. Il. James Marshall. Crown, 1974. $5.95. Dinosaur's friends throw a party for him when he relocates in New York and give him gifts, one of which is a peace poster. An unmemorable book. Additional purchase. Ages 4-7.

93. — *If I Had My Own Way*. Il. Ray Cruz. Pantheon, 1974. $5.19. Four-year-old Ellie imagines what life would be like if she were in charge of her parents. Nicely done, with a winning theme, although a bit too long. Ages 4-7.

94. — *A Train For Jane*. Il. Miriam Schottland. Feminist Press, 1975. $3.50. Jane is emphatic in her request for a train despite suggestions for traditional "girl's toys". In verse on soft grey paper with Victorian-style illustrations and bright red freckles on our unkempt heroine, the book is attractive and fun to read. There is a discrepancy, how-

ever, between poem and pictures. Jane is already shown
playing with trucks, balls, sling shots, and fishing poles;
why are mom and dad so shocked by her wish? Ages 3-8.

95. Krahn, Fernando. *Sebastian and the Mushroom*. Il. by
author. Delacorte, 1976. $3.95. A pleasant, wordless
dream fantasy about a small boy out mushroom gather-
ing who has an adventure with a strange chap he finds
busy painting a mushroom. A drop of paint falling on the
child from the tall mushroom sends him into an adventure: space travel to a mushroom planet, a fall from a
motor star, and a return home to a safe bed via the kindly
moon. The small book is illustrated in soft blacks and
white; a nice bedtime world for parent and child to ex-
plore together. Ages 3+.

96. Kraus, Robert. *Bunya the Witch*. Il. Mischa Richter. Dutton/
Windmill, 1971. $1.25. Tired of being tormented by the
village children who call her a witch, Bunya tries to prove
she has no magic powers but to her surprise turns the
children into frogs and their parents into pigs. Then she
happily uses her new found powers to travel the world
on her broomstick. After reversing her spell, of course.
Colorful illustrations, lively text, and a great old woman.
Ages 3-7.

97. Krauss, Ruth. *Monkey Day*. Il. Phyllis Rowand. Bookstore
Press, 1973. (c. 1957.) $1.95. An offbeat tale about a girl
who loves monkeys and gives each of her pets a monkey
of the opposite sex. The monkeys wed and their marriages
are celebrated with songs, more gifts, and, later, lots of
monkey babies. The illustrations in black, white, and
monkey brown are fanciful and decorative, and the tale
is so anti-sexist that it is hard to believe it was first published in 1957. Recommended for ages 4-8.

98. Kroll, Steven. *That Makes Me Mad!* Il. Hilary Knight. Pantheon, 1976. $3.95. Cartoons illustrate the 13 kinds of
everyday annoyances that get young Nina's goat: when
no one listens; when she's blamed for something baby
Tony did; when she tries hard and it does not come out
right, and so forth. At the end, Nina makes peace with
mother, who is wise enough to let Nina express anger.
Children will identify with Nina's frustrations, and the
book can initiate discussions at home and in schools. Ages
3-6.

99. Levine, Joan Goldman. *A Bedtime Story*. Il. Gail Owens. Dutton, 1975. $5.50. Young Arathusela of Brooklyn is boss tonight and puts her exhausted and difficult ("I've had it! I'm on the brink!") parents to bed. Similar to *If I Had My Own Way* (No. 93). Children and parents will enjoy the strong identification they are bound to feel. Ages 3-8.

100. Levy, Elizabeth. *Nice Little Girls*. Il. Mordicai Gerstein. Delacorte, 1974. $4.95. Jackie has trouble being accepted as a girl at her new school because of her short hair and jeans. A humorous ending sets the sexist teacher and her classmates straight. A bit long for story hour but the end is worth waiting for. Ages 5-8.

101. — *Something Queer at the Ball Park: A Mystery*. Il. Mordicai Gerstein. Delacorte, 1975. $5.95. When Jill's lucky baseball bat disappears, her would-be-sleuth friend, a girl of unlimited disguises, sets a trap for the culprit. A sophisticated picture book/early reader with girls and boys on a baseball team together; and many uninhibited, humorous drawings. Ages 5-8.

102. — *Something Queer Is Going On. (A Mystery)*. Il. Mordicai Gerstein. Delacorte, 1973. $4.95. Gwen, the would-be sleuth and Jill, owner of a lovable basset named Fletcher, existed before No. 101. In *this* caper, Fletcher is kidnapped by a famous producer of cheap television commercials and Jill and Gwen relentlessly track him down. Clever and fun. Ages 5-10.

103. Lewis, Richard, ed. *In A Spring Garden*. Il. Ezra Jack Keats. Dial, 1965. $1.75. A collection of 23 classic Japanese haiku beautifully illustrated in watercolor and collage. Celebrating nature and life, the wise and gentle poems, along with Keats's double-spread visual treats, create a stunning moment in children's literature. Ages 4+.

104. Low, Joseph. *Boo to a Goose*. Il. by author. Atheneum, 1975. $5.95. Afraid of a mean old goose, six-year-old Jimmy and his farm friends practice building up his courage to face the nasty bird. Humorously illustrated with drawings in golds and browns, the tale ends on a happy note.

Jimmy has the power to frighten the old bird, but decides not to use it. "Maybe I won't scare Gus after all. Maybe he can't help being what he is." Ages 3-6.

105. McDermott, Beverly Brodsky. *Sedna: An Eskimo Myth.* Il. by author. Viking, 1975. $5.95. The mother of all sea creatures, Sedna, tells how she became a powerful but unhappy water spirit, able to control the animal sea life and to cease providing food for the hungry Inuit tribe. McDermott succeeds in creating a cool and magical atmosphere in violet and indigo. I do wish, however, that Sedna was drawn to look as terrifying as the text describes her. G K-3.

106. Mack, Stan. *10 Bears In My Bed: A Goodnight Countdown.* Il. by author. Pantheon, 1974. $2.50. A little boy rids his bed of too many teddy bears in this variation of a children's song, "Roll Over." The toy bears wear the boy's hats but do not appear to be any particular gender. Unfortunately, in children's books, if an unclothed animal does not have a bow in its fur, we too quickly assume it's male. Ages 3-6.

107. Maestro, Giulio. *Where Is My Friend? A word concept book.* Il. by author. Crown, 1976. $6.95. While looking for her friend, Harriet the white elephant introduces the reader to location words; up, under, through, etc. The book is most attractive: bright, bold colors serve as the background for Harriet's adventurous search, and the large black print puts the location word in still darker type. Harriet finds her pal, a tiny mouse, IN FRONT OF her nose, which is exactly where you should be holding this entertaining and educational title. Ages 2-5.

108. Maestro, Betsy. *A Wise Monkey Tale.* Il. Giulio Maestro. Crown, 1975. $5.95. When Monkey, preoccupied with her lunch, falls into a deep hole, she successfully uses her wit to escape. With bright, large illustrations and humor, the book is quietly non-sexist. Monkey, minus a bow (a miracle!), meets four other animals in her adventure: a female zebra, a female elephant, a male lion, and a snake of undisclosed gender. A wise male gorilla is also mentioned. A logical proportion of animals by sex is rare in children's books. Well done and highly recommended. Ages 3-8.

109. Mahy, Margaret. *Ultra-Violet Catastrophe! Or the Unex-pected Walk With Great-Uncle Magnus Pringle.* Il. Brian Froud. Parents, 1975. $4.95. Sally (alias Horrible Stum-per, the tree pirate) prefers outdoor adventures to visiting the soap-and-water fanatic, Aunt Anne Pringle. On one such reluctant visit, Sally finds soul mate in Great-uncle Pringle, Anne's elderly father. Together they set out for a walk, tunnel through bushes, wade, build a dam, and escape the horns of an angry cow. Dirty and disheveled, the two return home to face the livid Anne. Magnus in-vites Sally to his home where readers know that pirate heroines can seize the day. Full page water color illus-trations add to the country adventure. Ages 4-10.

110. Mangi, Jean. *A B C Workbook.* Il. Kathie Abrams. Femin-ist Press, 1975. $1.95. Twenty-six pages to color with sim-ple alliterative descriptions: "My name is Ann. I am an absolutely great astronaut." The children are multi-cul-tural by appearance and name. The drawings are very well done, large, and fun to color. Divinely democratic for darlings of 3-10.

111. Manushkin, Fran. *Baby.* Il. Ronald Himler. Harper & Row, 1972. $3.50. Not newly published, but new to me, is this clever and lively book about a fetus who refuses to be born - much to the distress of mother and family. Baby is finally convinced to join the world in this warm, unusual picture book. Himler's simple black and white drawings show an attractive family and an active, amusing baby girl with a mind of her own. A sort of Ramona Quimby in utero. Ages 3-8.

112. — *Bubblebath!* Il. Ronald Himler. Harper & Row, 1974. $4.50. Two dirty little sisters take a fun-filled bubblebath together and tickle, wash, hug, dry, and yell at each other. The amusing pink and green illustrations are just right for the domestic tale. Beginning readers might en-joy this as a first challenge, and younger children (2½-4) will identify with and envy the two active bathers. Ages 2-6.

113. — *Shirleybird.* Il. C. Stuart. Harper & Row. $5.95. Shirley is a little girl who wants to be "special." So she sprouts wings and flys off to the sun with Herbertbird, a boy artist who also turned special. She can be seen carrying

a thermos of mama's soup and not promising to marry
Herb: "I don't know if it's special enough." Non-stereotyped and very non-special. Ages 5-8.

114. — *Swinging and Swinging.* Il. Thomas di Grazia. Harper
& Row, 1976. $5.95. A perfect blend of writing and illus-
trating create a stunning fantasy about a girl whose
swing ride attracts a cloud, which sits on her head, the
sun, the moon, and "a shower of stars." Simple, special, a
real high; this book was a huge success in my class visits
with children K-2. Ages 2-8.

115. Marceau, Marcel. *The Story of Bip.* Il. by author. Harper &
Row, 1976. $6.95. Bip, who yearns to be a magician,
sprouts wings and soars into the universe. There among
the stars, moon, and sun he experiences wondrous fear,
and longs to be part of the earth again. Once returned,
he has a need to tell people about love, joy, and common
spirit. Shy in crowds, Bip finds his opportunity as a circus
mime where "with an enormous gesture, I caressed the
empty air and embraced the world." The story has flaws:
sugar-coated, rambling plot, and some overwriting. The
illustrations, in brilliant colors, match the phantasma-
goric mood. With all the flying around they even manage
a Chagall look. I recommend this title and am certain
that if Bernard Waber had been a co-author, it would
have been a four star work. Ages 6-adult.

116. Marshall, James. *The Guest.* Il. by author. Houghton Mifflin, 1975. $5.95. Mona is a large, grey, moosey looking
animal who wears long, stylish skirts and shoes, works
at Flora's cafe, plays the piano and lives alone - until
Maurice, a French snail, comes for a visit. Their friendship is described in a simple text and bright, neatly exe-
cuted drawings. The effect is good: more animal and less
Richard Scarry. Ages 3-7.

117. Martel, Cruz. *Yagua Days.* Il. Jerry Pinkney. Dial, 1976.
$5.95. When Adan Riera, a young Manhattan boy, visits
his father's family in Puerto Rico, he has good times on a
finca (plantation). Especially appealing are the *yagua*
days, when adults and kids alike slide down a hill into
the river on a *yagua,* the outer covering of a sprouting
palm frond. Many customs are introduced and there is a
Spanish word list at the end of the story. A worthwhile
additional purchase to help balance ethnic areas. Ages
5-9.

118. Maury, Inez. *My Mother the Mail Carrier./ Mi mama la
     cartera.* Il. Lady McCrady. Feminist Press, 1976. $3.50.
     My mother is tall, loves colors, likes her work, is strong,
     brave, wise, says four-year-old Lupita about her single
     parent, who works as a postal carrier. Lupita and her
     mother are sensitive, supportive, and good to each other.
     A humane story and one of many rare virtues: bilingual,
     multi-cultural, anti-sexist, and honest. It treats the two
     characters as *people* first, girl child and female adult,
     second. Attractively illustrated and fun to read - in both
     languages. Ages 5-10.

119. Mayer, Mercer. *Liza Lou and the Yeller Belly Swamp.* Il.
     by author. Parents, 1976. $5.50. Way down South in the
     Yeller Belly Swamp lived a little Black girl who used wit
     to outsmart an old Confederate Swamp Haunt, a wicked
     swamp witch, a slithery gobblygook, and a swamp devil.
     It is no secret that children adore monster tales and will
     love these fantastic swamp scenes, lush with fauna, flora,
     and nasty creatures. *However:* there is something not
     quite right in the portrayal of Liza and her home. Liza
     is a pretty little girl with a variety of short sundresses.
     But each dress is more ragged and patched than the last.
     Momma, the cottage curtains, the rag doll, etc. are equal-
     ly tattered. I question the need for all this shabbiness.
     What must have seemed "cute" to Mr. Mayer looks sus-
     piciously "pickaninny" to me. The Southern dialect and
     Liza's pet (which I mistook to be a large, pink rat) sadly
     interfere with the portrayal of a young Black heroine.
     Read before purchasing. Ages 5-10.

120. — *There's a Nightmare In My Closet.* Il. by author. Dial,
     1968. $1.75. " 'Go away, Nightmare, or I'll shoot you,' I
     said. I shot him anyway." Sleeping with a toy cannon,
     wearing a four star army helmet, and carrying a toy shot-
     gun, Mercer's small fry successfully intimidates a polka
     dot monster with an incredibly humorous face. To say
     this title is not popular with parents and children would
     be untrue, and the illustrations are perfect for the tone
     of this dryly humorous fantasy. The violence, however,
     makes me uncomfortable, and the sight of a coy little guy
     in an army helmet and pajamas is not appealing to me.

121. — *What Do You Do With a Kangaroo?* Il. by author. Parents, 1974. $5.95. A little girl refuses to take any nonsense from a variety of selfish animals who invade her privacy. Lovely illustrations and a spunky girl triumph over a flat ending. G 2-3. Read aloud to younger children.

122. Miles, Betty. *Around and Around - Love.* Knopf, 1975. $4.99. Perfect for a Valentine's Day preschool story hour is this free verse poem about the many aspects of love. Photos show people of all ages, races, and sexes engaged in expressing love and tenderness. Cozy and reassuring. Ages 3-7.

123. Morrow, Barbara. *Well Done.* Il. by author. Holt Rinehart, 1974. $5.95. A folk tale in which clever women save their husbands' hides when a duke's castle is besieged by an angry king. Fair: *ACL* 11/74; Poor: *Kirkus* 5/15/74.

124. *Mother Goose Nursery Rhymes.* Il. Arthur Rackham. Viking, 1975. Originally published, 1913. A collection of 162 nursery rhymes (two of which are inexcusable) with twelve full page color plates. An attractive book with a good variety of nursery rhymes. Anyone familiar with the history of Mother Goose knows that political and social meanings fill these seemingly innocent verses. I recommend *The Annotated Mother Goose* (Random House, 1962) for an interesting historic analysis of nursery rhymes. Many of the more sexually suggestive or political variants of these rhymes are not appropriate for a young children's collection. Read the anti-Semitic verse from the Viking collection:
> Jack sold his gold egg
> To a rogue of a Jew,
> Who cheated him out of
> The half of his due.

Two more verses in this rhyme continue to stereotype the Jewish person as a greedy culprit who would do anything for money. The second inappropriate verse reads:
> See, saw, Margery Daw
> Sold her bed and lay upon straw,
> Was not she a dirty slut,
> To sell her bed and lie in the dirt!

To call a girl a dirty slut in a book meant for very young children is tasteless. Not recommended.

125. Nakatani, Chiyoko. *My Teddy Bear*. Il. by author. Crowell, 1975. $4.95. A perfectly lovely and simple book about a small boy and his toy bear. A brief text accompanies large, colorful illustrations on heavy matte finish paper. The perfect choice for the youngest child not quite ready to sit still. (It broke the ice for my active two year old.) Ages 2-4.

126. Paterson, Diane. *Eat!* Il. by author. Dial, 1974. $4.95. After Martha is harassed by her parents to eat! eat! eat!, she proceeds to stuff her pet frog in a like manner. The illustrations of chubby Martha steal the show in this picture book which may attract guilty parents and older siblings more than the typical picture book audience. Ages 6+.

127. Pearson, Susan. *Monnie Hates Lydia*. Il. Diane Paterson. Dial, 1975. $5.50. All week Monnie had been planning for her older sister's birthday. She had baked a cake, planned a surprise party with dad, a loving single parent, and set a beautiful breakfast table. As the day unfolds, however, Lydia gets nastier and nastier until Monnie is driven to a desperate act. An interesting and realistic story. Ages 5-10.

128. Pelavin, Cheryl. *Ruby's Revenge*. Il. by author. Putnam, 1972. $4.29. Soft, earthy water colors and a lively text show Ruby the student-skunk acquiring the power of making her disagreeable teacher and classmates disappear. A lot of fun. Ages 5-8.

129. Pinkwater, Manus. *The Three Hogs*. Il. by author. Seabury, 1975. $6.95. Clever drawings and a bright contemporary mood. Three domestic pigs, abandoned by the farmer, are forced to find a new home. Rejecting urban life (the sight of the butcher shop reduces them to a neurotic state) the three nervous pigs escape to the forest and become happy, independent, wild hogs. I regret the stereotyped woman who opened the door to the pigs and emitted the age-old see-a-mouse shriek: "EEEEK!" Recommended for ages 3-8.

130. Plath, Sylvia. *The Bed Book*. Il. Emily Arnold McCully. Harper & Row, 1976. $5.95. This poem about wonderful, far-out beds was written by the tragic American poet in one of her happy moments as a young mother. You can be sure that each bed, charmingly illustrated by Ms.

McCully, is "Not just a white little/ tucked-in-tight little/ nighty-night little /turn-out-the-light- little bed." Ages 4-9.

131. Polushkin, Maria. *Bubba and Babba*. Il. Diane de Groat. Crown, 1976. $5.95. Translated and adapted from a Russian folk tale. When two lazy bears, who constantly bicker about chores and work, make a bargain that the first one up must do last night's dishes, the stubborn and bored twosome stay in bed until evening. Attractively illustrated by the artist of *Little Rabbit's Loose Tooth*. Large and colorful pictures, along with the simple tale, will appeal to other lazy little "bears" of 3-8.

132. Pomerantz, Charlotte. *The Piggy In the Puddle*. Il. James Marshall. Macmillan, 1974. $4.95. A nonsense story in tongue twisting rhyme and cheerful pictures about a pig whose love for mud puddles upsets her parents and little brother. A great hit at my story hour. Ages 4-8.

Powell, Ann. *Strange Street*. See No. 88.

133. Preston, Edna Mitchell. *Horrible Hepzibah*. Il. Ray Cruz. Viking, 1971. $3.00. Nice Mr. and Mrs. Smith had high hopes for their new daughter. She would be sweet and dainty, be named after an old rich aunt, and make them rich. Hepzibah is ugly, mean, and tough - not at all like Beautiful Vanilla, the girl next door - but she finally finds happiness with her rich old aunt, who is just as mean and nasty. Kids will cheer for this holy terror who resists tiresome daintiness. Humorous black and white drawings. G 2-3. Read to children 4-10.

134. Quin-Harkin, Janet. *Peter Penny's Dance*. Il. Anita Lobel. Dial, 1976. $7.47. Peter, an English sailor who lives to dance, promises his captain that he will dance around the world and return within five years to wed the captain's daughter. He risks danger, starvation, and execution on his journey but easily conquers these threats by dancing into the hearts of African warriors, an angry Chinese emperor, grateful American Indians. Making money and friends along the way, Peter returns home in the nick of time to wed Lavinia. The long text moves nicely and the illustrations are majestic and lively. If it bothers you that once again the Anglo male is the magical hero, at least he conquers by *dancing*. Ages 5-8.

135. Ramage, Corinne. *The Joneses*. Il. by author. Lippincott, 1975. $4.95. While Mr. Jones stays at home with his 31 children, Mrs. Jones takes submarines on dangerous expeditions. Disasters occur simultaneously under water and in the Jones house one day, and two worlds meet when Mom rescues her children and destroys a sea monster. The only attraction in this wordless tale is the reversed sex roles, but only the sexes are changed; the demeaning roles are the same. Ages 5-8.

136. Rice, Eve. *What Sadie Sang*. Il. by author. Greenwillow, 1976. $4.95. A gentle, cozy tale about a toddler girl and her mama strolling through the neighborhood to the East River. Sadie, who prefers a carriage ride to walking today, sings a private, merry tune "gheee, gheee, gheee" all the while. The grocer may think it's a toothache, but mama "knew a song when she heard it." Street scenes remind one of the 1950's. Illustrated in wintry greys, browns, and reds, the tiny book will fit perfectly into small hands - and into those of bigger people (like me, I guess) who know a good memory when they see it. Ages 3-7.

137. Roach, Marlynne K. *The Mouse and the Song*. Il. Joseph Low. Parents, 1974. What a rare treat to see a female mouse without a bow on head or tail! A very pleasant story based on entries in Thoreau's journal concerning a mouse who loved to hear him play his flute and who lived in the cellar of his cabin at Walden Pond. Heavily illustrated with water colors, the tale is told in a leisurely, lucid style. Ages 4-8.

138. Rockwell, Harlow. *My Nursery School*. Il. by author. Greenwillow, 1976. $6.95. Lois Lenski, eat your heart out! Large, colorful, and lucid illustrations, accompanied by simple declarative sentences in big, clear print tell the story of a girl's preschool day and her pride in the accomplishments of herself and her friends. Rockwell creates a multi-racial, role-free environment without the usually heavy hand. Some scenes show a male teacher distributing snacks, and a seed a girl planted actually growing taller than one planted by a boy! Perfect for children looking forward to or just beginning nursery school, and for those who need to be reassured after a long vacation. Highly recommended. Ages 2½-5.

139. Rogers, Fred. *Mr. Rogers Talks About Going To the Doctor, Going To School, The New Baby, Haircuts, Moving, Fighting.* Photographs by Myron Papiz. Platt & Munk, 1974. $4.95. In simple and direct language, accompanied by profuse and appealing color photographs, Mr. Rogers talks heart to heart with young children about common fears. Very nicely done. There are other titles in the "Mr. Rogers Talks About" series. Ages 3-7.

140. Rogers, Helen Spelman. *Morris and His Brave Lion.* Il. Glo Coalson. McGraw Hill, 1975. $5.95. It was a strange sight: a grown woman crying over a picture book! Books for young children are getting very poignant and realistic indeed. The story of how four-year-old Morris comes to accept his parents' divorce fully expresses fresh, raw pain felt by the child and his parents. A toy lion, bought after a visit to the zoo, symbolizes the bravery and strength that young Morris has to acquire to adjust to every day life without dad. The attractive pictures are by the woman who beautifully illustrated *On Mother's Lap* (McGraw, 1972). Non-stereotyped and with the added attraction of an integrated neighborhood. Ages 4-8.

141. Ross, Pat. *Hi Fly.* Il. John C. Wallner. Crown, 1974. $3.50. I find it difficult to be objective about picture books dealing with flies and ants, especially in mid-summer, but Pat Ross's wordless story about a little girl who sees a fly on the kitchen ceiling, magically shrinks to its size, and proceeds to have all sorts of humorous adventures, made me forget my dislike for a few moments. The black and white line drawngs are clever and the story is jovial. But I *don't* like the girl's ridiculous floppy hair bow. Ages 4-8.

142. Sachs, Marilyn. *Matt's Mitt.* Il. Hilary Knight. Doubleday, 1975. $4.95. The story of Matt and his glorious career, which he owes to a magic blue mitt received as a baby gift. Matt plays first with the neighborhood teams, marries "the first lady umpire," and ends up in the hall of fame - along with his glass-cased mitt. Humorously written and conventionally illustrated. No girls are seen in any baseball games, and the first woman umpire is shown serving Matt in her umpire suit and frilly apron. No word is mentioned of her career; she is shown fondly gazing at hubby's scrapbook. *Matt's Mitt* is no home run. Ages 4-7.

143. Sandberg, Inger. *Let's Play Desert.* Il. Lasse Sandberg. Delacorte, 1974. $4.95. A nursery school girl and boy pretend that their sandbox is a desert and they are the explorers. Bright, attractive illustrations but a dull story line. Ages 3-6.

144. Schlein, Miriam. *The Girl Who Would Rather Climb Trees.* Il. Judith Brown. Harcourt Brace, 1975. $4.95. Melissa, an active girl, does not know what to do with the doll given to her. Reluctant to hurt the gift givers, but bored with the toy, she comes up with the perfect solution. "Shhh," she says. "Dolly's asleep." And she's off to climb trees. The book obviously hopes to convince us that dolls and girls are not natural playmates. Poor Melissa even hurts her tooth on the doll's hard cheek. Light in tone and nicely illustrated in black and white line drawings, the book leaves a question in my mind. Isn't there a place for dolls, even in the lives of the most active and liberated children? Ages 3-7.

145. Sexton, Anne and Maxine Kumin. *The Wizard's Tears.* Il. Evaline Ness. McGraw Hill, 1975. $5.95. A novice wizard comes to Drocknock, and turns the people into frogs by underestimating the powers of his tears. Ness's wizard is a 12-year-old boy in short pants and big glasses; the town's mayor is a plucky older woman who wears the city's keys around her neck (even as a frog). The town's people may still need wizards to cure chicken pox and drought, but they enjoy telephones and motor bikes. A lively story that mixes myths and modern touches, with a strong sex-role-free attitude. Attractive illustrations in greens, reds, and blacks. Ages 4-10.

146. Sharmat, Marjorie. *I'm Not Oscar's Friend Anymore.* Il. Tony DeLuna. Dutton, 1975. $5.95. A young boy has a fight with his best friend Oscar, then imagines the loneliness and anguish Oscar must be feeling. And Oscar? Well, he does not even remember the disagreement. Homey illustrations in warm browns and golds. Ages 4-7.

147. — *Morris Brookside is Missing.* Il. Ronald Himler. Holiday, 1974. $3.95. When Morris the dog is wronged by his masters and disappears, his owners are aided by a kindly policewoman to find the missing "someone." A pleasant story with cozy illustrations for young dog lovers. Ages 4-8.

148. — *Walter the Wolf.* Il. Kelly Oechsli. Holiday, 1975. $6.95. Walter is a gentle young wolf who enjoys playing the violin, until Wyatt the fox convinces him that the biting business is more satisfying. Happily, gentleness wins out; Walter learns that violence is no fun. An entertaining tale with cheerful illustrations. Ages 4-8.

149. Sherman, Ivan. *I Am a Giant.* Il. by author. Harcourt Brace, 1975. $5.95. Bright, bold illustrations in pinks, yellows, and reds tell the story of a young girl who sees herself as a giant. ("They have to milk thirteen cows to fill my cup.") The self-assured giant sees the world around her as a miniature playground for her make-believe games. It's good to see an assertive girl giant, although she keeps her aproned mother busy. First graders may enjoy the easy text, and pre-schoolers will identify with the desire to reduce the power of usually towering adults. Ages 3-7.

150. Shulvitz, Uri. *Dawn.* Il. by author. Farrar Straus, 1974. $5.95. A boy and his grandfather share the beauty of the sunset in this quiet, beautiful picture book. Ages 3-8.

Singer, Yvonne. *Sara and the Apartment Building.* See No. 89.

151. Skorpen, Liesel Moak. *Bird.* Il. Joan Sandin. Harper & Row, 1976. $5.95. The story of a young farm boy who discovers a fallen baby bird and spends the summer teaching it to fly, and becoming very attached to it. Bird flies South for the winter and returns to the farm to hatch her eggs. When one egg falls from the tree, the boy joyfully discovers Bird's return. The gentle story is nicely told and the countryside pictures are pleasant. The mother is a totally gloomy, negative character, and we are told three times that the boy hid his face to hide his feelings - be they good or bad. Additional material for young animal lovers. G 2-3; read aloud to ages 4-7.

152. Steptoe, John. *My Special Best Words.* Il. by author. Viking, 1974. $6.95. A day in the life of Bweela, a three-year-old Black child; Javaka, her one-year-old brother; their loving single parent; their caring baby sitter; and their very special words: ILOVEYOU, PICKMEUPDADDY. An appealing story showing a close, loving family. Everyday words and functions (toilet training scenes) are balanced by haloed and unusually colored (emerald green) people. Ages 3-7.

153. Tapio, Pat. *The Lady Who Saw the Good Side of Everything.*
Il. Paul Galdone. Seabury, 1975. $6.95. A woman and her
cat travel on a log halfway round the world after a storm
sweeps their house out to sea. The woman, who is un-
named, finds good in every mishap, and ends up in China,
happily brewing tea in her new house. Galdone's illustrations are the best thing in the book: his sea scenes and
the drawings of the cat's pessimistic personality. Unfortunately the little old lady is a stereotype, with a little
hat and gray bun. For contrast see No. 168. I identified
with the cat. Ages 3-6.

154. Terris, Susan. *Amanda the Panda and the Redhead.* Doubleday, 1975. $4.95. Talkative Amanda, upset that her
redheaded baby brother gets too much attention, refuses
to talk for one day in protest. Realistic, humorous dialogue and illustrations complement the non-stereotyped,
warm family scenes. Reads well aloud. Ages 4-7.

155. Thomas, Ianthe. *My Street's a Morning Cool Street.* Il.
Emily McCully. Harper & Row, 1976. $4.95. A young
Black boy on his way to P.S. 3 in New York City tells
us about the multitude of sights and sounds in the early,
busy downtown neighborhood. The text is brief, lucid,
and poetic, enhanced by illustrations in soft yellow, blues,
and greys. (I do wish the illustrator had drawn some
Black women behind store windows and in work clothes.)
Ages 4-8.

156. — *Walk Home Tired, Billy Jenkins.* Il. Thomas Di Grazia.
Harper & Row, 1974. $4.95. A lovely book about a small
Black boy who is too tired to walk home from the park,
but luckily, has an older sister, Nina, who invites him on
plane, train, and boat rides (". . . but not too fast. You
won't get sick on this ride.") The excellent charcoal illustrations in soft browns realistically depict crowded urban
scenes which contrast with Nina's less confined adventuring. The writing is poetic, succinct and the images are
positive and loving. Ages 4-8.

157. Trompert, Ann. *Little Fox Goes To the End of the World.*
Il. John Wallner. Crown, 1976. $6.95. Very attractive il-
lustrations show Little Fox telling her mother about
some future daring journey she plans to take, with dan-
gers which she easily overcomes. "Is the mother really

such a moron?" my seven-year-old daughter asked, when on page after page Mother Fox screamed, gasped, shivered, and covered her head with her apron in response to her daughter's narrative. "No," I said. "She's just playing with Little Fox." But it bothered me that Jennifer's focus was on the mother's behavior and not on the more interesting (to me) imaginative Little Fox. Ages 4-8.

158. Van Leeuwen, Jean. *Too Hot For Ice Cream.* Il. Martha Alexander. Dial, 1974. $4.95. Sara takes her mischievous younger sister to the park by herself. Mom is busy writing a poem and dad is unavailable. Everything is realistic except the spotless city streets. A pleasant story. Ages 4-8.

159. Van Woerkom, Dorothy. *The Queen Who Couldn't Bake Gingerbread.* Il. Paul Galdone. Knopf, 1975. $5.50. I have already adapted this terrific picture book into a puppet play, performed with my daughter on the last day of kindergarten. A king who wants a wife who is beautiful, wise, and a fabulous gingerbread baker, marries a woman who not only can't be bothered about baking, but desires a man who can play the slide trombone. The king cannot. They agree not to mention their shortcomings, until one day their suppressed desires leap out. After several days of misery the king emerges victorious with his own freshly baked gingerbread, and the queen with her glorious sounding trombone. Illustrated with humor and bright colors. P.S. The Editor Who Couldn't Bake Gingerbread Either passed out store-bought cookies after the performance. Ages 4-10.

160. — *The Rat, the Ox, and the Zodiac.* Il. Errol Le Cain. Crown, 1976. $6.95. In assigning the twelve animals their place in the Chinese zodiac, the Emperor has to settle the problem of Ox and Rat - both want first place. Ox claims the prize for his strength and Rat for his intelligence. As in all such fictional contests brain is victorious over brawn, and Rat earns the exalted position. The illustrations are exceptionally attractive. Of the twelve animals, only three (small ones) are female. The two protagonists are male. I was really hoping for a she-dragon! Recommended G K-4.

161. Varga, Judy. *Circus Cannonball*. Il. by author. Morrow, 1975. $5.95. Mrs. Morelli, wife and mother of circus performers, yearns for her own excitement. Her hot-tempered husband insists "woman's place is in the home," but she tries various dull circus jobs. Bored with them, she returns home to cook spaghetti for her happy husband, The Great Morelli. His hot temper has, however, caused his assistant to quit; his act cannot go on. He is a human cannonball and there is no one to mix the shooting powders. Mrs. M. steps into the breach, adds a secret ingredient of pepperoni seeds, and the act is a wild success. She is now her husband's new assistant! Oh, well, behind every great man there is a woman. The book masquerades as non-stereotyped, but while Morelli and his son perform great feats of daring, the daughter Lola wears pretty costumes and gets sliced in half (an act, of course). Mrs. M. is always trying to please her self-involved husband . . . I could go on. This book is intended to please both traditional and feminist parents, but it has not the sparkle or cleverness to please the children of either. The illustrations, although rather too sweet, are better than the text. Ages 4-9.

162. Velthuijs, Max. *The Painter and the Bird*. Trans. R. Broehel. Il. by author. Addison-Wesley, 1975. $4.12. An attractive and bright picture book about an artist who has sold his favorite painting, a scene with a lovely bird. The bird, missing the artist, (who is also forlorn) flies out of the painting and back to the painter. Ages 4-8.

163. Viorst, Judith. *Rosie and Michael*. Il. Lorna Tomei. Atheneum, 1974. $5.95. There are no limits to the humorous friendship between Rosie and Michael; the two pals try and try and try (it does go on and on) to top each other in loyalty. Books about friendships between the sexes are so rare that this is sure to capture the attention of many kids. It does compare unfavorably, however, to Marjorie Sharmat's *Gladys Told Me To Meet Her Here* (Harper & Row, 1970), a book with the same theme. Ages 5-8.

164. Waber, Bernard. *I Was All Thumbs*. Il. by author. Houghton Mifflin, 1975. $6.95. Legs is an octopus (of undisclosed gender) who resents being forced from happy life in Captain Pierre's laboratory to return to the sea. Legs eventually readjusts to the natural environment. This

book is witty and wonderfully illustrated; excellent to read aloud to children 4-10. Its funny that "Legs" seems to be a male name. We seem programmed to think that anything not specifically drawn as female (hairbow, long eyelashes) must be male. If Legs were named "Twinkle-Toes" we would probably think of "Toes" as being female. Ages 4-10.

165. — *Lyle Finds His Mother*. Il. by author. Houghton Mifflin, 1974. $5.95. Lyle, a performing crocodile, leaves his cozy New York City home to search for his long-lost mother. The unladylike creature he discovers is not what he expected at all. Well-written, humorously drawn, and fun to read. Lyle lives in a non-stereotyped environment. Ages 4-7.

Wallace, Jan and Angela Wood. *The Sandwich*. See No. 90.

166. Wells, Rosemary. *Morris's Disappearing Bag*. Il. by author. Dial, 1975. $4.95. Morris, the youngest of four in a rabbit family, feels excluded on Christmas day when his sisters and brothers refuse to share their toys with him, dismissing him as "too young" for the beauty kit, chemistry set, and hockey outfit. Fortunately, Morris discovers one more gift, a disappearing bag, and once Betty, Rose, and Victor are happily tucked inside, Morris plays with their toys until bedtime. Simple and charmingly illustrated. A good tale for Christmas nostalgia all year round. I would be more comfortable with the beauty kit if it had been given to the younger sister only until she outgrew such nonsense and wanted a chemistry set like her older sister. However, the author has all four bunnies play with it. Ages 3-6.

167. Williams, Barbara. *Albert's Toothache*. Il. Kay Chorao. Dutton, 1974. $4.95. Star reviews: *Kirkus* 8/15/74 and *SLJ* 11/74. A toothless turtle complains that his tooth hurts and the family is baffled until grandma comes. There is nothing nontraditional about the characters. Dad leaves for work while mom stays home, aproned and *worried*. The turtle-kids are named, dressed, and characterized according to human stereotypes, e.g. sister Marybelle is very fashion-conscious. If you can ignore all this, you will appreciate the clever and sincere treatment of a child's pain. Ages 4-8.

168. — *Kevin's Grandma.* Il. Kay Chorao. Dutton, 1975. $5.50. Two youngsters compare grandmothers — one bakes cookies, the other skydives. The Gray Panthers would say "Right On!" to Kevin's grandma. Ages 4-7.

169. — *Someday, Said Mitchell.* Il. Kay Chorao. Dutton, 1976. A gentle story about a two or three-year-old who tells Mommy about all the things he will buy her when he is big: a magic vacuum cleaner, a mansion filled with fat dust-free chairs, etc. Mommy responds that she does not need these things right now, but she needs a little person to help her with her chores. The illustrations, in soft greens and lilac, are lovely. But the book is too much the author's "little son" fantasy. I doubt that a two-year-old could describe all those labor-saving devices. Not for parents who do not like the idea of waiting to be taken care of by their grown sons.

170. Williams, Jay. *Everyone Knows What a Dragon Looks Like.* Il. Mercer Mayer. Four Winds, 1976. $7.95. A well-told and splendidly illustrated book. A city just outside China is menaced by the Wild Horseman of the North. The city elders can only pray for salvation to the Great Cloud Dragon. When he obligingly turns up, only the young sweeper, Han, can believe that this small, fat old man could be the mighty dragon. (Each elder had thought that the great one would resemble himself.) The fat man saves the city to please Han, and the leaders are properly humble. The illustrations are an art show in themselves, and the story has the touch of sly wit that always distinguishes William's fairy tales. Do not expect a non-sexist tale, however. This one goes stag. Ages 6+.

171. Williamson, Jane. *The Trouble With Alaric.* Il. by author. Farrar Straus, 1975. $4.95. Alaric is a dog with an identity problem. He insists on being treated like a human being and refuses even to bark for "his best friend, who was a person." When the friend insists that if Alaric is not a dog he must get a job and share household tasks, Alaric does work for an exhausting day, and then barks enthusiastically the next morning. This simple tale, illustrated with child-like black and white line drawings, will amuse people 4-8.

172. Wolde, Gunilla. *Betsy and the Chicken Pox*. Il. by author. Random House, 1976. $2.95, $1.95. See Nos. 173, 174. 175. These little Betsy books, translated from the Swedish, are charming and non-sexist. In No. 173, Betsy has all the young child's familiar feelings of joy, anger and fear when her baby brother arrives. In this book Betsy is jealous of her parents' attentions to her brother when he is sick. Here we meet Betsy's father for the first time. The books are simply illustrated in bright watercolors. They should be in all home/school libraries for children. Ages 2-6.

173. — *Betsy's Baby Brother*. Random House, 1975. $2.95, $1.95. See No. 172.

174. — *Betsy's New Day At Nursery School*. Random House, 1976. $2.95, $1.95. See No. 172.

175. — *This Is Betsy*. Random House, 1975. $1.95. See No. 172.

176. Wood, Joyce. *Grandmother Lucy in Her Garden*. Il. Frank Frances. Collins, 1975. $4.91. A pleasant but trite trip through the pretty woods belonging to Grandmother Lucy and her cat, Tom. Pretty illustrations match the simple text about granddaughter's visit. A friendly tale. Ages 2-6.

177. Yolen, Jane. *Milkweed Days*. Photos by Gabriel Amadeus Cooney. Crowell, 1976. $5.95. Three children romp through a field of milkweeds and contemplate the magic and fun that these plants and the majestic countryside bring. Together with the large, beautiful black-and-white photographs of three happy children and their lovely environment, the poetic text makes the reader long for some milkweed days of her own. Ages 4-8.

178. Young, Miriam. *So What If It's Raining*. Il. Carol Nicklaus. Parents, 1976. $5.50. In a role-free atmosphere, Jennifer and Jason spend a rainy day together playing fantasy games. Anyone who has ever listened to five-year-olds play ("Pretend that I . . ." "No. Make-believe I . . .") will recognize the reality of the children's behavior. My own Jennifer, however, picked up a flaw in the assertive characterization of Jennifer. When Jason suggests: "Let's

both be cowboys riding the range," my daughter felt that his liberated buddy should have insisted on being called a "cowgirl." Not spectacular, but a colorful, lively story which should go well in pre-school story hours. Ages 3-6.

179. Zalben, Jane Breskin. *Basil and Hillary.* Il. by author. Macmillan, 1975. $6.95. When the farm animals help two pigs (in love) build a house, the rain comes and washes it away. But nothing bothers lovers: Hillary happily waddles in a new puddle, exclaiming, "What a perfect place we have to live in!" Sweet and simple (and expensive). Nice for ages 2-3.

180. Zolotow, Charlotte. *May I Visit?* Il. Erik Blegvad. Harper & Row, 1976. $4.95. When recently-wed big sister visits mother, little sister is entranced by her neatness and grown-up ways. After she leaves, the child asks mom if she too may visit when grown "if I don't spill talcum on the bathroom floor." Mom assures her that future visits will be fine even if she never changes her ways at all. Blegvad's simple, pretty pictures in brown, black, and green fit the homey, loving mood, but this book is not memorable or exciting enough for a recommendation. Ages 4-8.

181. — *When the Wind Stops.* Il. Howard Knotts. Harper & Row, 1975. $4.50. The story, written in simple lyrical prose, of a small boy at bedtime who is sorry to see the day end and is reassured by mother that "Nothing ends. It only begins in another place or in a different way." Attractive black and white sketches of the book's country setting with seasonal changes add to the cozy and comforting tale. Ages 3-6.

182. — *The Summer Night.* Harper & Row. $4.95. Originally published in 1958 as *The Night Mother Was Away,* this story about a father putting his young daughter to sleep is still cozy but now updated. Good: *Kirkus* 10/15/74.

CHAPTER VI

EASY READERS

183. Alexander, Sue. *Witch, Goblin, and Sometimes Ghost.* Il.
Jeanette Winter. Pantheon, 1976. $3.95; $4.99. Six easy-
to-read stories about three round-faced children who are
respectively, a witch (with her little apron on), a goblin
in striped hose, and a cute ghost in white hooded garb,
wearing glasses. The stories vary from flat to mildly
amusing. The book may be popular, however, because of
the appeal of the Halloweenish characters. Additional
purchase. G 2-3.

184. Armstrong, Louise. *How to Turn Lemons Into Money: A
Child's Guide To Economics.* Il. Bill Basso. Harcourt
Brace, 1976. $4.95. A simple lesson in basic business
economics which introduces concepts and jargon.
Through the example of a girl's success in opening a lemo-
nade stand, we learn about labor, marketing and invest-
ment. All this is done with a humorous touch and
amusing yellow and black cartoons. (Unfortunately, Mr.
Basso, like most other children's book illustrators, cannot
refrain from plopping a hair ribbon on each female head.)
The book might even help a youngster to understand why
teacher is on strike. G 2-5.

185. Bach, Alice. *The Most Delicious Camping Trip Ever.* Il.
Steven Kellogg. Harper & Row, 1976. $5.95. When two
brother bear cubs prepare for a camping trip with Aunt
Bear, it is obvious that each is expecting a different experience. Ronald wants to investigate wild life and Oliver
wants to feast. When their resourceful aunt teaches them
the art of "accommodation," the two cubs not only get
what they came for but have a good time cooperating.
A clever story of 42 pages with perfect line drawings. Put
this book in your pack when you go camping with your
own little cubs. G 2-4.

186. Berenstain, Stan and Jan. *He Bear. She Bear.* Il by authors.
     Random House, 1974. $3.37. ("A Bright and Early
     Book"). For the beginning reader, a book with a message
     about two little bears. As they gaily make their way
     through bear village, we see male and female bears en-
     gaged in a multitude of professions and activities. "We
     can do all these things, you see, whether we are he OR
     she." Certainly not as memorable as a Lobel work, this
     deserves a place on library shelves because of its lively
     illustrations, easy flow of words, and alternative (to text-
     books) message. G K-2.

187. Berkin, Carol & Elizabeth James. *I'd Rather Stay Home.*
     Color photographs by Heinz Klultmeier. Children's
     Press, 1975. $6.60. The fears and anticipation of starting
     school. The protagonist is a Black boy who attends a
     multi-racial non-sexist classroom, and happily makes a
     friend by the end of the day. Bibliotherapy at its finest
     with a simple text in large print and excellent full-page
     color photographs. Ages 5-8.

188. — *Sometimes I Hate School.* See No. 187. The feelings of
     two five-year-old boys who shy away from school when
     Ms. Kimball, their teacher, leaves them with a substi-
     tute for several days. Mr. Coleman, however, becomes a
     great hit and will do just fine (the boys think) until Ms.
     Kimball returns. Ages 5-8.

189. Bonsall, Crosby. *And I Mean It, Stanley.* Il. by author. Har-
     per & Row, 1974. $2.50. An outspoken little girl dressed
     in old jeans builds a junk sculpture while holding a one-
     sided conversation with her mysterious non-friend, Stan-
     ley. A very successful early reader. G K-2.

190. Bunin, Catherine and Sherry Bunin. *Is That Your Sister?
     A True Story About Adoption.* Pantheon, 1976. $4.95.
     The Bunin family are two white parents, their two natu-
     ral sons, and two adopted Black daughters. Told by six-
     year-old Catherine (with her mother) are some of the pro-
     cedures of adoption, her feelings about her own adoption
     and that of her younger sister. Also discussed is the sen-
     sitive issue of a mixed racial family. Photographs of this
     solid, happy family offer proof of Catherine's story that
     "real" parents are the "mom and dad who take care of
     me and love me." An excellent book, non-sexist and thor-
     oughly honest. G 2-4. Read aloud to K+.

191. Carrick, Carol. *Old Mother Witch*. Il. Donald Carrick. Sea-
      bury, 1975. $5.95. When young David and his friends
      are Trick or Treating they dare him to ring the bell of
      his neighbor, a cantankerous elderly person they call
      "Old Mother Witch." (Earlier that evening they had
      drawn a picture of "an old hag" on the sidewalk in front
      of her house.) On his way to her door, David stumbles
      over something — Mrs. Oliver, dead! Actually she has
      had a heart attack, and after the ambulance comes,
      David feels terrible about his mean thoughts. The two,
      however, never can confront each other. When she re-
      covers, Mrs. Oliver quietly leaves a bag of cookies on his
      doorstep while David peeks shyly through the curtains.
      The unexceptional story is easy to read; all the treats
      are in the terrific illustrations of a Halloween night in
      the country. G 1-3.

192. Coerr, Eleanor. *The Mixed-Up Mystery Smell*. Il. Tomie De
      Paola. Putnam, 1976. $4.69. A delightful easy reader
      about two sisters and their male friend, Nobby, who in-
      vestigate the mysterious odor coming from an old, scary
      house. What they mistake for a witch beating a living
      creature, is really a kindly old woman baking bread for
      her business. She gives her recipe to the enthralled trio
      who promptly turn their own detective headquarters into
      a bake shop. Mrs. Birdie's special recipe is written out for
      the readers too. The illustrations are charming in blue,
      brown, and white. Grades 1-3.

193. Cohen, Barbara. *Where's Florrie?* Il. by Joan Halpern.
      Lothrop Lee, 1976. $4.95. A story set in New York in the
      1930's. Young Florrie receives a toy cast-iron stove for
      her birthday and her very strict father warns her against
      EVER starting a fire in it. ("But how else can I cook?"
      falls on deaf ears.) When a friend convinces her to dis-
      obey orders, an explosion occurs which sends father out
      onto the fiery sidewalk and frightens Florrie into run-
      ning away. A traveling carousel in the neighborhood
      soothes the troubled heroine until father discovers her
      and gently brings her home. Suspenseful, and entertain-
      ing, with very attractive black and white line drawings.
      G 2-3, read aloud to ages 4+.

194. Delton, Judy. *Rabbit Finds A Way*. Il. Joe Lasker. Crown, 1975. $4.95. Rabbit, on his way to Bear's house for some beloved carrot cake, meets Duck (he's hanging laundry) and helps Squirrel (she's building a porch). He turns down their invitations for lunch in anticipation of Bear's cake. To his great disappointment, Bear has slept late and there is no cake. Once home Rabbit decides to bake his own cake — dozens of carrot pastries. Easily doubling as an early reader, *Rabbit Finds A Way* gently teaches the lesson of self-reliance. Homey and warm illustrations. Grades 1-3.

195. — *Two Good Friends*. Il. Giulio Maestro. Crown, 1974. $4.50. Bear is a wonderful cook, but messy. Duck is tidy, but dislikes preparing meals. They help each other out in this easy-to-read book. Excellent: *SLJ* 9/74 and *Kirkus* 4/74. G 1-2.

196. — *Two Is Company*. Il. Guilo Maestro. Crown, 1976. $4.95. Duck and Bear are best friends and we all know what happens when a third person seems to be teaming up with one of the duo. Bear feels put out when Duck extends hospitality to Chipmunk, his new neighbor. It is not until Chipmunk helps Bear with a job she is good at that Bear learns the value of friendship. Maestro's drawings (as usual) are entertaining and enhance the tale. Not a nontraditional story, (the smaller, more helpless animal is female) but nonetheless the friendships ring true. G 1-3.

197. Dines, Glen. *John Muir*. Il. by author. Putnam, 1974. ("A See and Read Biography") $3.96. What I shall remember about this easy-to-read biography of the great conservationist is Muir's fascination with machines before he fell in love with Yosemite Valley, California. For example, he "made a desk that opened and closed the books so he could read faster." (I want one.) In addition, he "made a bed that stood him on his feet in the morning." (That I don't need.) John also had a crabby mother and a seasick sister, but his dad and brother were swell. Easier to read, but not as satisfying as "A Crowell Biography," this book could interest young or reluctant readers. G 2-4.

198. Egypt, Ophelia Settle. *James Weldon Johnson.* Il. Moneta Barnett. Crowell, 1974. $3.95. ("A Crowell Biography") James Weldon Johnson was a talented Black songwriter and poet. The Johnson brothers created grand entertainment for Americans in the 1920's. Johnson was also a devoted civil rights activist who fought in the battle against lynchings. A well-written, attractively illustrated biography. Grades 2-4.

199. Freedman, Russell. *Animal Fathers.* Il. Joseph Cellini. Holiday House, 1976. $4.95. This book should help to get the apron off every mother animal in picture books and offer youngsters a different perspective on animal sex roles. The book describes the intense involvement of fifteen animal fathers in the care of their young. The Common American Seahorse, for example, reverses biological procedures (as we know them) with the female pushing a tube through a small opening in the father's pouch and squirting the eggs into it. "After that," writes Freedman, she turns around and swims away." (Sigh.) Although the other males are not as biologically involved, their behavior after the birth of their young is vital to the survival of the babies. Well illustrated and smoothly written. A worthy purchase for every children's collection. G 2-4. Read to K+.

200. Gackenbach, Dick. *Hattie Rabbit.* Il. by author. Harper & Row, 1976. $3.95. Two short stories for early readers about a young rabbit named Hattie. In the first story Hattie considers that Elephant, Chicken and Giraffe are more distinctive-looking mothers than her own, but she finally decides that Mother Rabbit is best of all. In the second story Hattie sells crummy items to her friends and makes profits but no pals. Repentant, she spends all her profits on a bag of candy and wins her friends back by sharing it with them. The drawings are lively and mildly humorous. The stories, although not unusual, will hold the interest of a very young reader. Gackenbach unfortunately makes all his animals into human sex-role stereotypes. In the first story the role of nurturer is given to four female parents. The mothers are dressed alike, in long dresses, aprons and fluffy caps. In the second tale, Hattie's two male friends wear slacks while the females wear dresses and hair ribbons. This book is not really sexist, but it is no different from the usual animal book written for early readers. G 1-2.

201. Gauch, Patricia. *This Time, Tempe Wick?* Il. Margot Tomes. Coward McCann, 1974. $5.95. A genuine American legend about a girl who outwits the Revolutionary soldiers involved in the 1781 mutiny of Pennsylvania. The story is enhanced by the attractive illustrations of early America which Ms. Tomes does so well. G 2+.

202. Glovach, Linda. *Let's Make a Deal.* Prentice Hall, 1975. $5.95. The friendship between a Black and white boy is unselfconsciously presented in this tale about Tom and Dewey, their shared treehouse and dog. No innovative writing or illustrations, but a warm story about two children from lower middle-class families living in and near New Orleans. G 1-3.

203. Goldman, Susan. *Grandma is Somebody Special.* Il. by author. Whitman, 1976. $3.75. A realistic but warm look at a young girl's pleasant visit to Grandma, a city woman. Although Grandma works and goes to school, we see her giving lots of time to her grandchild on this special visit. Pleasant water colors make this a nice additional early reader for your library. Ages 4-7.

204. Gordon, Shirley. *Crystal Is The New Girl.* Il. Edward Frascino. Harper & Row, 1976. $4.79. Susan's new classmate Crystal irritates Susan with her antics at first. Looking a bit like Little Lulu she finally wiggles her way into Susan's affections, so that even when they both must go to the principal's office because of Crystal's behavior, Susan is still devoted to her. When the girls must part for the summer, many readers will feel a sympathetic pang. The red, black and white cartoons are clever and mostly non-stereotypic. The principal of the school is a Black woman, and one of the schoolteachers is a man, a welcome change. Still, most of the girls sport hair ribbons of all sorts. G 1-3.

205. Gordon, Sol. *Did The Sun Shine Before You Were Born?* Third World Press, 1974. $4.95. Il. Vivien Cohen. A sex education book for young children, multi-ethnic, non-sexist and done in good taste, with attractive black line drawings. Can be read to younger children. G 1-3.

206. Hart, Carole. *Delilah*. Harper & Row, 1973. $3.79. Delilah is a spunky sports-loving 10-year-old whose family life is free of sex role stereotypes. A collection of well written short stories. G 2-3.

207. Hoban, Lillian. *Arthur's Pen Pal*. Il. by author. ("I Can Read Book") Harper & Row, 1976. $3.95. Arthur, a boy chimp, has a neat pen-pal named Sandy and a bothersome little sister, Violet. It is not until he learns that his karate-chopping Indian wrestling friend is a Sandra and not a Sanford that he does some serious thinking about his attitudes toward Violet and girls in general. The humorous, easy to read yarn is accompanied by appealing illustrations which add humor despite some stereotyping. Violet and her baby-sitter are always shown in dress and apron and no girl chimp is every without the identifying hair bow. Recommended G 1-2.

208. Hurwitz, Johanna. *Busybody Nora*. Il. Susan Jeschke. Morrow, 1976. $4.95. Six stories about an outgoing 5-year-old girl who lives with her parents and younger brother in a New York apartment. The gentle humor centers around Nora's interest in her neighbors (about 200 of them) and in her desire to include them in her life. The children in the illustrations have gnome-like faces but the family looks real and relaxed. Not feminist, but not stereotyped. A pleasant read. G 1-3.

209. Jordan, June. *New Life: New Room*. Il. Ray Cruz. Crowell, 1975. $5.95. With dad's understanding and gentle guidance, two boys and their younger sister decide how they can fit themselves and the new baby in an already crowded flat. This story of three Black children who enjoy being together and working things out is well-written and cozy, if a bit too optimistic. It offers traditional sex roles for children: little sister is already knee-deep in housekeeping toys and feminine attitudes. She is mocked at first for this by her brothers, who later resign themselves to her toys and interests. Nonetheless, the book is a worthy addition to easy reading shelves. G 2-4.

210. Keller, Beverly. *Fiona's Bee*. Il. Diane Paterson. Coward McCann, 1975. $4.69. Fiona is a shy girl who longs for friendship, yet is afraid to make a direct approach. Instead, she buys a dog dish, fills it with water, and hopes that a dog and its master will come along and stop for a bit. When Fiona rescues a bee drowning in the dish, and the bee insists on drying off on Fiona's shoulder, Fiona makes a cautious journey to the park to tempt the clinging bee with a tasty floral dinner. On the way to the park Fiona gathers young admirers and new confidence as neighborhood children wonder at her ability to train a bee. With charm, humor, and excellent characterization, the easy-to-read title is highly recommended. G 1-3.

Levison, Irene. *Peter Learns To Crochet*. See No. 226.

211. Lobel, Anita. *King Rooster, Queen Hen*. Il. by author. Greenwillow, 1975. $5.95. Good early readers are hard to find and I highly recommend this book. Unfortunately it contains a smattering of sexism. (The rooster wants the hen to become "his" queen not "the queen.") A rooster decided that he and "his" queen shall travel to the city and sit on the throne. They meet several animals on the way who are willing to be in their service, until a sly fox sends them dashing back to the farm. Funny and well done. G 1-2.

212. Lobel, Arnold. *Frog and Toad All Year*. Il. by author. Harper & Row, 1976. $3.95. Five seasonal tales which show Frog and Toad having a sled ride, an autumn leaf cleanup, a search for spring, an ice cream orgy, and a merry Christmas. Wise and entertaining brief stories for early readers. Cozy illustrations in Lobel's familiar browns, greens, and white add the perfect touch. G 1-3.

213. — *Owl At Home*. Il. by author. Harper & Row, 1975. $2.95. Only a genius could create "literature" using a first grade reading vocabulary. Lobel, the creator of the Frog and Toad books, has managed to do just that. Several short stories about an owl who is as vulnerable to mistakes and confusion as the next person, are written with great simplicity and humor. Good illustrations of Owl and his cozy home add to the charm. Highly recommended. G K-2.

Olderman, I.S. *My Body Feels Good.* See No. 224.

214. Pettigrew, Shirley. *There Was An Old Lady.* Il. Steve Henry. Coward McCann, 1974. $4.50. An easy, entertaining introduction to poetry. Twenty verses describe the adventures of a lively old woman. G K-3.

215. Pinkwater, Manus. *Blue Moose.* Il. by author. Dodd Mead, 1975. $5.25. Mr. Brenton loves to cook and his restaurant is a big success, only folks up at the edge of the Northeastern woods don't talk much (or compliment any) and Mr. Brenton feels lonely and unappreciated. Then a very intelligent talking blue moose moves in and becomes headwaiter. With simple and attractive illustrations, a yarn as refreshing as the first Maine snowflake. G 1-3.

Rizzo, Ann. *The Strange Hockett Family.* See No. 227.

216. Ross, Pat. *What Ever Happened To The Baxter Place?* Il. Roger Duvoism. Pantheon, 1976. $4.95. Sort of a fictionalized documentary about how time and "progress" reduce the large flourishing Baxter farm located in rural Maryland to a small plot of land surrounding an old farmhouse. The Baxter family, described in strongly nonsexist terms, own nearly 300 acres of thriving land; but money needs, age, and the diverse interests of the daughter and son necessitate the sale of their fields to developers. The illustrations clarify the story of the slow and steady suburbanization of the land. Factual enough for a lesson in American history, yet lyrical and sensitive. G 1-4.

217. Russell, Solveig P. *Rozy Dozy.* Il. Dora Leder. Abingdon, 1975. $3.95. Rozy Dozy is Fred's younger sister. Whenever they play detective, Rozy is the escaped (male) convict. She's good at hiding. One day while visiting Uncle Pete's horse farm, Rozy overhears two thieves plotting to steal a prize horse. After the capture of the thieves by the police, Fred, who is amazed at "Dopey Rozy Dozy's" victory, offers her a chance to be the detective next time. Rozy rejects his offer, preferring to remain the "hider." Typical "little sister": lazy, quiet, passive, and making no gains at the end of the tale. G 1-3.

218. St. George, Judith. *By George, Bloomers!* Il. Margot Tomes. Coward McCann, 1976. $4.69. An easy-to-read tale about a little girl anxious to exchange her cumbersome dress for the newly created "bloomer" outfit advocated by 19th century dress reformers. Mother, shocked at Hannah's "tomboyish" ways, gives in to the request when Hannah rescues her brother from a steep roof. It is obvious that this rescue was made possible only by the fact that Hannah was wearing bloomers custom-made from a torn skirt. This pleasant feminist tale is reminiscent of *Phoebe's Revolt* by Natalie Babbit (Farrar-Straus, 1968), a more literary book. Cheerful illustrations. G 1-3.

219. Shick, Eleanor. *Neighborhood Knight.* Il. by author. Greenwillow, 1976. $5.95. A small fatherless city boy has a secret. He is really a knight who "protects" his mother and older sister, the Queen and Princess, and who fights imaginary battles to let off steam. The lovely, soft-penciled illustrations of his urban environment contrast beautifully with his fantasies of medieval life, and the writing is well above average. It is all so charmingly done that one can almost enjoy the message, until one realizes that the idealization of boys who protect women and who must fight to prove their worth is dangerous and destructive in the long run.

220. Schulman, Janet. *The Big Hello.* Il. Lillian Hoban. Greenwillow, 1976. $5.95. A little girl depends on her doll as a security symbol when she moves to California, and is upset when she loses it during unpacking. Dad brings home a dog, however, and the child discovers her doll being fed by the child down the street; life looks brighter. Six brief chapters written simply and illustrated appealingly constitute this pleasant, uneventful tale, with its ordinary kind of little girl "heroine". G 1-2.

Siegel, Beatrice. *Living With Mommy.* See No. 225.

221. Silverstein, Shel. *The Missing Piece.* Il. by author. Harper & Row, 1976. $5.95. "It" is looking for its missing piece. As It searches high and low, It has adventures, both good and bad. When the missing piece is finally found, It discovers that pure happiness did not come with it, and so It disregards the small triangle with a dot for an eye. It then goes off singing once more about Its missing piece. Clever proof that a humorous and "philosophical" tale can be told with few words and simple images. Ages 6-adult.

222. Simon, Nora. *All Kinds Of Families*. Il. Joe Lasker. Whitman, 1976. $4.25. The families in this book are multiethnic, single parent, older married couple, etc. "Family" is not limited to blood relatives or legal adoptions. A sensitively written, supportive book. A few of the illustrations, of families being separated, are unnecessarily dark and grim.

223. Stevens, Carla. *Stories From A Snowy Meadow*. Il. Eve Rice. Seabury, 1976. $6.95. These four short stories are about Mole, Shrew, Mouse and their dear old friend, Vole. These friends learn about sharing, anger, illness and finally death, when they lose Vole. Tender and well-written, with black and white illustrations as a gentle complement. G 2-4. Read aloud to K-2.

Storypack. Feminist Press. $2.50. Five short storybooks illustrated in black and white. With teacher/parent manual:

224. *I. My Body Feels Good*. By I.S. Olderman/ R. Maceiras. Pleasant feelings that come from things like swinging and making mud-pies to things like thumb-sucking and masturbation. No literary or artistic merit here. This is pure bibliotherapy. If you need it, buy it.

225. *II. Living With Mommy*. By Beatrice Sigel. For some reason stories of pre-schoolers in divorced families move me more than Solzhenitsyn does. This is about a child who must adjust to daily life without father. It still seems like bibliotherapy to me, but some children might need it. Ages 3-6.

226. *III. Peter Learns To Crochet*. By Irene Levison. An elementary school boy wants to learn to crochet; a friendly male teacher shows him how. This is the most successful story in this packet. Ages 4-7.

227. *IV. The Strange Hockett Family*. By Ann Rizzo. One evening Jane and her rather stuffy grandparents find themselves in a house exactly like theirs, but the grandparents who live there play reversed sex roles. This strange experience shakes up grandma and grandpa, opening their minds to new ideas and insuring Jane a less stereotypic future. A discussion starter. Ages 6+.

228. *V. When It Flooded The Elementary School.* By Elenea Yatzeck. A super-girl rescues everyone during a flood. She even talks the boys out of drowning themselves. The great thing about this story is that the ten-year-old author has such a high opinion of herself and of her sex. And that's about it. Ages 5-8.

229. Talbot, Toby. *A Bucketful Of Moon.* Il. Imero Gobbato. Lothrop Lee, 1976. $5.95. The moon's reflction is magic in this folk tale-like book, and it fools a "sprightly old woman" into riding terrified goats, climbing windmills, throwing rocks through windows and even more, in order to capture the moon. This old woman, wearing shawl, nightcap and wooden shoes, is tough and dauntless and idiotic, of course. The illustrator catches the bounce and character of the old lady. Entertaining. G 1-3. Read aloud to ages 4+.

230. Tarcov, Edith. *The Frog Prince.* A retelling of the story by the Brothers Grimm. Il. James Marshall. Scholastic, 1974. $4.95. A lively text and very funny illustrations tell the story of the haughty princess who is forced to befriend a frog who rescued her golden ball from a well. Highly recommended. G K-3. Read aloud to preschoolers.

231. Thomas, Ianthe. *Eliza's Daddy.* Il. Moneta Barnett. Harcourt Brace, 1976. $4.95. Eliza's Daddy has left her and her Mommy and lives across town with his new family, which includes a little girl Eliza's age. Eliza imagines that Daddy's new daughter is superior to Eliza in every way. Finally one Saturday (Daddy's day), Eliza gets her courage up and asks to see the new family. Mandy, the new daughter, turns out to be a perfectly pleasant and ordinary child like Eliza herself. Daddy takes them both out for the day. Well written. Soft pencil sketches match the mood. G 2-4.

232. Tobias, Tobi. *Arthur Mitchell.* Il. Carole Byard. Crowell, 1975. $4.50. A very good biography which emphasizes the professional side of the Black dancer, founder of the Dance Theater of Harlem. We learn about his industrious youth, the physical difficulties of ballet training, and his strong desire to provide work for other Black dancers. G 2-4.

233. Van Woerkom, Dorothy. *Becky And The Bear*. Il. Margot Tomes. Putnam, 1975. $4.69. When Father and Ned go hunting one morning in Colonial Maine, Becky does her chores reluctantly, grumbling that she would rather do something "brave". Soon she gets her chance: she must save herself from a huge bear, and she does, in a funny, clever way. Few of these books for early readers have female protagonists. A fun way to learn about life in the Colonies. Attractive, warmly colored illustrations. G 1-3.

234. — *Meat Pies and Sausages*. Il. Joseph Low. Greenwillow. 1976. $5.95. Three stories for the beginning reader about a clever fox and her enemy the mean wolf. They are clever and fast-moving. They all end with the wolf being physically hurt, in case you object to that sort of thing. G 1-2.

Yatzeck, Elena. *When It Flooded The Elementary School*. See No. 228.

CHAPTER VII

FICTION, GRADES 3-10

235. Alcott, Louisa May. *Trudel's Seige*. Il. Stan Skardinski. McGraw Hill, 1976. $5.95. Alcott might just as well disguise herself again, because the four terrific melodramatic stories in *Behind A Mask: The Unknown Thrillers Of Louisa May Alcott* (Morrow, 1975), which were published under a pseudonym, beat this little piece of sugar and spice by a mile. Skardiniski chose this story from Alcott's first book. A little Dutch girl keeps her aged, depressed and dying relatives from starvation by selling precious trinkets, doing odd jobs, and finally, by warning the rich but kindly and generous local landowner that unemployed rascals are planning to ruin his crops. (Shirley Temple would have been perfect for the little girl). Good for a large or historical collection. This is non-sexist but saccharine and out of place in our cynical times. G 3+.

236. Alexander, Lloyd. *The Wizard In The Tree*. Il. Laszlo Kubinyi. Dutton, 1975. $7.50. Mallory, a poor kitchen maid who believes in fairy tales, rescues the cynical enchanter Abrican, and ends up as mistress of a large estate after outwitting an unscrupulous squire. Well written, with action and thought stimulation enough to attract readers from grades 4 up. A good read-aloud for the family. G 3-6.

237. Amoss, Berthe. *The Chalk Cross*. Seabury, 1976. $6.95. Stephanie Martin enters an old New Orleans art school run by nuns, and begins a strange journey back and forth from the present to an earlier identity: she was Sidonie Laveau, daughter of the Voodoo Queen. In this earlier life, she witnesses the cruel effects of slavery, the conflict between voodoo and the Church, and even the plague. The modern Stephanie is horrified at being switched back and forth. An engrossing novel. G 6-8.

238. Anderson, Mary. *F.T.C. Superstar.* Il. Gail Owens. Atheneum, 1976. $6.95. The author, who is an actress, tells about an ordinary cat who suddenly wants to be a great actor. He adores summer stock in New Jersey! Emma, an intellectual pigeon, coaches Freddie, the cat. Emma would rather read than anything else. She is struggling to get out from under the wing of her overbearing husband. Neil Simon himself would like this story: it has sophisticated humor and child-like charm, for all ages G 3+

239. Annett, Cora. *How The Witch Got Alf.* Il. Steven Kellog. Watts, 1975. $4.95. A farm donkey, jealous of the affection given to the family cat and dog, goes to great and ridiculous lengths to be noticed. Humorous and touching, this story will strike a responsive cord in brothers and sisters who feel that they too deserve more attention. No sex-role stereotypes are overcome: the man works outside, the woman in the house; she does her best to boost his ego, etc. But the feelings of this male donkey are tender and genuine, and both story and illustrations are very good. G 1-4.

240. Arkin, Allen. *The Lemming Condition.* Il. Joan Sandin. Harper & Row, 1976. $4.95. One lone lemming, Bubber, questions his family and friends' determination to make a mindless journey to mass suicide. Females are traditionally cast in this short, entertaining tale, but it is nicely written and a good read-aloud. G 3-5.

241. Asbjornson, Peter. *The Squire's Bride.* Il. Marcia Sewall. Atheneum, 1975. $5.95. A spoiled old squire tries to force a young peasant woman into marriage in this entertaining Norwegian folk tale. The reluctant bride engineers a misunderstanding, and the astonished squire finds himself at the altar with a bay mare all dressed in white. The wedding guests have a good time, and so does the reader. Illustrated in attractive pencil sketches. G 2+. Read aloud to ages 4+.

242. Babbitt, Natalie. *The Devil's Storybook.* Il. by author. Farrar Straus, 1974. $4.95. A collection of humorous stories about a devil who loves to see folks suffer, but often ends up as his own victim. Shades of Oscar the Grouch: Sesame Street graduates will roar at this anti-hero. G 4+.

243. — *Tuck Everlasting.* Farrar Straus, 1975. $5.95. In 1881 a lonely eleven-year-old has an adventure neither you nor she will ever forget. She is kidnapped by the immortal Tuck family, when they find her trying to drink from their spring. The water would have kept her eleven years old forever. Winnie guards the Tucks' secret and rescues these unhappy people, who have been accidentally locked into immortality. A wonderful story, enchantingly written. G. 4+. Read aloud to G 2-3.

244. Bach, Alice. *The Meat In The Sandwich.* Harper & Row, 1975. $5.95. A sports story, with strong family scenes, competently written. Mike, a fifth grade would-be super jock, almost realizes his dreams when his pal Kip, compulsively competitive and a male chauvinist, helps him train for the soccer team. Back at home, Mom tries to parcel out chores to leave herself time to paint. Conflict arises when Mike decides that he is the meat in the sandwich and his two sisters are slices of bread. Good solid work which should attract both sexes. G 4-7.

245. Baker, Betty. *The Spirit Is Willing.* Macmillian, 1974. $4.95. Fourteen-year-old Carrie, who dislikes domestic chores and ladylike behavior, lives in a mining town in 19th century America. A mummy display in a saloon sets Carrie off into an adventure as a spiritual medium. Good spirits for all in this well-written, entertaining book. G 4-6.

246. Beatty, Patricia. *By Crumbs, Its Mine!* Morrow, 1976. $6.95. In 1882, When Damaris Boyd and her family are travelling by train from St. Louis to their new home in the Arizona Territory, the savage cry of "Gold!" is heard. All the men, including papa, scramble off to the goldfields, leaving mama and the three children stunned and alone. Damaris, "a terror on two feet," builds a thriving business, wins back money Dad lost at poker, and even brings Dad himself back from the goldfields. All the characters in the book are colorful, and the women are individual and independent. This book is not as impressive as No. 247, but it is highly recommended. G 4-7.

247. — *How Many Miles To Sundown?* Morrow, 1974. $4.95.
An adventure story set in the Southwest in the 1880's.
A 13-year-old girl, who is independent and brave, is the
heroine. The author surpasses herself in this entertaining saga with its great cast of independent women. G 5-9.

248. — and John Beatty. *Master Rosalind.* Morrow, 1974. $5.95.
In the late 16th century, Rosalind, who is 12 years old,
disguises herself as a boy in order to act in Shakespeare's
plays. Well-written adventure story, with mystery and
high spirits. G 7-9.

249. — *Something To Shout About.* Morrow, 1976. $6.95. This
author's novels are always something to shout about:
they are historical novels with strong adventuresome
girls and women. This is no exception, although it is not
one of her best. The story is set in a gold-mining town in
the Montana Territory in 1875. The women turn the town
on its ear when they begin to collect money from saloon
customers for a new school. A dramatic confrontation
occurs between a young apprentice doctor and a brash
saloonkeeper. The doctor turns out to be a woman dis-
guised as a man, the funds are raised by the women, who
are jailed several times for their principles, the 12-year-
old narrator is proud of her sex, and the reader gets a
good feeling for the customs of gold-mining days. G 4-8.

250. — and John Beatty. *Who Comes To King's Mountain?* Morrow, 1975. $5.95. Young Alex MacLeod joins the Red-
coats, who have come back to South Carolina in 1780.
Alex hates killing in any form, and when he sees his
grandfather hanged, his friend murdered and his father
beaten, he undergoes a conversion. He leaves the
MacLeod women to protect their home and joins the
American cause. Well-written, and highly recommended
for its realistic picture of war. G 6+.

251. Behrman, Carol. *Catch A Dancing Star.* Dillon, 1975. $5.95.
This novel about ballet defends the right of boys to be
ballet dancers or at least to study ballet. Good review:
SLJ 4/75. G 5-9.

252. Bell, Frederic. *Jenny's Corner.* Random House, 1974. $4.99.
Jenny is desperately concerned with the safety of the
deer on her parents' farm. This brief, poetic tale, set in
the 19th century, will please animal lovers. G 4-7.

253. Bennett, Jay. *Say Hello To The Hit Man*. Delacorte, 1976. $5.95. Although the women are stereotyped, professors are stereotyped, organized crime is stereotyped, and the victim — a mobster king's son, whose life is threatened — is a stereotypic straight good guy, the book is entertaining and keeps your attention. The plot is implausible, but the mystery about who is tormenting college student Fred Morgan, and why, hooks you (when you are not counting the author's use of the word "gentle"). Without giving it away, I'll tell you that the butler did not do it. Grades 8+.

254. Blume, Judy. *Forever*. Bradbury, 1975. $6.95. Although the jacket blurb calls this a novel for adults, it is really a teenage romance. A high school senior progresses date by date toward sexual intercourse, and gets the technique down pat. She realizes then that her promise of "forever" was a little premature. Blume writes in the style of her books for fourth graders. The great thing about this book, however, is its abolition of the double standard, and its plea for the education of girls in contraceptive techniques. An encounter between the heroine and a Planned Parenthood physician is described in detail. This book should knock Daly's *Seventeenth Summer* off the shelf. Recommended. Grades 9+.

255. Bolton, Carole. *The Search For Mary Katherine Mulloy*. Nelson Hall, 1974. $5.95. Young Mary immigrates to America in search of her lover after most of her family dies in the Irish potato famine. Unfortunately the book is reminiscent of an old movie with John Wayne and — anyone, Lana Turner? You name it. The lover solves the problem. G 6+.

256. Branscum, Robbie. *The Three Wars Of Billie Joe Treat*. McGraw Hill, 1975. $5.95. During World War II, a 13-year-old boy carries on a personal war with his stingy mother on their Arkansas farm, and with his sadistic teacher, who turns out to be a Nazi spy. Billy goes on a hunger strike to protest Mom's scanty portions of food, and he and his friends must cope with the unpleasantness of Mr. Marshall's class in school and the misery of losing loved ones in the war. Billy's war with Mom and the relations with the hill people is most successfully done, and the book is full of action. The females are traditional (the girls in school even scream together), but Billy is sensitive and caring and his portrayal refreshing. G 4-7.

257. Bulla, Clyde Robert. *Shoeshine Girl*. Il. Leigh Grant. Crowell, 1975. $5.95. Sarah, ten years old, is mad at the world. She is sent to Aunt Claudia's for the summer because her parents feel they cannot cope with her any longer when her best friend is caught stealing. She is refused pocket money by her parents, so she gets a job as a shoeshine girl. When her boss is hit by a car, Sarah keeps the shoeshine stand open by herself. She must reluctantly leave the job when her mother becomes ill. She is fond of her boss, and her job has given her financial independence and a sense of personal achievement. Sarah is a heroine rarely found in children's books, except perhaps those of Cleaver and Beatty. Highly recommended. G 3-4. Read aloud for ages 6-8. Bravo!

258. Cameron, Eleanor. *The Court Of The Stone Children*. Dutton, 1973. $5.50. Fantasy and mystery are skillfully combined when Nina, an aspiring museum curator, solves a murder mystery by communicating with the dead. Well written. The San Francisco setting is enchanting. G 4-8.

259. Cavanna, Betty. *Ruffles And Drums*. Morrow, 1976. $5.95. This is the story of Sarah Devotion, a teenager during the Revolutionary War. Although Sarah is allowed to feel a pang or two about her passive female role in life, this book is only a formula romance: the adventure goes to the male, while Sarah does the "growing up", which means she "adjusts" to a lacklustre life. G 4-6.

260. Cawley, Winifred. *Gran At Coalgate*. Il. Fermin Rocker. Holt Rinehart, 1975. $6.50. This novel is a Cut Above others, and might take a special reader too, to appreciate its special qualities. It is set in a British coal-mining town in the 1920's. The dialect might be difficult, but a glossary is included. Jinnie, eleven years old, is anxious to win a scholarship to a school of education. Just before the Great Strike of 1926, she is sent to visit her beloved grandmother in Northumberland. Gran lives in a mining town there. Jinnie has all sorts of new experiences, all of which her father, a small shopkeeper, considers sinful: dancing, films, and Labour talk. The print is small, but the characters are well-developed and the settings are excellent. A cannie (nice) book! Winner of the 1974 Guardian Award; it had been published in England by Oxford University Press. G 5-9.

261. Chittum, Ida, ed. *The Princess Book*. Random House, 1974. $4.95. Nine modern fairy tales by female authors about princesses who achieve varying degrees of liberation. On the whole, the stories are unimaginative and lifeless. In addition, the fluff and flounce of the princesses in the illustrations do not suggest any strength or independence. For large collections. G 4-7.

262. Clapp, Patricia. *King Of The Dollhouse*. Lothrop Lee, 1974. This is the first book I've encountered which is loaded with female chauvinism. A miniature royal family moves into Ellie's dollhouse. King Borra Borra stays home with his 12 children while Queen Griselda goes off adventuring. The King prefers domestic life. Why then is it only the Queen who can remember the children's names? The Queen alone recognizes the symptoms of teething and must be summoned home by the frantic, helpless King. The King, hiding from Ellie's mother, panics at the sound of her footsteps. The Queen leads the flustered King and babes into hiding. Surely no one could *enjoy* bustling anxiously about brushing crumbs and straightening surfaces as the King does. Its nice to see a non-traditional dollhouse family. But there's nothing nice about making one parent into a bungling idiot so that the other parent can look heroic. Neither plot nor style are impressive here. G 3-4.

263. Cleary, Beverly. *Ramona The Brave*. Morrow, 1975. $5.50. Ramona, notorious pest and well-meaning troublemaker, is now in the first grade and trying to mend her ways. Many of the sexist attitudes and stereotypes found in the earlier book, *Ramona The Pest,* have been dropped from this one. Ramona is a distinct individual, who will attract the interest of children. A genuinely funny book, written cleverly. Good for older, reluctant readers. G 2+.

264. Cleaver, Vera and Bill Cleaver. *Dust Of The Earth*. Lippincott, 1975. $6.95. The Drawn family is poor: fourteen-year-old Fern Drawn's Grandfather Bacon has called them "the dust of the earth". But much worse to Fern is her realization that the family do not love one another. They are nagging and cold. When her grandfather dies and they move into his tumbledown farm in the South Dakota hills, where Fern herds sheep, the family learns to depend on and to enjoy one another. Lucidly written and moving. G 4+.

265. — *Me Too*. Lippincott, 1973. $5.95. Lydia, twelve years old, tries to teach things to her retarded twin sister, in order to spite her cold father. Excellent characterization and a poignant story. G 4-8.

266. Clifton, Lucille. *The Times They Used To Be*. Holt Rinehart, 1974. $4.95. A short poetic novel built about two Black girls in a rural area after World War II. They discuss their lives: the people they know and the things that happen, and especially the frightening (to them) mystery of menstruation. Beautiful. G 6+.

267. Cohen, Barbara. *Thank You, Jackie Robinson*. Lothrop Lee. 1974. $4.50. A Black man and a fatherless white boy make friends in the 1940's. They are devoted to the Dodgers and to each other. Moving and sensitive, a story for both sports fans and bookworms. G 4-7.

268. Collier, James Lincoln and Christopher Collier. *The Bloody Country*. Four Winds, 1976. $6.95. The authors inject a strong dose of reality into juvenile American history material. Both this book and their earlier *My Brother Sam Is Dead*, are often painful and startling to those of us brought up on American myths. A Connecticut family is torn apart by the violence of the American Revolution. When the family opens a mill in the Wyoming Valley of Pennsylvania, some earlier settlers, called Pennamites, claim the land and join with the British and the Indians to drive the more recent Valley immigrants away. Father insists on staying, even after his wife and son-in-law are murdered, because he says, a man without his own land is like a "low-down slave". Son Ben can't understand then why Dad won't free their own slave, Joe Mountain, who eventually escapes to a free part of Pennsylvania. A good story and an eye-opener. G 6+.

269. Colman, Hilda. *Nobody Has To Be A Kid Forever*. Crown, 1976. $4.95. Mom leaves home to find herself after twenty years of marriage, leaving thirteen-year-old Sarah in a disintegrating family: Dad is talking of realizing his old dream of becoming an artist and older sister has gone off to Boston with her boyfriend. Sarah manages to get it all together. Written as Sarah's journal, the book reads easily. G 4+. For reluctant readers G 5-8.

270. Cone, Molly. *Dance Around The Fire.* Houghton Mifflin, 1974. $5.95. Joanne Ruben, upset that her parents do not practice Judaism, falls into the hands of anti-Israeli terrorists in Italy, on her way to Israel. This book is not well written and the plot and characterizations are mediocre. It does give a picture of Jewish religious customs, and older reluctant readers might enjoy the up-to-date settings.

271. Conford, Ellen. *Dear Lovey Hart, I Am Desperate.* Little Brown, 1975. $5.95. A high school freshman writes an anonymous Lonely Hearts column and makes an unread school newspaper into a best seller. At first Carrie answers her letters shrewdly and wisely, even helping a lonely student, recovering from drug addiction, to make new friends. But troubles mount: her grades drop, she falls in love with the paper's editor, the boy next door is amorous, her pesty sister threatens to reveal her identity. Father, the school guidance counselor, ignorant of the writer's identity, hates the column. Ultimately Father Knows Best, which unfortunately is what this book could be subtitled. The column must be dropped, the editor responds to affection, sister gets the attention she has been craving and tune in next week. G 5-9.

272. Corcoran, Barbara. *The Winds Of Time.* Atheneum, 1974. $5.95. A miracle ending, but a frightening beginning for Gail, left alone when Father deserts her and Mother must be institutionalized. Star review: *Kirkus.* G 6-8.

273. Danziger, Paula. *The Cat Ate My Gymsuit.* Delacorte, 1974. $5.95. A fast-moving and entertaining novel for young teens. Marcy Lewis is chubby and insecure and fights many battles at once. She protests the school's decision to fire an innovative teacher, struggles against her tyrannical father, and finally becomes just plain comfortable in her own (fat) skin. No deep psychology here, but a satisfying story. G 6-9.

274. Darke, Marjorie. *A Question Of Courage.* Crowell, 1975. $5.95. The story of the fight for Woman Suffrage in Britain is a dramatic one. The violence of the Suffragists' tactics, and the cruelty of the Government response of imprisonment and forcible feeding for hunger strikers, makes this a fascinating subject for writers. This is a

good-fast-moving novel about a 17-year-old seamstress who becomes involved with a radical arm of the movement because she likes one of the leaders, who is young, wealthy and enthusiastic, and has a handsome, cynical older brother. The seamstress, Emily Palmer, becomes one of Mrs. Pankhurst's bodyguards. Her romance with Peter does not detract from the book's reality. Well done. G 6-9.

275. Degens, T. *Transport 7 — 41 — R*. Viking, 1974. $5.95. A thirteen-year-old becomes a heroine when she makes a dangerous journey in post-World War II Germany. An engrossing novel which describes the difficult, often heartbreaking conditions survivors of war have to face. G 7+.

276. Dixon, Paige. *The Search For Charlie*. Atheneum, 1976. $4.95. Jane flies home to Montana from her college in the East in order to find her brother Charlie who is missing from the family ranch. Jane successfully trails him, with the aid of Vic, a young Indian. The violence dormant in all of us rises to the surface when Jane is unable to control her gun because of her hatred of the kidnapper. As a result she nearly kills Vic. The theme of this successful book is well-integrated, and the chase through the Montana forests is exciting. Fast paced and neatly written, this is a good short book for older reluctant readers. G 4-8.

277. Dizenso, Patricia. *Why Me? The Story Of Jenny*. Avon, 1976. A quiet high school student attempts to put her life back together after she is raped at knife point by a young man whom she has met at the local hang-out. After reading three paragraphs, one realizes that this is poorly written. Two problems prevent it from being as useful a book as it should be: Jenny is not an individual but a composite of reactions and problems; and, more important, Jenny appears to bear the blame — she accepted a ride from him, didn't she? The blame is never where it belongs: on the subjection of women, and on the sick mind of the rapist himself. Jenny is sympathetically portrayed, and many of her reactions have the stamp of reality, but the book is only a marginal effort. G 9-+.

278. Donovan, John. *Family.* Harper & Row, 1976. $5.95. A story of a laboratory colony of apes, told from their point of view. The narrator, Sasha, reveals much about human nature, while ostensibly talking about apes. Ironically, the subjects are observing the scientists who are observing them. Like Robert O'Brian's *The Rats of Nimh*, in this book Sasha and three friends escape to a mountaintop where they regain their natural behavior and habitat. Skillfully written, and readable, this novel has an unusual viewpoint that could generate much discussion. G 5-8.

279. Doty, Jean Slaughter. *The Crumb.* Greenwillow, 1976. $5.95. This above-average story about horses explores the often corrupt world of horse-racing, where misuse of drugs is one of the biggest problems. Narrated by Cindy, a lively inquisitive teenager, the fast-moving story has much appeal for children. G 4-6.

280. Edmonds, Walter D. *Bert Breen's Barn.* Little Brown, 1975. $6.95. In upper New York state in the early 19th century, Tim Dolan, a poor youth, struggles to purchase a barn, in which he later finds a buried treasure. Characters seem to be paired off in a Tweedledum and Tweedledee way: the badly behaved French Canadian brothers who work at the mill meet Tom's well-behaved sisters. Pairs are indistinguishable from each other. Much too much is made of the "prettiness" of Tom's mother, with her brightening eyes and blushing cheeks. She seems like Tom's sister instead of his mother. She is capable and dependable: her prettiness excuses this. But the descriptions of nature are superb. This book is by the author of *Drums Along The Mohawk*. A solid, leisurely read. Recommended. G 5-9.

281. Ellis, Mel. *Sidewalk Indian.* Holt Rinehart, 1974. $5.95. A Native American teenager, falsely accused of murder, escapes to a reservation where he begins to learn about his heritage. The book ends with his death in an organized protest. Reviews warn that the characters are either all good (the Native Americans) or all bad (the white people). Good review *ACL* 10/74; Fair review: *SLJ* 9/74; Poor review *Kirkus* 5/1/74. G 9+.

282. — *The Wild Horse Killers*. Holt Rinehart, 1976. $6.50. The summer after her freshman year in college, Sandra Bradford fights to save the wild horses in her Western valley from hunters who sell the bodies to pet food companies. Sandra leads the horses over desert, mountain, highway and field to a place where Federal law will protect them. An exciting adventure story, with some lapses into sentimentality. Its theme is an important one, and its heroine is competent. G 6-9.

283. First, Julia. *Flat On My Face*. Prentice Hall, 1974. $4.95. Athletic Laura has high practice scores but low popularity. Her mother does not think a girl should play baseball or much of anything else. Laura becomes her own person when she befriends a handicapped boy and brings his entire school to a baseball game. Quick and light. G 4-6.

284. Fitzhugh, Louise. *Nobody's Family Is Going To Change*. Farrar Straus, 1974. $5.95. A well-to-do conservative Black family faces the decision of the daughter to become a lawyer and the son to study the dance. The style is more successful than the plot but the book is interesting, dealing as it does with a Black family's struggle with sex role rigidity. By the author of *Harriet The Spy*. Fitzhugh died soon after publication of this book. Harriet will live forever. G 6-9.

285. Flory, Jane. *The Liberation Of Clementine Tipton*. Houghton Mifflin, 1974. $5.95. A tale about women's rights in 19th century Pennsylvania. Good: *Horn Book* 12/74; Poor: *Kirkus* 11/1/74; Recommended: *Ms* 12/74. G 4-5.

286. Gathorne-Hardy, Jonathan. *Operation Peeg*. Lippincott, 1974. $5.95. Two girls and a fanatic housekeeper find the island which houses their boarding school suddenly drifting in the Atlantic. Star reviews: *SLJ* 10/74, *Kirkus* 10/1/74. *Kirkus* disapproves of the stereotyped housekeeper. G 4-8.

287. Gauch, Patricia Lee. *Thunder At Gettysburg*. Il. Stephen Gammell. Coward McCann, 1975. $5.95. Tillie Pierce witnessed the Battle of Gettysburg and wrote a book about it in 1889. Her story is retold here. She changed in three days from a child who thought the Civil War was

an exciting game between bad greys and good blues to a young adult shocked into pacifism. Written with dignity and compassion. Format is handsome with black and white sketches. Valid literature and history. G 3-8.

288. George, Jean Craighead. *Going To The Sun.* Harper & Row, 1976. $5.95. Here's a winner! This story, exquisite in style and plot, is a plea for the conservation of the endangered Rocky Mountain goats of the Mission Mountains in Montana. The story revolves around Melissa and Marcus, childhood sweethearts who secretly marry and set up a research camp high in the mountains to study the goats. Marcus's father, who is a hunter, refuses to consider that the goats are an endangered species; he helps Marcus get the research center only in order to find the goats and make money as a hunter's scout. Marcus must deal with his father, and there is further conflict with Melissa, who is a strong protagonist, loving, capable and forthright. All the characters are drawn with sensitivity. This novel, which is partly an attack on hunting and the consequent destruction of native wildlife, is moving and timely. G 6+.

289. Gonzalez, Gloria. *The Glad Man.* Knopf, 1975. $4.95. Melissa and her young brother Troy discover an old man living with his dog in a broken-down bus in the middle of the city dump. When the city finds out about this, attempts are made to evict him. Melissa organizes a huge campaign to save the old man's house. Well-written and amusing. Melissa is twelve, and loves baseball while Troy is sensitive and book-loving. Unfortunately Troy is ridiculed for being a bookworm, and Mom frets a lot about household sloppiness: two common stereotypes. Similar in theme to John Krumgold's *Onion John,* this book should have wide appeal. It is entertaining, with individualized characters and a good plot. G 3-6.

290. Greene, Bette. *Philip Hall Likes Me. I Reckon. Maybe.* Dial, 1974. $5.95. Beth is a lively, intelligent Black girl who lives happily with her family on a farm. Beth has a crush on Philip, and she wants to believe he is superior to her. But whatever they do — raising prize calves or organizing consumer protests — Philip always takes second place. In the end — unprecedented in children's litera-

ture — the delicate male ego is unprotected by the competing female. Beth acknowledges that she is indeed smarter than Philip. And they can still like each other. G 4-8.

291. Greene, Constance. *I Know You*. Il. Byron Barton. Viking, 1975. $5.95. A best friend (nameless) narrates the story of Al: her worries about her non-existent menses, Mom's new boyfriend, and Dad's reappearance after eight years with a wedding invitation. Al is real and likeable and the dialogue is crisp. But the author seems confused about her attitude toward the women's movement. One mother is a "wierdo but nice" because she's against an early marriage for her daughter and because she wants to take back her maiden name. Another woman is ridiculed for being a stuffy old lady "who gives the men her full attention." But the book is entertaining. G 4-6.

292. Greenfield, Eloise. *Sister*. Crowell, 1974. $4.95. Family relationships are explored in this well-written story of a year in the life of a Black teenager. Mother is having problems with her rebellious, unhappy older daughter. Very good. G 6-9.

293. Grossman, Mort. *The Summer Ends Too Soon*. Westminster, 1975. $6.50. Can a Gentile girl find lasting love with a Jewish boy whom she meets at a Jewish camp? Maybe. But the real question here is: how can a Jewish man write such anti-Semitic nonsense about Jewish women? Anyone can write a bad book, so we will not quibble about that. But we quote Izzie, the camp director about Diane, the Gentile girl: " . . . her movements were very soft, very feminine. Her neatness was a direct contrast to the way most of the counselors dressed . . ." He gushes, "I love you . . . There's a decency and goodness about you that is foreign to Camp Ramble Lane." Sharon, the only attractive counselor has "a long and aquiline nose." The author appears as enchanted as Portnoy with the golden "shiksa" ideal. Grossman is no Roth and because of the stereotypes and the sappy sentiments, the complaint here is mine. G 6-9.

294. Hale, Janet. *The Owl's Song*. Doubleday, 1974. $4.50. Billy White Hawk faces despair on his reservation and prejudice from white and Black people in the city. *SJL*

writes that the author is unsympathetic to characters other than Native Americans. Good: *SLJ* 9/74 and *Kirkus* 4/1/74. G 7+.

295. Hamilton, Virginia. *M.C. Higgins the Great*. Macmillan, 1974. $6.95. A Black boy must choose between moving from his beloved mountain home and facing the danger that hangs over his family. Although parts of the novel are difficult to understand and the book might not attract mass readership, it is powerfully written. A fine literary achievement. G 5+.

296. Harris, Christie. *Mousewoman And The Vanished Princess*. Il. Douglas Tait. Atheneum, 1976. $6.95. The author's love for Northwest Indian lore is transformed here into a fine collection of entertaining stories all centered around the same theme. Mouse woman is a small supernatural creature who loves young people. The six stories are diverse and fun to read, but only the princess in the first story really rescues herself. Recommended nonetheless. G 4+.

297. Haynes, Betsy. *Cowslip*. Nelson, 1973. $4.95. Cowslip (named for the wild free flower) is a thirteen-year-old Kentucky slave who comes to realize that slavery is not willed by God but is an unnatural and terrible institution. Cowslip cares for three small children on Colonel Sprague's plantation. She learns to read and write, sees a friend beaten and murdered, and finds out about the Underground Railroad. The story is not free of stereotypes, but it is moving and adequately written. Readers will sympathize with Cowslip's plight and cheer her determination to become "wild and free." G 4-6.

298. Hentoff, Nat. *This School Is Driving Me Crazy*. Delacorte, 1976. $6.95. Sam, the son of the stern headmaster of Bronson Alcott School, is a sixth grade clown with a heart of gold. He gets into trouble when he promises a friend not to reveal the names of three bullies who are shaking him down. In an attempt to write realistic dialogue, Hentoff relies heavily on swearing. One finds oneself waiting for each new swear word as one waits for "you know" from people who say it all the time. The writing is smooth and there are some funny, dramatic moments. On the whole, however, it is didactic: Father knows best after all. G 5+.

299. Herman, Harriet. *The Forest Princess.* Il. Carole Dwinell. Over the Rainbow Press, 1974. $2.95. A princess, who has grown up isolated in a forest tower, canot adjust to the sexism she finds at the castle of a prince whom she visits. Banned from his kingdom for attempting reforms, the princess continues to travel and begins happily to notice improvements in the treatment of women. Attractively illustrated. Can be colored. Not Hans Christian Anderson, but not Grimm either. Ages 4-10.

300. Ho, Minfong. *Sing To The Dawn.* Lothrop Lee, 1975. $5.95. Dawan, a Thai country girl, wins a scholarship to a city school and has to convince her family that learning is respectable for a female. This is not poorly written, but it is more social protest than art. The characters are mouthpieces for viewpoints. The author is a Thai woman who is donating her royalties to a girls' scholarship fund. This book was awarded first prize by the CIBC, and it is a worthwhile addition to a collection because of its passionate plea for an idea whose time has come. G 4-8.

301. Hodges, Margaret. *The Freewheeling Of Joshua Cobb.* Farrar Straus, 1974. $5.95. Crane substitutes for her sister on Joshua's camping trip. Joshua's ideas about girls change when this brave inquisitive heroine becomes his comrade. Star review: *Kirkus.* G 5-8.

302. Hoover, H.M. *Treasures Of Morrow.* Four Winds/Scholastic, 1976. $6.95. Above-average science fiction: descendants of two cultures survive a nuclear holocaust, and two children are genetically linked to both societies. The people, not subtly described, are primitive, nasty military people, and sensitive intellectuals who descend from the industrialist Simon Morrow and his staff who built "Lifespan". Tia and her young brother Rabbit were born on the military base but possess Morrowan E.S.P. They will live in Morrow but return to the base to study the primitives. Tia is brave and intelligent, although she goes to pieces at the end and is "gathered up" by her lover. Fast-moving and well-written but a bit black and white for my greyish tastes. (A similar theme is found in Jay William's *People Of The Ax.*) G 4-6.

303. Houseman, Laurence. *The Rat-Catcher's Daughter*. Atheneum, 1974. $5.95. Here is a literary dilemma. On the one hand, imaginative fairy tales in lyrical prose and with engrossing plots; on the other, an endless procession of dazzlingly beautiful female characters, whose looks determine their fates. In none of these twelve tales does a woman have an adventure. There are a boy artist, a boy deserted in a magic castle and men who fight for crowns or weave magic spells. The women are simply "beautiful things". This book is beautifully written and enchanting to read — alas! G 4+.

304. Howard, Moses L. *The Ostrich Chase*. Il. Barbara Seuling. Holt Rinehart, 1974. $5.95. Khuana, an adolescent girl of the Kalahari Bushpeople, defies the taboo on females hunting, because she wants to kill a nesting ostrich and take the prized egg. Her defiance causes an accident in which her grandmother is wounded. Khuana stays with her in the merciless desert until she is well enough to join the nomadic tribe. When they rejoin the astounded family, who never expected them to survive, the resourceful heroine has the satisfaction of offering an ostrich feast. Fairly exciting and attractively illustrated. A good non-sexist tale. G 4-6.

305. Hunter, Mollie. *The Kelpie's Pearls*. Il. Stephen Gammell. Harper & Row, 1964. New ed. 1976. A wise old woman, Morag MacLeod, befriends a kelpie in the Scottish Highlands. The kelpie is supernatural and Morag is forced to give up her simple life when the neighbors begin to suspect her of witchcraft. The characters are colorful and the text is enchanting and gentle, with fine descriptions of the north bank of Loch Ness. Children will like it who liked Natalie Babbitt's *Tuck Everlasting*. Nicely illustrated too. G 3-6.

306. Hutchins, Pat. *The House That Sailed Away*. Il. Lawrence Hutchins. Greenwillow, 1975. $5.95. During a London storm Morgan's house is swept off its street and away to an island in the South Pacific. There they (Morgan's family) encounter pirates and cannibals. The plot is bad, and so is the characterization. Let this one sail right by.

307. Johnstone, Norma. *Of Time And Seasons*. Atheneum, 1975. $7.95. Bridget, whose family is wealthy and brilliant, lives in New Jersey in the middle of the last century. Her beautiful eighteen-year-old sister, Delilah, is suffering from brain damage because of a childhood fall. The family situation is interwoven with the beginnings of the Civil War to create a complicated story. Mother wants a career as a writer, Delilah dances in the moonlight and is attacked and made pregnant, an older brother flees the army and goes to Canada, and, primarily, Bridget herself works out her personal attitudes. A rich saga for the leisurely reader. $ 6+.

308. Karp, Naomi J. *The Turning Point*. Harcourt Brace, 1976. In 1938 twelve-year-old Hannah moves from the Bronx to a suburb in Queens to find that anti-Semitism has infiltrated her new home. The problems are a little too neatly resolved: one neighborhood Nazi goes to a mental hospital, and a prejudiced coach sees the error of his ways. But the story is entertaining and the heroine is attractively strong. The mother is a "typical" Jewish mother, a nag and a worrier, but at this point I am not sure how many choices Jewish culture offers women, so I hesitate to call this an empty stereotype. (I wish I could). G 5-9.

309. Kelley, Sally. *Troubles With Explosives*. Bradbury, 1976. $6.95. Sally Banks, in the fifth grade, has lots of problems: Dad is in plastics and is constantly having to move house, Mom is super-organized, the new teacher is a tyrannical sadist, and Sally stutters. (Small wonder). Sally finds her own solutions to these problems in a fast-moving story that should really attract reluctant readers. She is a likeable heroine and the classroom scenes are realistic. Unfortunately a stereotyped feminist is included, the "NOW" mother (!) of a friend. Here reality stopped. G 3-5.

310. Kennedy, Richard. *Come Again In The Spring*. Il. Marcia Sewall. Harper & Row, 1976. $4.95. Death comes calling for Old Man Hark one winter day. He wants to live until spring so that the birds he feeds will not starve. He makes a wager with Death, a sharp-nosed man in a great bearskin coat. Hark must remember special moments in his early childhood and even his birth. The impossible

is done, with the help of the beloved birds. A gentle story with a special ending. Attractive black and white drawings. Recommended. G 3+. Read-aloud to ages 6+.

311. Kerr, Judith. *The Other Way Round.* Coward McCann, 1975. $7.95. A sequel to *When Hitler Stole Pink Rabbits* (1972). Anna and her family, Jewish refugees, live in London. Anna grows up and develops a love for art and for her middle-aged, married art teacher. She also begins temporary work as a stenographer. Her youth and enthusiasm are bright against the dark background of bombs, prison camp news and illnesses. Successfully written, with a strong feeling for the era. As in all war stories I have read, here too the men are desperate to be busy and the women are just desperate. Recommended. G 6-10.

312. Kerr, M.E. *Is That You, Miss Blue?* Harper & Row, 1974. $6.50. This novel is set in a boarding school where Miss Blue, a religious fanatic, is driven mad by people who will not accept her eccentricity. Flanders, fifteen-year-old, narrates the funny, sad, crazy events of the story. Pointed and intriguing sketches of various kinds of misfits, well done. G 6+.

313. — *Love Is A Missing Person.* Harper & Row, 1975. I am disappointed in this author's newest book. I am a great fan of hers. But this book appears to be more an exercise in sketching eccentrics than an attempt at an integrated novel of characters and ideas. Suzy Slade is fifteen. She lives in Long Island with her wealthy family, and worries about her radical chic sister Chicago, while associating with a ludicrous middle-aged librarian who is still in love with her World War II sweetheart. Suzy's dad is married to a flaming dingbat, unfortunately named Enid. There is also Roger, a Black super-brain, super-jock, who alternates between Chicago and Suzy's friend Nan. Valid questions are raised here. But the characters are too far-out to be authentic. G 6-12.

314. — *The Son Of Someone Famous.* Harper & Row, 1974. $4.95. The son of a "Kissinger-type" of man, and the daughter of a "Why-can't-you-act-like-a-girl?!?!?!?!" woman become close friends. A wonderful novel. With humor and pathos, the point is made that people should be allowed to be themselves. G 7+.

315. Killens, John Oliver. *A Man Ain't Nothin' But A Man: The Adventures Of John Henry.* Little Brown, 1975. $5.95. A novel based on the life of the legendary hero, John Henry, a powerful Black man who gave his life in a match with the despised steam hammer. Written in tall-tale Southern style, the book concentrates on John's love life, and his belief that every man must be treated with dignity. John's love was Polly Anne, a tiny, beautiful woman whom he couldn't live without. The other women in John's life were loose and wild. Mother warned him about these gals. The story is well told; John evolves as part human, part legend. The author tends to get too sentimental about John and Polly's lovemaking, but does a really nice job in describing his steel driving contests and the final match. Recommended. G 7+.

316. Klein, Norma. *Blue Tree, Red Sky.* Il. P.G. Parker. Pantheon, 1975. $4.95. An easily read and smoothly written book about Valerie, her younger brother, their traditionally sex-role oriented sitter, Mrs. Weiss, and their widowed artist-mother. Valerie would prefer an unemployed mother, and between laughter about penises and vaginas, sadness at the anniversary of dad's death, and sibling rivalry, Valerie comes to understand that mother works because she loves her profession. Politically right, the book lacks the spark of life that makes us believe in the characters. Not one of this author's best. G 2-4.

317. — *Naomi In The Middle.* Dial, 1974. $4.95. A liberal urban family is awaiting the birth of a third child. Smooth and easy to take, but I found this title more a clever and glib slice of life than a morsel of literature. G 3-6.

318. — *Taking Sides.* Pantheon, 1974. $4.95. Twelve-year-old Nell's experience with her parents' second divorce from each other and her own adolescent changes make for above average, fast moving drama. The themes of divorce, illness, alcoholism, sex, handicapped and obese people, and feminism are introduced. And it works. This is one of the author's best books. G 6+.

319. Knudson, R.R. *Fox Running.* Harper & Row, 1975. $5.95. Two women athletes become friends in this novel about the sport of running. Fox Running is an American Indian who was trained in the fields by her deceased grand-

father, and the story of how she was recruited (kidnapped, really) by the track coach of a local university is most implausible. But the book's good features are the realism and detail given to the vivid sport scenes and the rare portraits of powerful women athletes in action. G 5+.

320. — *You Are The Rain.* Delacorte, 1974. $5.95. A close and loving relationship develops between two young women who are trapped in a hurricane. I could not get into the book, but it received a good review from *SLJ* 10/74. G 8+.

321. Konigsburg, E.L. *Father's Arcane Daughter.* Atheneum, 1976. $5.95. The reappearance of Caroline, Winston's half sister, kidnapped from college seventeen years ago, enables this aloof, lonely adolescent and his mentally handicapped sister to escape from their own stifling environment. A nice mixture of intrigue and sophistication. Something different from the author's usually breezy, comic style, although there is much wit in Winston's intelligent comments. G 6-9.

322. — *The Second Mrs. Gioconda.* Atheneum, 1975. $5.95. Salai, servant to Leonardo da Vinci, tells how the Mona Lisa came to be painted. The author asks why Leonardo should have chosen to paint the portrait of a wife of a second rate merchant, when Europe's nobility wished to pose for him. The clues lie in the characters: the Duke of Milan and his plain, profound young Duchess, Beatrice, the haughty Isabella, and the complicated personalities of Leonardo and his dishonest apprentice. We never really know Mona Lisa, but this story is rich and wonderful. G 6-12.

323. Lampman, Evelyn. *White Captives.* Atheneum, 1975. $6.25. Based on Olive Oatman's life, this book about her kidnapping by the Apaches in Utah in 1857 explores the vastly different cultures of the white and Native American people. Excellent: *SLJ* 5/75; Good: *Kirkus* 3/15/75 and Children's Book Review Service "Spring Supplement: 1975."

324. Lattimore, Eleanor. *The Taming of Tiger.* Morrow, 1975 $4.95. A nervous mother insists that her family move to the country after her son is punched by Tiger, a local bully. Unfortunately, Tiger visits his cousin who lives

very close to Benjamin's new house. Tiger is "tamed" after a fight with Benjamin and a close encounter with the police. No alternatives to fighting are suggested; Dad applauds B's successful attempt to slug Tiger. Very traditional plot, style, and characterization. Mother is distraught, Father is resourceful. And girls? Well: "The boys Benjamin's age didn't usually play with girls, but they noticed the pretty ones." "Pretty" and "little" is the way Nell, B's contemporary, is described EVERY time. The author talks down to her readers. G 2-4.

325. Lawrence, Mildred. *Touchmark*. Harcourt Brace, 1975. $7.50. More than anything Nabby wants to become a pewterer. But things do not look too promising in Boston in 1776 for an orphaned girl who wants to enter a male profession. How Nabby, who is resourceful, physically strong and sharp-tongued, manages to earn the apprenticeship and help the Sons of Liberty, is told with rich historical detail and at a fast pace. G 4-7.

326. Levy, Elizabeth. *Lizzy Lies a Lot*. Il. John Wallner. Delacorte, 1976. Do I detect an autobiographical admission in this humorous, sympathetic account of a little girl who discovered the pitfalls of lying? Lizzie shares her home with a sarcastic, nagging grandmother, who is realistically portrayed. Since she has a fertile imagination, Lizzie finds it as easy to lie as to breathe. Fortunately Lizzie's parents help her to break her destructive habit. Well done. G 3-6.

327. McCannon, Dindga. *Peaches*. Lothrop Lee, 1974. $4.50. An enthusiastic Black 9th grader, Peaches, who is growing up in Harlem, is determined to become an artist and to keep her virginity. Entertaining but not memorable. G 5+.

328. McHargue, Georgess. *Stoneflight*. Viking, 1975. $6.95. One summer in New York when Janie Harris's parents are quarreling and she is lonely for her vacationing friends Janie is drawn to the stone griffin on the roof of her apartment house. She enters a fantasy world and finds herself flying over the city on its back. Her troubled family life is drawn so well that I found myself thinking that the fantasy was in her own mind only. But that's O.K. Some readers might prefer to believe that Janie did "quicken"

Griff to life and only narrowly escaped being turned to stone herself. This book is reminiscent of Eleanor Cameron's *Court Of The Stone Children*. A fine mixture of art history, fantasy and realism. Highly recommended. G 5-9.

329. Manley, Seon and Gogo Lewis. *Ladies Of The Gothic: Tales Of Romance And Terror By The Gentle Sex*. Lothrop Lee, 1975. $6.95. A collection of ten tales by British and American authors of the last two centuries, with a good introduction to the genre. Thoroughly entertaining, except for the title. G 6+.

330. — *Sisters Of Sorcery: Two Centuries Of Witchcraft Stories By The Gentle Sex*. Lothrop Lee, 1976. $7.95. As in No. 329, the title is the only objectionable thing about this book. "Sweet things" included are writers like Doris Lessing, Dorothy Sayers and Lady Gregory. There are twelve tales. See Nos. 329 and 331. G 8+.

331. — *Women Of The Weird: Eerie Stories By The Gentle Sex*. Lothrop Lee, 1976. This includes stories by E. Nesbit (a personal favorite of mine), Edna St. Vincent Millay and Shirley Jackson. See Nos. 329 and 330. These collections are not necessary purchases for small libraries on tight budgets, but teachers will find that reluctant high school readers will like them. G 8+.

332. Mann, Peggy. *My Dad Lives In A Downtown Hotel*. Il. Richard Cuffari. Doubleday, 1973. $4.50. Joey learns that his parents' recent separation is not his fault and that his father still loves him. The raw pain alleviated, Joey is happy to realize that he sees more of his dad than before and he knows that many children grow up with his problem. Aside from a put-down of girls by Joey and the rather cold portrayal of Joey's Dad (who ignores his pathetic wife's attempt to pretty herself up for his visits to Joey), the book is very successful. Good illustrations and a fast-moving style combine to show the agony of divorce from the perspective of a ten-year-old boy. G 3-6.

333. Mathis, Sharon Bell. *The Hundred Penny Box*. Il. Diane and Leo Dillon. Viking, 1975. $5.95. A poignant, brief look at the loving relationship between young Michael and his 100-year-old great-great aunt. Our culture is repelled by

old age. But here Michael, a young Black boy, adores and fights for the dignity of his old, precious aunt. Illustrated in warm browns and golds by water color applied with cotton. G 3-6.

334. — *Listen For The Fig Tree*. Viking, 1974. $5.95. A competently written and stirring novel about Muffin, a blind Black girl, trying to get her despondent mother through the first Christmas season without her murdered husband. Many vital characters are portrayed, as well as the interesting Kwanza, a Black African celebration. My only complaint concerns the reason a male character gives Muffin for an attempted rape: "You know why this happens to Black women? . . . All of you — each one, nobody left out — are so incredibly beautiful, profoundly beautiful . . . Ageless, incredibly perfect love. And, see — people like to touch that. Want to hold that." Rape is not an act of love. It is an act of disgust and hate. Surely Black women and young readers deserve a more truthful, if more painful, explanation of what this girl went through. G 6-9.

335. Melwood, Mary. *Nettlewood*. Seabury, 1975. $8.95. This book needs a special reader. A child who loves long, old-fashioned stories with sensuous writing (one can smell the English countryside in which it takes place), and who will enjoy a junior *Upstairs, Downstairs* plot of family intrigue and mystery. All sorts of characters meet 12-year-old Lacie when she is forced to spend some time at her older cousins' tumbledown, quiet village in the 1920's. These heroines won't inspire young feminists, but this is a pleasant, leisurely tale. G 6+.

336. Miles, Betty. *Just The Beginning*. Knopf, 1976. $5.95. Cathy has several problems: Mom has taken a job as a cleaning woman; she herself faces a strong possibility of being expelled from school for breaking a rule, and Big Sister is just about perfect. Cathy resolves these problems and begins to build up some confidence in herself in this light, sensible tale. Mom ends up organizing with the other cleaning woman to get fairer wages and better working hours. G 4-6.

337. — *The Real Me.* Knopf, 1974. $5.99. When Barbara tries to reform the P.E. department of her new school, and demands also the right to take a newspaper route, she learns that hard work often comes before success. Fast moving and light, with a strong message. Many 6th grade girls will identify with Barbara's struggle to become her own person. G 4-6.

338. Minard, Rosemary. *Womenfold And Fairy Tales.* Houghton Mifflin, 1975. $5.95. Eighteen traditional tales with "a girl or woman as the moving force." The lively heroines include Mollie Whuppie, Clever Grethel and Kate Crackernuts. Hostile review *NYT Book Review* 4/13/75 by Susan Cooper, who questions the idea behind this book. Girls identify as strongly with male heroes like Jack the Giant-Killer as boys do, Cooper says, and do not need female protagonists of this sort. She goes on to attack words like "Ms" and "chairperson." Nevertheless this collection is highly recommended. G 4-8.

339. Mohr, Nicholasa. *El Bronx Remembered: A Novella And Stories.* Harper & Row, 1975. $5.50. Twelve stories about Puerto Rican people living in the Bronx from 1946 to 1956. Some of the subjects are death (of a pet, of a school friend), marriage (a pregnant teenager and a middle-aged homosexual) and friendship (between a Puerto Rican and a Jewish girl). The first story "A Very Special Pet" is one of the most realistic portraits I have ever read of a mother and her pre-school children. The book is powerful and entertaining. Highly recommended. G 6+.

340. Murray, Frances. *The Burning Lamp.* St. Martin's, 1974. $6.50. Young Phemie Witherspoon, inspired by Florence Nightingale, opens a hospital in Colorado in the 19th century, battles prejudice against women and makes peace between fighting men. Good: *SLJ* 9/74. G 5+.

341. Myers, Walter Dean. *Fast Sam, Cool Clyde, And Stuff.* Viking, 1975. $6.95. Puerto Rican and Black young adults share friendships, with good times and problems. Excellent: *CIBC,* Vol. 6, no. 8, 1975.

342. Naylor, Phyllis. *Walking Through The Dark*. Atheneum, 1976. $6.95. A pleasant period piece about young Ruth Wheeler growing up during the Depression. Things go from bad to worse; Father loses his job and the family must adjust to poverty. This is a sensitive and realistic portrayal of the problems involved in coping with a new kind of life. The book has dull stretches, but Ruth emerges as a capable, sensitive and independent individual. G 4-6.

343. Obukhova, Lydia. *Daughter Of Night: A Tale Of Three Worlds*. Macmillan, 1974. $5.95. This science fiction tale is built on the theory that our planet was developed by advanced interplanetary beings. Lilith, Adam's first wife, is a symbol of the search for knowledge, and a strong female figure in her own right. The book uses masculine language, however: "mankind," "Man," and masculine pronouns. In the developed planets, inhabited by intelligent beings, scientists are masculine and women are considered only as maternal or sexual creatures. Lilith, the lone strong female, walks in a male-oriented verbal scene.

344. O'Connell, Jean S. *The Dollhouse Caper*. Il. Erik Blegvad. Crowell, 1976. This is an entertaining fantasy about a dollhouse family, owned by three brothers, which saves the brothers' home from a disastrous burglary. The author seems to understand little boys: one, for example, has the nasty habit of stuffing poor Mr. Dollhouse head first into the toilet. The dolls are sex-stereotyped: "Mr. Dollhouse sprang off the sofa and stood listening in the parlor. Mrs. Dollhouse sat up, looking confused. Todd went to the window, where he could see the driveway. Ruth clutched her quilt about her." G 3-5.

345. O'Daniel, Janet. *A Part For Addie*. Houghton Mifflin, 1974. $5.95. A mystery set in Albany in the 19th century with witchcraft, murder and Addie Trimble, a right-on heroine. Excellent: *SLJ* 1/75; Fair: *Kirkus*, 12/1/74. G 5-8.

346. O'Dell, Scott. *Child Of Fire*. Houghton Mifflin, 1964. $5.95. This story of a sensitive Chicano who martyrs himself for a cause received mixed reviews. Star reviews: *SLJ* 10/74; *Kirkus*, 8/1/74. Poor: *Horn Book* 12/74; *NYT Book Review* 11/3/74. I agree with *NYT* critic that the book

is a bad introduction to Chicanos. The Anglo narrator stereotypes the men: "Chicanos are good mechanics." The women have no identity except their appearance and the hero's macho problems are blamed on a young waitress. This author is talented but this book misses the mark. G 6+/

347. Oppenheim, Shulamith. *The Selchie's Seed*. Bradbury, 1975. $5.95. Il. D. Goode. An injured white whale floats into the cove near an island off Scotland where the Sinclaire family lives in a cottage. Fifteen-year-old Marian falls in love with the whale and wishes to join it. Marian's mother is discovered to be a selchie, a descendant of sea creatures who shed their skins in the moonlight and dance on the shore. The whale brings Marian a magical sealskin belt. She wears it and becomes a selchie, whose destiny is the sea. Beautifully written and illustrated, with traditional sex roles. Based on Scottish legend. G 4-6.

348. Orgel, Doris. *A Certain Magic*. Dial, 1976. Eleven-year-old Jenny discovers a diary kept by her Aunt Trudi when she was a lonely eleven-year-old refugee living with a British family just before World War II. A curse on snoopers is in the diary, but Jenny reads it anyway. Her later trip to London is almost ruined by guilt and fear but the curse is a blessing in disguise. Recommended. G 4-5.

349. Peck, Richard. *Representing Super Doll*. Viking, 1975. $5.95. A fourteen-year-old farm girl accompanies her friend, a beauty contest winner, to New York for a three day promotional trip. Entertaining, with witty dialogue and a fast-moving plot. It's easy to make fun of this kind of beautiful but very stupid girl, and of beauty contests. But the author makes no attempt to sympathize with his characters, or to explain their behavior. The picture of a young woman named Moon, who is concerned with social issues, is distorted to the point of caricature. The heroine is a resourceful girl. G 6-10.

350. Perl, Lila. *The Telltale Summer Of Tina C*. Seabury, 1975. $6.95. Twelve-year-old Tina has a great deal to think about: her divorced parents' new loves, and her own interest in boys and in beauty hints. Tina begins to feel sorry for herself when she is teased by a boy she knows,

and feels better when another boy becomes her friend. The characters often make speeches rather than chat, and the writing is frequently mannered: "I hoped the 'glow' of my experience with Johann was going to last . . ." Disappointing. By the author of *Crazy April.* A soap opera for the pre-teen set. G 4-6.

351. Pevsner, Stella. *A Smart Kid Like You.* Seabury, 1975. $6.95. Nina, who is twelve, has to cope with her parents divorce, with having her new stepmother as a math teacher, with new stepbrothers, and with her own mother, who does not treat her as nearly grown up. Nicely written, with good characterization. But why does the supposedly sensitive father not introduce his new family to Nina informally, instead of letting them stumble upon each other by accident?

352. Pfeffer, Susan. *The Beauty Queen.* Doubleday, 1974. A satire of the Miss America contest. G 6-9.

353. — *Marly The Kid.* Doubleday, 1975. $5.95. A sequel to No. 352. Marly turns to her divorced father and her stepmother for assurance and love. This author appears to be a feminist. Excellent: *CIBC* 7/75. G 6-9.

354. — *Rainbows And Firewords.* Walck, 1973. Twin sisters grow closer to each other after they move to the country. G 5-9.

355. — *Words You Want To Hear.* Walck, 1974. An articulate young woman's first sexual adventure. G 9-11.

356. Platt, Kin. *Chloris And The Freaks.* Bradbury, 1975. $6.95. Jennifer, twelve years old, becomes confused and disillusioned when her mother's second marriage falls apart, at the same time that a friend's parents are getting a divorce, and her science teacher is having trouble with his alimony payments. The theme of astrology is much in evidence. This book attempts to explain the inexplicable: why people fall in and out of love. Well written, and a solid story that has received excellent reviews. The author appears to be very hard on his female adult characters, who are petty, immature and flirtatious. The males fare better, even one who deserts his wife after childbirth. The expression "women's lib" is used with ironic intent. G 7+.

357. Polese, Macia and Dorothea Wender. *Frankie And The Fawn*. Abingdon, 1974. $4.50. Two country children whose mother is a veterinarian, nurse a wounded fawn back to health. The mother is especially well-drawn and the whole family is non-sexist. An old-fashioned tale, with a happy ending. Good for animal lovers. G 3-5.

358. Rabe, Bernice. *Naomi*. Nelson Hall, 1975. Eleven-year-old Naomi has her fortune told one day in rural Missouri in the 1930's. When she is told she will die before her fourteenth birthday, she panics and takes advice from everyone about how to live longer. Finally, disgusted, she decides to be her own woman and, at a ime when girls marry early, chooses to become a doctor. The book ends on her fourteenth birthday. Beautifully written, funny, and touching, with a wonderful heroine. G 6+.

359. Raskin, Ellen. *The Tatooed Potato and Other Clues*. Dutton, 1975. $7.50. Humor, mystery, puns, and delicious characters. When Dickory Dock (sister of Donald), an art student, goes to work for Garson, a wealthy portrait painter, she becomes a witness to murder, monsters, and intellectual escapades. Fabulous. G 6+.

360. Rock, Gail. *A Dream For Addie*. Knopf, 1975. $5.95. Addie Mills is a lively and resourceful 12-year-old girl in a small Nebraska town in the 1940's. Aspiring to be an artist, she understands sensitivity and befriends a town celebrity — an unsuccessful actress who drinks too much. Entertaining. G 5-7.

361. Rodgers, Mary. *A Billion For Boris*. Harper & Row, 1974. $4.95. More adventure from the cast of *Freaky Friday* (Harper & Row, 1972). A television set shows the next day's news, and Boris plans to improve his undependable, artistic mother. Very funny at first, but eventually there is something irritating about the idea of a teenaged boy choosing a psychiatrist and a mink coat for his mother. G 4-8.

362. Rosen, Winifred. *Cruisin For A Bruisin*. Knopf, 1976. $6.95. Glib and fast-moving story of the sexual awakening of a Jewish adolescent in New York. The upper middle-class girls of today may relate to this precocious heroine of the fifties, but it is hard to believe that twenty years ago

Winnie Simon actually lay nude with her blonde boy
friend and went for joy rides with a troubled male, one
of her psychiatrist-father's patients. A *Cosmopolitan* for
the younger set. G 7+.

363. St. George, Judith. *The Girl With Spunk*. Putnam, 1975.
$6.95. Seneca Falls in 1848 was an exciting place to be.
Josie, a young servant who finds her life restricted, is
ripe for the first Woman's Rights Convention. Fair to
good: *Kirkus*, 12/1/75. G 5-7.

364. Searcy, Margaret. *Ikwa Of The Temple Mounds*. U. of Ala-
bama, 1974. $5.50. Through the story of a twelve-year-
old Indian girl we learn about the culture of the Indian
Mound Builders, who lived in the Southeastern United
States over eight hundred years ago. Women's roles are
emphasized. Good: *Booklist* 2/1/75 and *SLJ* 2/75.

365. Sharmat, Marjorie. *Maggie Marmelstein For President*. Il.
Ben Shecter. Harper & Row, 1975. $4.11. When Thad,
running for president of the sixth grade, turns down Maggie's generous offer to be his campaign manager, she announces her own candidacy. The ensuing battle of egos
is fought without consideration of any real issues. Noah,
nice and intelligent, wins in a write-in upset. Relieved,
the two losers resume their friendship. Smoothly written,
humorous and engaging. Recommended. G 3-6.

366. Shaw, Richard. *Shape Up, Burke*. Nelson Hall, 1976. $6.95.
An ex-cop turned private detective wants to build up his
weakling son, and without worrying about the opinion of
his meek wife, enrolls Pat for the summer at a survival
camp, and then in a military school. The boy escapes the
camp and leads Dad a merry chase. The characters are
stereotyped and the mesage too loud, but the story is funny and exciting, and one of the few in which Boy rebels
against Macho Knows Best. Good for the reluctant
reader. G 4-9.

367. Singer, Issac Bashevis. *A Tale Of Three Wishes*. Il. Irene
Lieblick. Farrar Straus, 1976. $4.95. Legend says that on
the holy night of Hoshanah Rabbach for one moment the
sky will open and wishes will come true. Three children
make the dark journey to the synagogue to try their luck.
It would seem that their wishes for wisdom, wealth and
beauty are too grand for their years, but they do grow up

deservedly blessed. Need I tell you which one of the children (two boys and a girl) wished for beauty? Would you be surprised to learn that one of the children later married "the daughter of an important man"? The author is a fine storyteller, and his Esther does grow up "learned and virtuous" as well as beautiful. Colorful illustrations match the appealing mood. G 2-4. Read aloud to ages 4+.

368. Sleator, William. *Among The Dolls*. Il. T.S. Hyman. Dutton, 1975. $6.50. Vicky wants a ten speed bike for her birthday, but gets an antique dollhouse instead. Disappointment turns to morbid fascination. One day she becomes part of the doll family and is trapped in the house. The dolls are what she has pretended they are: meek father, whiny sister, mean aunt and timid brother. And they remember the terrible things she has done to them. The brother eventually saves Vicky, because he is a male, though flawed. Characters are stereotyped, but nonetheless this is an exciting story with excellent, suitable creepy illustrations. G 4-6.

369. Smith, Beatrice. *Don't Mention Moon To Me*. Nelson Hall, 1974. $5.95. Seventeen year old Holly goes from California to Europe for two weeks and becomes involved in smuggling. Humorous and light, the mystery holds your interest without any big surprises. Drawback: Holly smuggles a vial of moon dust in her padded bra and goes from 32A to 38C (rags to riches?). Too much emphasis on bras. G 6-9.

370. Smith, Nancy Covert. *Josie's Handful Of Quietness*. Abingdon, 1975. $4.95. The adolescent daughter of Mexican-American migrant workers wants to stay in one place to make friends and to do well in school. Her dreams come true with the help of an old lonely Anglo man who hires her family to manage his small farm. Josie is a good, intelligent character. Her family's problems (Dad must overcome Macho tendencies) make a good story. G 4-6.

371. Sortor, Toni. *The Adventures of B.J., Amateur Detective*. Abingdon, 1975. $3.50. Betty Jane's mother owns a detective agency inherited from her late husband. B.J., trying to solve a case, bumbles the job; Sammy, who wasn't even involved, solves it. Sammy is a little sexist and B.J. is a ineffectual, but the book gives a good picture of the heavy demands on a working widowed mother. Mom is the best character. Easy to read. G 3-5.

372. Steele, Mary Q. *Because Of The Sand Witches There.* Il. Paul Galdone. Greenwillow, 1975. $5.95. In E. Nebit's *Five Children And It,* "It" is a sand fairy, who turns children's dreams into nightmares. In this book Mildred and her obnoxious younger brother are led into trouble by a sand witch. But they gain an understanding of themselves. The adults are better drawn than the children here: unusual in a childrens' book. The women are strong and well-rounded and the beaches in winter are vividly described. No Nesbit, but entertaining. G 4-6.

373. Steele, Mary & William Steele. *The Eye In The Forest.* Dutton, 1975. $6.95. A legendary band of ancient Indians search for their lost homeland and find it with the help of Neeka, a brave female hunter. Excellent: *SLJ* 5/75. G 7-9.

374. Steptoe, John. *Marcia.* Il. by author. Viking, 1976. The attractive, intelligent 14-year-old Black heroine faces tough decisions: her boyfriend wants her to sleep with him. She is tempted but frightened. He threatens to leave her and after a soapbox speech to Mama, who agrees that early sex is inevitable, off they go to a doctor to equip Marcia for her new activities. The style and dialogue are easy and entertaining. I wonder whether boys who threaten girlfriends with abandonment in order to get sex are worth the effort to keep them. This book was written by a man. Read before purchase. G 6+.

375. Sullivan, Mary W. *What's This About Pete?* Nelson Hall, 1976. $5.95. An adolescent boy enjoys fine sewing. Mom is a dressmaker. Dad does not like it and a school coach openly calls Peter a homosexual. A school counselor and a sympathetic girlfriend help Peter to stick to his needle. An unusual theme and a good choice for the older reluctant reader. G 4-7.

376. Taylor, Mark. *Jennie Jenkins.* Il. G. Rounds. Little Brown, 1975. $4.95. A modern American folk tale built around the song "Will You Wear White, Oh My Dear Oh My Dear?" Jennie hates parties and dressing up and vows to get even with her sisters for forcing her to go to the Nettle Bottom Ball. Clever and funny. G 2-4.

377 Terris, Susan. *No Boys Allowed.* Il. Richard Cuffari. Double-
     day, 1976. $4.94. Tad, eight, is tired of being bossed by
     four older sisters. One day he takes off alone on a bus to
     downtown San Francisco to buy a birthday gift for Mom.
     He spends all his money and has to walk home in the
     growing darkness. He finally reaches the apartment to
     find a calm father, reading, and a nervous mother, tele-
     phoning. The book begins well, with a boy who needs to
     assert his independence, but the final message seems to
     be that females will worry you out of the house and then
     worry like fools when you're gone. Early readers will
     enjoy the realism of the scarey walk home. An easy to
     read book with good illustrations. G 2-4.

378. — *The Pencil Families.* Greenwillow, 1975. $5.95. Emily's
     parents go on vacation, leaving her with a disinterested
     brother, an odd cousin, an overactive imagination and a
     collection of pencils. Strange things happen when she
     discovers a gold pencil next to a dead man. The brother
     is forced to become interested in Emily and to respect her
     when she finally solves the mystery. The plot is good and
     fast moving, although the ending is rather anticlimatic.
     Emily has her points, but is really just a typical little
     sister. G 3-6.

379 — *Whirling Rainbows.* Doubleday, 1974. $4.58. The fat,
     blue-eyed adopted half-Indian daughter of Jewish intel-
     lectuals seeks to find her identity in a summer camp near
     Indian territory in Wisconsin. Her clever Mom who has
     an "Environment is everything" philosophy says,
     "Women have no characters at all." Recommended for
     girls who like sport stories but don't object to books with
     no character at all. G 5-8.

380. Titiev, Estelle, and Lila Pargment. *How The Moolah Was
     Taught A Lesson And Other Folk Tales From Russia.*
     Dial, 1976. Il. Ray Cruz. $5.95. In two of these four tales
     a poor man must meet certain challenges in order to keep
     his wife from abduction by a powerful and wicked noble.
     The nobleman is punished in each case: respectively by
     drowning, by public humiliation, and by being eaten by
     a witch. The first three stories are fun to read aloud, being
     filled with suspense and wit. The last story, "Of Oskus-
     Ool and His Wise Wife", is the least successful, although

the wife is instrumental in her husband's victory. It has
a confused plot. On the whole the book, illustrated in
black and white, is attractive and interesting. G 3-5. Read
aloud to G 1+.

381. Tobias, Tobi. *The Quitting Deal*. Il. Trina Schart Hyman.
Viking, 1975. $5.95. Together Jennifer and Mommy try
to quit bad habits: thumb-sucking for one and cigarettes
for the other. They try holding hands, eating candy,
paying fines, and finally decide cutting down is the only
answer. Good line drawings by the art director of *Crickett*
Magazine. One critic commented that Mommy looks
spacey all the time. G 2-4.

382. Turnbull, Ann. *The Frightened Forest*. Seabury, 1975.
$6.95. Gillian unintentionally frees a witch from a de-
serted railway tunnel and embarks on a frightening
supernatural adventure. Although this book lacks convincing characterization, both sexes can enjoy its mysterious adventures. G 4-6.

383. Underwood, Betty. *The Forge And The Forest*. Houghton
Mifflin, 1975. $6.95. Bernadette's guardian is a stern,
handsome pastor. She rejects his ideas about original sin
and the submission of women, in this story set in the
1830's, but respects his fiery abolitionism. The pastor's
wife goes mad from two tragic births and no birth con-
trol except abstinence. Bernadette is a strong character,
but the book is uneven: possibly the author attempted to
temper her feminism with sentimentality. However, the
Abolitionist movement is brought to life and we applaud
Bernadette's decision to use her artistic talents to
reveal the miseries of slavery. G 6-10.

384. Ungerer, Tomi. *A Storybook*. Il. by author. Watts, 1974.
$4.95. Many of these tales were favorably reviewed by
Eve Merriam. "Petronella" is included, by Jay Williams.
Watch out for Red Riding Hood: she marries the wolf.
Good: *NYT Book Review* 11/3/74. G 1+.

385. Van Stockum, Hilda. *The Borrowed House*. Farrar Straus,
1975. $6.95. When this story begins, in rural Germany
during World War II, twelve-year-old Janna is an avid
member of the Hitler Youth. When it closes, she has set
fire to a house to hide the fact that she has hidden a
Jewish youth there, among other clandestine anti-Nazi

operations. This book is similar in theme to Norma Johnston's *Of Time And Season*. Heroines in both books are dependent on male moral support and cry a lot. Does love do this to girls? Or does this reflect the writer's desire to let us know their strong heroines are really "women" at heart? Anyway, this is a successful mixture of history, romance and mystery. G 4-7.

386. Vestly, Anne-Catherine. *Hello, Aurora*. Translated by Jane Fairfax. Crowell, 1975. $5.50. The neighbors disapprove when Aurora's Dad becomes temporarily house-spouse and Mom, a lawyer, goes out to work. Pleasant Norwegian family tale, with a heroine kids can relate to. G 3-4.

387. Watson, Simon. *No Man's Land*. Greenwillow, 1976. $6.95. It's Boy Vs. Machine in this exciting science fiction tale about a sterile, mechanical future in which old people are forced into retirement homes, and village life is replaced by the concrete labyrinths of city "projects." Alan, the young hero, vows to aid two old people hiding from authorities in a country town. He learns that the town is to be destroyed by a moody, powerful machine, Giant, and successfully sabotages the beast. He then goes into forced exile, apprenticed to a doctor. A well-written story with an intelligent protagonist battling overwhelming odds. G 6-10.

388. Wells, Rosemary. *None Of The Above*. Dial, 1974. $5.95. An ordinary girl must adjust to her stylish new stepmother and brilliant stepsister. With bare description, but a skillful blend of vivid dialogue and quiet introspection, we are taken through Marcia's teenage years and her struggle to set her own modest goals. G 7+.

389. Wheeler, Ruth. *Bright Sunset: The Story Of An Indian Girl*. Lothrop Lee, 1974. $5.50. A girl is frightened of tribal initiation into womanhood. Good: *SLJ* 10/74. G 4-6.

390. Wilkinson, Brenda. *Ludell*. Harper & Row, 1975. $5.95. Black life in Georgia. Ludell is twelve years old. Her teachers are real characters, and so are her neighbors, friends and her loving grandmother. She has good times and bad times, and even falls in love. When we first meet

her, her big dream is that Mama, who works in New York, will send her a TV set. When we leave her, two years later, she is happily preparing to become a professional writer. Highly recommended. G 4+.

391. Williams, Jay. *The People Of The Ax.* Walck, 1974. $5.95. The adventures of teenagers Frey and Arne who live in a primitive time after an atomic holocaust. They fight sub-human creatures without souls: these Croms are greedy, evil and reproduce at a great rate. Frey and Arne live in a tribe where women have their share of leadership. The sexism of the Croms is considered a sign of barbarism. A slow-starting but entertaining adventure story, which should appeal to both sexes. G 6-10.

392. Wolitzer, Hilma. *Introducing Shirley Braverman.* Farrar Straus, 1975. $5.95. In 1944, while war rages in Europe, Shirley, a twelve-year-old in Brooklyn, has her own problems. She wants to win a city-wide spelling contest, to become friends with her older sister Velma, and to make a "mensch" of her nervous six-year-old brother. This story is entertaining and authentic. Shirley and her plucky pal Mitzi are well worth meeting. G 4-7.

393. Yolen, Jane. *The Magic Three Of Solatia.* Crowell, 1974. $5.95. This fantasy is reminiscent of *The Tempest* and *Alice In Wonderland.* It is the story of Sianna: her magic, her romance and her heroic son. When she is young, Sianna is carried off by a wave and meets the dread mer-witch, Mary. Mary teaches Sianna her sea magic in exchange for learning Sianna's songs. The story is divided into four books. The son's adventures are not as engrossing as Sianna's but dazzling dream-like imagery and unusual adventures make this book captivating. G 5-9.

394. — *The Transfigured Hart.* Crowell, 1975. $5.95. A bookish boy and an active girl try to capture an albino hart which they believe is the last unicorn. Only virgins can tame unicorns, so Heather, twelve years old, agrees to act as bait. If she is not pure, the unicorn's horn will dismember her. Heather wonders if having kissed a boy counts. The children successfully save the animal and the author successfully keeps the double standard alive. Disappointing. G 4-6.

395. Young, Miriam. *No Place For Mitty*. Four Winds, 1976. $5.95. In San Francisco in the 1880's, ten-year-old Mitty's father becomes an Evangelist, wrecking the family's finances and affections. A divorce is the result and the fatherless family moves across the Bay to grandparent's farm. Here Mitty can run and jump with her brothers until a rich aunt takes her to Berkeley to make a lady of her. Elocution, sewing and piano lessons stifle poor Mitty; her grandmother, an unusual strong female, notices her dampened spirits. Mitty is a satisfactory feminist rebel. The book is predictable and written in a mechanical style, but it is readable. Because of the dearth of strong lively heroines, it might be worth consideration. G 4-6.

CHAPTER VIII

NON-FICTION, GRADES 3-10

396. Adoff, Arnold. *My Black Me: A Beginning Book Of Black Poetry.* Dutton, 1974. $4.95. Fifty brief selections from the work of Black poets. Excellent: *Kirkus* 4/15/74.

397. Alderman, Clifford. *Colonists For Sale: The Story Of Indentured Servants In America.* Macmillan, 1975. $7.95. A study of the indentured servitude of Irish, German, and other non-English colonists in America. *Kirkus* notes the author's bias in favor of the oppressed groups but recommends (4/75). Good: *SLJ* 5/75. G 5-8.

398. Ancona, George. *And What Do You Do?* A Book About People And Their Work. Il. photos. Dutton, 1976. $6.95. A good, simple introduction to twenty-one jobs that do not require a college degree: air-traffic controller, optician, TV production assistant, etc. Attractive photographs of nine women and fifteen men busy at their jobs accompany short descriptions of the training and duties their work entails. The author says these people "feel that the work they do is important to others — important enough to be paid for it." What is his opinion of homemaking? G 3-5.

399. Anticaglia, Elizabeth. *Heroines of '76.* Walker, 1975. $5.83. Divided into two parts: I. Heroines in Battle, and II. Heroines in Work. Fourteen biographies of patriots and royalists, writers, artists, settlers, spies, and soldiers. Part I succeeds: dramatic events carry the story. Part II is flat and artificial. The characters are merely props in an historical pageant. I object to the put-down of Phyllis Wheatly's deserter-husband, with no denunciation of the slave owners who trained this intellectual to be a performing poodle. G 2-5.

400. Arnold, Adele. *Red Son Rising*. Dillon, 1974. $5.95. The biography of Carlos Montezuma, an Apache Indian captured by a white man and raised as his son, who became a physician and an advocate of Indian rights. Good: *SLJ* 2/75. G 4-7.

401. Axelbank, Albert. *Soviet Dissent: Intellectuals, Jews And Detente*. Watts, 1975. $6.95. American and Russian views of the Soviet dissidents: people like Solzhenitsyn and Panov. Good: *Kirkus* 2/15/75. G 6-12.

402. Bacon, Margaret Hope. *I Speak For My Slave Sister: The Life Of Abby Kelley Foster*. Crowell, 1974. $5.50. A "Woman of America" series biography of the leader of the most radical Abolitionist faction. Stirring, fascinating history. Highly recommended. G 5+.

403. — *Rebellion At Christiana*. Crown, 1975. $5.95. The story of escaped slaves who resisted arrest in Pennsylvania and killed the man who attempted their capture under the Fugitive Slave Act. Starred review: *SLJ* 2/75; Excellent: *CBRS* 2/75. G 7-12.

404. Baker, Jim. *Billie Jean King*. Grosset & Dunlap, 1974. $3.99. A look into this athlete's personal and professional life, with much emphasis on the famous match with Bobbie Riggs. Fair: *SLJ* 5/74. G 3-5.

405. Balducci, Carolyn. *A Self-Made Woman. Biography Of Nobel Prize Winner Grazia Deledda*. Houghton Mifflin, 1975. $6.95. This writer, born in an impoverished section of Sardinia in the 19th century, won the Nobel Prize in 1926. Detailed pictures of her childhood and family life reveal much about Southern Italian culture. Scholarly, well-written and entertaining. With a 5-page bibliography. G 8+.

406. Belloc, Hilaire. *The Yak, The Python And The Frog: Three Beast Poems*. Il. Steven Kellog. Parents, 1975. $4.95. A little girl's elderly papa takes her shopping for the "rare and strange pet" she has requested. These humorous poems are accompanied by fantastic illustrations, greatly detailed. Although this is a picture book, it seems too sophisticated for children under six. G 2+.

407. Belting, Natalia. *Whirlwind Is A Ghost Dancing*. Il. L. & D. Dillon. Dutton, 1974. $7.50. A collection of poems about North American Indians. Sources and locations are given for each selection. Illustrations are acrylic and pastels. Recommended: *BCCB* 3/75. G 4+.

408. Bendick, Jeanne. *How Animals Behave*. Il. by author. Parents, 1976. $4.96. A clearly written, well-organized introduction to the study of animal behavior. Explanations are given for instance, for instinct, imprinting, learning by experience and reasoning. Behavior patterns are examined in animals varying from one cell organisms to human beings. Non-sexist, but the illustrations are really cartoons: they verge on racial caricature. Recommended for school assignment. G 2-4. Read aloud to K+.

409. Berg, Jean Horton. *I Cry When The Sun Goes Down: The Story Of Herman Wrice*. Westminster, 1975. $6.95. This Black leader is best known for having worked with the Young Great Society of Mantua, Pa., a civil projects group of ex-gang leaders and troubled youths. The people and events which turned Wrice from a poor West Virginia mountain youth into an organizer are described here, with enough fictionalized dialogue to keep things moving. Children will probably need to learn something about Wrice's current activities before caring enough about him to read about his past. G 6+.

410. Blair, Ruth Van Ness. *Mary's Monster*. Coward McCann, 1975. Mary Ann Anning was a 19th century British pale-ontologist. This fictionalized biography begins with a lively account of her childhood interest in fossils, but ends with a rather dry procession of scientific fact. Mary's character dissolves in mid-life. I was glad that she was not treated here as peculiar because of her interests. But alas! on page 58 we find that Mary was "an Exception to the Rule . . . Most young women were content to be housewives or governesses . . . In a few cases, they were writers like Jane Austen . . ." "Content"? How about "coerced"? Were there only "a few cases" of women not content to be domesticated? Recommended, despite this rather simple-minded attitude, for readers interested in women scientists and in fossils. G 3-5.

411. Brown, Dee. *Wounded Knee: An Indian History Of The American West.* Holt Rinehart, 1974. $6.95. Selected first-hand accounts of the history of four tribes. Good: *Kirkus,* 10/15/74. G 6+.

412. Bryan, Ashley. *Walk Together Children: Black American Spirituals.* Atheneum, 1974. $6.95. These beautiful songs were created by American slaves and preserved by Northern collectors. Recommended: *MS* 12/74 and *SLJ* 10/74. G 1-4.

413. Burchard, Marshall and Sue Burchard. *Sports Hero, Billie Jean King.* Il. photos. Putnam, 1975. $4.69. This is a large print biography. King biographies must be as numerous as books about Helen Keller. The authors just go through the motions. G 2-4.

414. Burchard, Marshall. *Sports Hero, Reggie Jackson.* Putnam, 1975. $4.99. The easy-to-read biography of the popular Black baseball star. Good: *SLJ* 2/76.

415. Burgess, Mary. *Contributions Of Women: Education.* Il. photos. Dillon, 1975. $6.95. Fifteen women educators are discussed: the lives of six Americans are given in detail, while nine others are briefly sketched. Excellent: *SLJ* 12/75.

416. Burt, Olive. *Black Women Of Valor.* Messner, 1974. $6.95. Brief biographies of Juliette Derricotte, social worker; Maggie Walker, bank president; Septima Clark, educator; and Ida Barnet, journalist. Fair: *Kirkus* 11/15/74. G 4-6.

417. Carrick, Malcolm. *Splodges.* Viking, 1976. $6.95. With humor and enthusiasm the artist-author demonstrates that "accidents" (a dripping line, a wayward brush) can lead to imaginative ideas. Youngsters can blot with toy blocks, draw with candles, or blow with a straw onto wet paint. A bright, entertaining craft book. G K-4.

418. Carter, Joseph. *Freedom To Know: A Background Book.* Parents, 1974. $4.95. A discussion of censorship, propaganda, news services and the question of the concealment of truth vs. the safeguarding of security. Star review: *SLJ* 1/75. G 7-12.

419. Childress, Alice. *When The Rattlesnake Sounds.* Il. Charles Lilly. Coward McCann, 1975. $5.95. Harriet Tubman is the heroine of this one-act play which takes place in the hotel laundry where she worked to raise money for the abolitionist cause. Harriet tells two co-workers about the Underground Railroad and her feelings and experiences. Highly readable and dramatic. Good for high school production. G 5+.

420. Chirinos, Lito. *Lito The Shoeshine Boy.* Translated and with photos by David Mangurian. Four Winds, 1975. $5.95. A touching, but unsentimental, portrait of a homeless nine-year-old Honduran boy, whose spirit and dignity have not yet been destroyed by poverty.

421. Chukovsky, Kornei. *The Silver Crest: My Russian Boyhood.* Transl. Beatrice Stillman. Holt Rinehart, 1976. $6.95. The famous Russian writer tells about the often sadistic world of his gymnasium in Odessa at the turn of the century, where children from 9 to 17 went if their parents could afford the fees. It reminds one of Robert Cormier's private boys' school in *The Chocolate War.* Kornei was eventually expelled because it was discovered that his mother was a washerwoman. He was forced to earn his living and educate himself. He describes the corruption of officials and the persecutions of the poor. This biography becomes a political statement: neither didactic nor self-righteous but direct, and written with the young reader in mind. A powerful memoir. Recommended for every collection. G 6-Adult.

422. Clapp, Patricia. *Dr. Elizabeth: The Story Of The First Woman Doctor.* Lothrop Lee, 1974. $4.95. A lively fictionalized biography written in the first person. Blackwell was the first woman to earn a medical degree. If only Clapp had tempered her use of exclamation points!!! Nevertheless, a good read. G 3+.

423. Clyne, Patricia E. *Patriots In Petticoats.* Il. Richard Lebenson. Dodd Mead, 1976. $4.95. Short biographies of female patriots, with guides to monuments and museums with relevant holdings. *Kirkus:* Women are not presented as strong and individual. The writing is stiff, and the title is unfortunate. (I agree). Below average. 1/15/76. G 4-6.

424. Coates, Ruth. *Great American Naturalists.* Lerner, 1974. $3.95. Biographies of 14 conservationists, male and female, from the 18th to the 20th centuries. Good: *SLJ* 1/75. G 4-9.

425. Coy, Harold. *Chicano Roots Go Deep.* Dodd Mead, 1975. $5.95. Chicano life, culture and history. Excellent: *Kirkus* 7/1/75.

426. *Daughters In High School: An Anthology Of Their Work.* Daughters, 1974. $3.80. Young feminists talk about growing up female in this collection of poetry and prose. Excellent: *SLJ* 3/75. G 8+.

427. Davis, Mary L. *Women Who Changed History: Five Famous Queens Of Europe.* Lerner, 1975. The times, personalities and governments of Eleanor of Aquitaine, Isabella of Spain, Elizabeth Tudor, Marie Antoinette and Catherine the Great. The author uses expressions like "green-eyed divorcee" and says sweepingly that Catherine "seduced every man she wanted". Useful for school assignments, perhaps, but not really successful. G 4-8.

428. De Pauw, Linda Grant. *Founding Mothers: Women Of America In The Revolutionary Era.* Houghton Mifflin, 1975. $6.95. A history of the social and legal position of American women in the 18th century. Diaries and letters are used to illustrate points. There are chapters on laws, employment and the military and on Black and Native American women. Well-known people are included, but the emphasis is on the ordinary unknowns who contributed to the country's development. Competently written and objective. With bibliography and index. G 6+.

429. Dobrin, Arnold. *A Life For Israel: Golda Meier.* Il. photos. Dial, 1974. $4.95. A biography combined with a historical picture of Israel. With chronology, bibliography and index. Good: *Kirkus* 11/1/74.

430. Dockery, Wallene. *Weather Or Not.* Il. Steve Laughbaum. Abingdon, 1976. $3.75. It's good to see a woman as a TV weather reporter, but this book is irritating rather than entertaining because of the gimmicky way the weather is explained to two young boys. The dialogue is forced and stiff. The boys' questions are so naive that they do not go well with the sophisticated answers they get. G 2-4.

431. Donahue, Parnell, M.D. *Germs Make Me Sick! A Health Book For Kids.* Il. Kelly Oechsli. Knopf, 1975. $2.95. This easy-to-read book will take the mystery out of childhood illnesses. Illustrations of children of many races in role-free settings. With glossary and index. G 3-8.

432. Dunnahoo, Terry. *Before The Supreme Court: The Story Of Belva Ann Lockwood.* Houghton Mifflin, 1974. This 19th century American lawyer was a civil rights activist, a colleague of Susan B. Anthony, and the first woman to present a case before the Supreme Court. Recommended: *MS* 12/74; Fair: *Kirkus* 5/15/74. See No. 437. G 6+.

433. Epstein, Sam and Beryl. *Jackie Robinson: Baseball's Gallant Fighter.* Il. V. Mays. Gerrard, 1974. $3.28. Easy-to-read fictionalized biography of the first Black Major League baseball player. Good: *SLJ* 4/75. G 2-4.

434. Faber, Doris. *Bella Abzug.* Il. photos. Lothrop Lee, 1976. $6.95. This lively biography gives us a full and entertaining picture of the famous politician, but it is marred by comments about Abzug's appearance. "She's also much better-looking than her pictures; on the heavy side . . . but very stylish . . ." That sort of thing. We are told even that she was once "gorgeous". This will do until something less sexist comes along. G 4+.

435. Felton, Harold W. *Nancy Ward, Cherokee.* Il. Carolyn Bertrand. Dodd Mead, 1975. $4.95. Half Cherokee and half English, Nancy Ward took the American side in the Revolutionary War and helped white captives escape from pro-British Indians. She was a pacifist, and introduced dairy farming to her people, to whom the American Government she supported did not bring justice, a fact she knew by the time she died in 1822. This biography is too brief to give adequate information about this unusual woman. G 4-6.

436. Fleming, Alice. *Contraception, Abortion And Pregnancy.* Nelson Hall, 1974. General and sketchy information. Mixed response. *Kirkus* 10/15/74. G 7+.

437. Fox, Mary Virginia. *Lady For The Defense. A Biography Of Belva Lockwood.* Harcourt Brace, 1976. $6.50. For another book on this topic see No. 432. A lively fiction-alized account of her life. Occasionally the author uses dialogue to feed us information. Belva's tough perso-nality comes through despite the author's comments on her "womanliness". Readable, but hardly the last word on this subject. G 4-9.

438. Friedman, Ina. *Black Cop.* Westminster, 1974. $5.25. A biography of Tilmon O'Bryant, the first Black assistant chief of police in Washington, D.C. *Kirkus* says that points about racial prejudice are well taken, but that there is too much idealization of O'Bryant. Fair: *Kirkus* 4/15/74. G 5-9.

439. Fufuka, Karama. *My Daddy Is A Cool Dude.* Il. Mahri Fufuka. Dial, 1975. $5.95. A collection of 27 poems sup-posed to be by children, about life in a Black ghetto. Soft pencil sketches tell us more about things than the poetry does. A pleasant introduction to joys and sorrows of Black urban life, but no talent like Nikki Giovanni. G 1-4.

440. Giovanni, Nikki. *Ego Tripping And Other Poems For Young People.* Il. George Ford. Lawrence Hill, 1973. $2.95. 23 excellent poems about Black life and feeling. The illustrations are powerful. This book catches the spark of life. G 6+.

441. Gleasner, Diana. *Women In Sports: Swimming.* Harvey, 1975. $4.95. Biographies of 5 champion swimmers: C. Loock, S. Babashoff, K. Heddy, G. Buzonas and D. Nyad. Fair: *ACL* 2/76. G 4-6.

442. Goldreich, Gloria and Esther Goldreich. *What Can She Be? An Architect.* Photos Robert Ipcar. Lothrop Lee, 1974. $4.50. Another title in the well executed "What Can She Be?" series. Susan Brody is the architect here: her work is well described and photographed. G 2-5.

443. — *What Can She Be? A Farmer.* Photos Robert Ipcar. Loth-rop Lee, 1976. $4.95. Althea and Natalie Ross are two sisters who have a dairy farm in Maine. Their daily lives are treated, seasonal changes and the deep satisfaction of their work.

444. — *What Can She Be? A Geologist.* Photos Robert Ipcar. Lothrop Lee, 1976. $4.95. Dr. Ina Brown is shown teaching, on field trips, and relaxing with her three sons. We learn a good deal about geology as well as about the life of a female scientist. G 1-6.

445. — *What Can She Be? A Musician.* Photos Robert Ipcar. Lothrop Lee, 1975. $4.75. Leslie Pearl is a teacher, conductor and composer. A simple text accompanies the photographs. Recommended for home and school. G 2-5.

446. — *What Can She Be? A Police Officer.* Photos Robert Ipcar. Lothrop Lee, 1975. $4.75. This is the sixth of this series, which shows women working in male-dominated jobs. Laura and Nancy Ames are sisters and New York City policewomen. Large print. Highly recommended. Ages 4-10.

447. Gordon, Sol. *Girls Are Girls And Boys Are Boys: So What's The Difference?* Il. Frank Smith. Stein & Day, 1974. $4.95. This book proceeds on the theory that biology is not destiny but the sex information given is too advanced for the picture book format and the tone of the prefatory pages. The illustrations unfortunately are reminscent of government pamphlets. G 2+.

448. — *You! The Psychology Of Surviving And Enhancing Your Social Life, Love Life, Creative Life, Etc.* Quadrangle, 1975. $6.95. This rather zany book contains friendly and supportive sex education, a healthy attitude toward life, and even room in its pages for the reader to write in thoughts and feelings. A perfect gift for teenagers. G 7+.

449. Greenfeld, Howard. *Gertrude Stein: A Biography.* Crown, 1973. Il. photos. $5.95. An attractively produced, well-written book for serious readers. G 7+.

450. — *They Came To Paris.* Crown, 1975. $6.95. A survey of the expatriots who gravitated to Gertrude Stein's salon in Paris in the twenties. Excellent: *BCCB* 2/76. With bibliography and index. G 8+.

451. Greenfield, Eloise. *Paul Robeson.* Il. George Ford. Crowell, 1975. $4.50. One in a series of "Crowell Biographies". Excellent: *Kirkus* 5/15/75. See No. 454. G 2-4.

452. Gurko, Miriam. *The Ladies Of Seneca Falls: The Birth Of The Women's Rights Movement.* Macmillan, 1974. $7.95. A highly readable, well-documented picture of the personalities of the first suffragists and the background of the birth of the suffrage movement. A handsome book, with bibliographies, index and many photos. A classic. G 6+.

453. Gurney, Gene and Claire Gurney. *Women On The March.* Abelard Schulman, 1974. $5.95. A guide to opportunities for women in the military. Good: *SLJ* 11/74; Mixed: *Kirkus* 10/15/74. G 5-12.

454. Hamilton, Virginia. *Paul Robeson: Life And Times Of A Free Black Man.* Harper & Row, 1974. $5.95. This son of a Black slave went on to become a lawyer, actor, singer and victim of anti-Communism. See No. 451. Good: *SLJ* 11/74. G 9+.

455. Harnan, Terry. *African Rhythm — American Dance: A Biography Of Katherine Dunham.* Knopf, 1974. $4.95. Il. photos. Good: *SLJ* 4/74; Fair: *Kirkus* 4/15/74. G 6-8.

456. Haskins, James. *Fighting Shirley Chisholm.* Dial, 1975. $5.95. The highlight of this book is its lively description of Chisholm's campaigns for N.Y. State Assembly and for the Congress. There is no explanation for the hostility between women's groups and Black men's groups during the Presidential campaign, although we read constant reference to a good deal of bickering. This lack of information is a major flaw in an otherwise excellent biography. G 6-12.

457. — *The Picture Life Of Malcolm X.* Watts, 1974. $3.90. Large print and many photos. Fair: *Kirkus* 1/15/75.

458. — *Ralph Bunche: A Most Reluctant Hero.* Hawthorne, 1974. $6.95. This remarkable man was a scholar, athlete, diplomat and winner of the Nobel Prize. See No. 490. Excellent: *SLJ* 9/74. G 7+.

459. Hautzig, Esther. *Life With Working Parents: Practical Hints For Everyday Situations.* Il. Ray Doty. Macmillan, 1976. $6.95. This book is more valuable in intent than in content. Although solid advice for emergency situations

is given, there are many pages of recipes and craft ideas which can be found in other books. However, the cheerful, optimistic tone of the text can certainly ease the mind of any child who is tense about having two employed parents, and the book is non-sexist. G 5-8.

460. Heaps, Willard. *Juvenile Justice.* Seabury, 1974. $6.95. How our system deals with young criminals. Good: *SLJ* 1/75; Fair: *Kirkus* 12/1/74. G 7-12.

461. Henderson, Nancy. *Circle Of Life: The Miccosukee Indian Way.* Messner, 1974. $5.95. Contemporary life and history of this Florida tribe. Good: *SLJ* 1/75. G 4-6.

462. Hilton, Suzanne. *The Way It Was - 1876.* Westminster, 1975. $6.95. Il. photos and prints. This handsome and informative book tells about daily life in America a hundred years ago; there are chapters on home life, sports, medicine, travel, school, etc. The treatment of women is not only treated in a separate chapter, but is a theme throughout. Only one error: Susan B. Anthony, who never married, is called "Mrs. Anthony." Entertaining and very readable. Highly recommended. G 6-Adult.

463. Hirsch, S. Carl. *He And She: How Males And Females Behave.* Lippincott, 1975. $7.95. A lively, well-written look into animal behavior and the scientists who study it. There appear to be varied relationships and patterns of behavior between the sexes of different species; thus the author rejects the idea that behavior can be predicted or assumed on the basis of sex. G 5+.

464. Hopkins, Lee Bennett. *On Our Way: Poems Of Pride And Love.* Photos David Parks. Knopf, 1974. $4.95. A selection of good poetry by well known Black writers. This attractive book includes biographical data. Highly recommended. G 4+.

465. Horvath, Joan. *What Boys Want To Know About Girls. &What Girls Want To Know About Boys.* Nelson Hall, 1976. $6.95. Two books in one volume about the biological and emotional changes of puberty and adolescence. Young teenagers are interviewed about their preferences, relationships, and sexual activities. Males only are asked about masturbation. The comment is repeat-

edly made that boys are more easily aroused sexually than girls, without any reason given for this, if it is true. But role-free relationships are favorably discussed, both sexes are treated with equal respect, and the positive and friendly approach may provide comfort and enlightenment for young teenagers. G 5+.

466. Horwitz, Sylvia. *Francisco Goya: Painter Of Kings And Demons.* Harper & Row, 1974. $5.95. Starred reviews: *Kirkus* 10/15/74 and *SLJ* 1/75. G 7+.

467. Jackson, Florence. *The Black Man In America: 1905-1932.* Watts, 1974. $3.90. A brief survey of Black political, artistic, organizational and economic history. Black women are hardly mentioned. There are three earlier volumes in this series. *1791-1861* (1971) has more information about women; *1881-1877* (1972) mentions few women; and in *1877-1905* (1973) we find the statement that "the 15th Amendment gave Black people the right to vote." Of course, it did not give Black women this right, and women are not counted as people throughout these books. G 4+.

468. Jackson, Gregory. *Getting Into Broadcast Journalism: A Guide To Careers In Radio And TV.* Hawthorn, 1974. $6.95. This detailed guide pays special attention to women and minorities. Good: *Booklist* 1/15/75 and *Kirkus* 12/15/74.

469. Jacobs, William. *Roger Williams.* Watts, 1975. $4.90. A brief discussion of the life and thought of the great early American dissenter. Excellent: *Kirkus* 1/15/75.

470. Johnson, Hannah L. *Let's Make Soup.* Photos Daniel Dorn. Lothrop Lee, 1976. $5.50. Step by step instructions about how to make beef and vegetable soup, a recipe for chicken soup, and storage and serving advice. The steps are easy to follow. Large photos show 3 children (ages 8-12) cooking. It's good that 2 boys make soup, but we are told "mommy can buy the meat." So can Daddy, Ma'am! G 2+.

471. Jones, Kenneth. *War With The Seminoles: Indians Fight For Their Freedom And Homeland (1835-1843).* Watts, 1975. $3.90. A description of the violation by the Government of its own treaties. Included is the story of Osceola, a War leader, and an account of Seminole life today. Good: *Kirkus* 1/15/75. G 5-9.

472. Katz, William Loren & Jacqueline Hunt Katz, eds. *Making Our Way: America At The Turn Of The Century In The Words Of The Poor And The Powerless.* Il. photos. Dial, 1976. $5.95. Fourteen personal accounts of experiences by people of various nationalities, many of them immigrants. We learn from their own words about a Polish Jewish woman who worked in a sweatshop at 16, a dedicated Irish cook and an anonymous farmer's wife. The most disheartening story is told by a Black sharecropper in Georgia. The editors have written an excellent introduction to the book, and brief forewords to each account. Highly recommended. G 6+.

473. Katz, William L. *Minorities In American History.* Watts, 1974. $3.95. Vol I: *Early America: 1492-1812;* Vol II: *Slavery To The Civil War 1812-1864.* This is a part of a planned set of six volumes, which demonstrate that the retention of original cultural traits was the best defense a minority had in an unfriendly environment. Fair: *Kirkus* 2/15/74. G 5-9.

474. Kherdian, David, ed. *Settling America: The Ethnic Expression Of 14 Contemporary Poets.* Macmillan, 1974. $6.95. The theme, by both famous and obscure poets, is "identity" and "finding oneself." Good: *SLJ* 2/75. G 10+.

475. Klever, Anita. *Women In Television.* Westminster, 1975. Il. photos. $5.95. Over 30 women are interviewed, from engineer to station manager. Their work is described, along with their feelings about working in a male-dominated profession. Their comments are revealing. One woman told her employer she would take a smaller salary than a man, and she is still getting a smaller salary. A director implies that her job resulted from an attack upon the studio by NOW. A news reader says the camermen alternate between the fear of upsetting her with gory stories and the fun of showing her corpses. The informal interview style of this book presents a personal picture that makes up for the lack of comprehensive information. G 5+.

476. Kraemer, James. *Your Future In Pharmacy.* Rosen, 1974. $4.80. This is one of the "Careers in Depth" series. It has a special chapter on women in this profession. Good: *SLJ* 5/75. G 7-12.

477. Landau, Elaine. *Woman, Woman! Feminism In America.*
Messner, 1974. $5.95. A general survey of sex discrimina-
tion, written from an optimistic standpoint. Fair: *Kirkus*
11/15/74. G 7-9.

478. Lengyel, Emil. *And All Her Paths Were Peace. The Life Of
Bertha Von Suttner.* Nelson Hall, 1975. $6.95. This paci-
fist and humanitarian (1843-1914) was a countess de-
scended from an Austrian military family. Her book
Die Waffen Nieder! (Lay Down Your Arms!) helped to
win her the Nobel Peace Prize, an honor she was instrumental in creating. This is a fast-paced biography, but
unfortunately too simplistic and idealised a portrait
emerges. A hidden heroine well worth rediscovery. G 6-8.

479. Levine, I.E. *The Many Faces Of Slavery.* Messner, 1975.
$4.95. A history. Fair: *SLJ* 5/75. G 7-12.

480. Levy, Elizabeth. *Lawyers For The People.* Knopf, 1974.
$4.95. Lively accounts of men and women who devote
their talents to the cause of human rights. Good: *SLJ*
11/74; *Ms* 12/74. G 6+.

481. Liebers, Arthur. *You Can Be An Electrician.* Lothrop Lee,
1974. $5.50. This contains a separate section on oppor-
tunities for women in this field. Excellent: *SLJ* 4/75. G
7-9.

482. Livingston, Myra Cohn, ed. *One Little Room An Every-
where: Poems Of Love.* Il. Antonio Frasconi. Atheneum,
1975. $5.50. A collection of poetry from different times
and countries divided into three parts: Hopes, Joys and
Sorrows. The tone is traditional, relying heavily on man's
worship of his lover's beauty and purity. The poems are
short. There is a balance between light romantic and
more serious verse. A modern or feminist addition would
have rocked the boat a little. Attractive woodcuts. G 6+.

483. Loeb, Robert. *Your Legal Rights As A Minor.* Watts, 1974.
$5.95. Answers to teenagers' questions. Good: *Kirkus*
4/1/74. G 7+.

484. Loeble, Suzanne. *Conception, Contraception: A New Look.*
McGraw Hill, 1974. $6.95. Il. charts, diagrams and
prints. A discussion of research in birth-control. Starred
review: *SLJ* 4/74. G 8+.

485. McDearmon, Kay. *Mahalia, Gospel Singer.* Il. Nevin & Phyllis Washington. Dodd Mead, 1976. $4.50. This famous and talented Black humanitarian and artist was a rare person. She never sold out to big band offers, nor allowed herself to become embittered by the prejudice she encountered. This book is adequately written, but the illustrations are distracting and unattractive. G 2-4.

486. McGovern, Ann. *If You Lived With The Sioux Indians.* Four Winds, 1974. $5.95. A question and answer story of the life of a Sioux boy in the 1880's. Good: *SLJ* 4/75; Fair: *Kirkus* 12/15/74.

487. — *The Story Of Deborah Sampson.* Il. Ann Grifalconi. Four Winds, 1975. This adventurous young woman, in male disguise, joined the Continental Army and became a respected soldier and, later, a pacifist lecturer. This book describes her difficult childhood as an indentured servant, her brief but eventful military career, and in less detail, her later years as a lecturer and wife and mother. Well-written, but not exciting. Fine line drawings in a handsome book with simple text. Recommended. G 2-4.

488. McHargue, Georgess, ed. *Little Victories, Big Defeats. War As The Ultimate Pollution.* Delacorte, 1974. $5.95. Anti-war excerpts from the work of Dos Passos, Vonnegut and Sholokov, among others. Starred review: *SLJ* 4/75. G 7+.

489. McHugh, Mary. *Law And The New Woman.* Watts, 1975. $5.90. Practical information about women in the legal profession, including a description of the types of jobs available, a list of approved law schools, a bibliography and other resource information. G 10+.

490. Mann, Peggy. *Ralph Bunche: U.N. Peacemaker.* Coward McCann, 1975. A detailed, subjective life. See No. 458. Fair: *Kirkus* 8/1/75.

491. Mayer, Ann. *The Two Worlds Of Beatrix Potter.* Children's Press, 1974. $4.95. A fictionalized biography in which we see the writer, restricted by society and by her family retreating to her private whimsical world of gentle animals. Good: *SLJ* 1/75. G 3-5.

492. Meade, Marion. *Free Woman: The Life And Times Of Victoria Woodhull.* Knopf, 1976. $6.95. This controversial 19th century feminist advocated complete sexual freedom, succeeded as a stockbroker and became a Presidential candidate. In this book her personality and ambitions as well as her family life are played against the customs of her times. However, we read that, unlike Woodhull, none of the other feminists "had suffered . . . poverty or physical drudgery." The other feminists are presented negatively as "pinched" or "distorted with rage." We do not read that Lucy Stone was born into poverty, that Lizzie Stanton had seven children and that Sojourner Truth had been a slave. These jabs at the other women are unfortunate in what would otherwise be a first-rate biography. Recommended. G 6+.

493. Meltzer, Milton. *The Eye Of Conscience: Photographers And Social Change.* Follet, 1974. $6.95. Ten photographers whose work explored social problems and inspired reform. Starred review: *SLJ* 10/74.

494. — *Never To Forget: The Jews Of The Holocaust.* Harper & Row, 1976. $6.95. A concise history of anti-Semitism in general, and in particular the events leading to Hitler's "final solution," with letters, diaries, newspaper stories, court transcripts, poems and ballads. Many examples are given of men, women and children who sacrificed themselves to hamper the Nazi program. The author's position is that blame cannot be put on one nation or one man, but on world apathy. "Indifference is the greatest sin," he says, adding that it can happen again. G 7+.

495. Merriam, Eve. *Rainbow Writing.* Atheneum, 1976. $4.95. Images of nature, word play, comment on our mechanized society, persistent cheerfulness, and thoughts about writing make this an entertaining book of poetry. From the poem "Ways of Composing":

> typewriter
> a mouthful of teeth chattering
> afraid to be quiet
> a pencil can lie down and dream
> dark and silver silences.

496. Meyer, Edity. *Not Charity, But Justice: Jacob Riis.* Vanguard, 1975. $5.95. A Danish immigrant, newspaper reporter, and photographer, Riis dedicated his life to making the public aware of slum conditions and the need for reforms. Excellent: *Kirkus* 1/15/75. G 6-10.

497. Milgrim, Shirley. *Haym Solomon: Liberty's Son.* Jewish Publication Society, 1975. $4.50. A fictionalized biography of an immigrant from Poland, who devoted his genius, energy, and money to the American Revolution. We see him telling his wife Rachael not to "worry your pretty little head" about financial matters. Her pretty little head availed her nothing, however, when Solomon died and the government reneged on his personal loans. Recommended. G 5+.

498. Mitchell, Joyce Slayton. *Other Choices For Becoming A Woman.* Knopf, 1974. $5.00. These essays by such diverse professionals as Margaret Meade and a male fashion designer urge high school women to open their minds to many options and raise their expectations. Good: *SLJ* 3/75. G 9+.

499. Molnar, Joe. *Elizabeth: A Puerto Rican-American Child Tells Her Story.* Il. photos. Watts, 1975. $4.90. The everyday life of a twelve-year-old ghetto child. Poor: *Kirkus* 1/15/75. G 3-6.

500. Morse, Charles and Ann Morse. *Evonne Goolagong.* Children's Press, 1974. $4.95. An easy-to-read biography in the Superstar Series. Good: *SLJ* 12/74. G 3-4.

501. Ness, Evaline. *Amelia Mixed The Mustard And Other Poems.* Il. by author. Scribners, 1975. $6.95. A superb selection of poetry about women, well illustrated in reds, browns, and oranges, from the works of Keats, Millay, Mother Goose, Nikki Giovanni and others. The females in the poems are as varied as the poets: Pandora, a greedy girl, an ancient queen, etc. Excellent source for felt-board stories and a good gift for child or adult. G 3+.

502. Noble, Iris. *Susan B. Anthony.* Messner, 1975. $5.95. A fictionalized, unreliable biography. My library colleague thought it was "fair". Poor: *Kirkus* 3/15/75. G 5-9.

503. Oliver, Dexter and Patricia Oliver. *I Want To Be.* Third World, 1974. $2.95. An occupational survey for Black children, which stresses the importance of Black history and of working for Black causes. *SLJ* called it political bibliotherapy and rated it "Poor": 2/75. G 4-6.

504. Ortiz, Victoria. *Sojourner Truth: A Self Made Woman.* Lippincott, 1974. $5.50. The story of the 19th century slave, freewoman, abolitionist and feminist is skillfully written. G 7+.

505. Pretlutsky, Jack. *Nightmares: Poems To Trouble Your Sleep.* Il. Arnold Lobel. Greenwillow, 1976. $6.95. Here is a painless way to interest children in poetry. Give them monsters: child-eating ghouls, werewolves stalking the streets, and witches waving "dessicated limbs." The folks most fourth graders are crazy about. The poems are clever, the pictures add a good, light touch, and the overall format is handsome. Recommended for every library open on Halloween. G 4-7, or read aloud to G 2+.

506. Raskin, Joseph and Edith Raskin. *Guilty Or Not? Tales Of Justice In Early America.* Lothrop Lee, 1975. $5.50. A lively, highly readable account of ten court cases which took place in Colonial times. G 4-6.

507. Reising, Robert. *Jim Thorpe.* Dillon, 1974. $4.95. A lightweight biography of the American Indian athlete. Good: *SLJ* 2/75. G 4-7.

508. Reit, Ann, ed. *Alone Amid All This Noise: A Collection Of Women's Poetry.* Four Winds, 1976. $6.95. "It is a good time to be a woman; it is a good time to be a poet." In the poems of Sappho, Kaga no Chiyo (Japan, 1703-1775), Jessie Sampler (Israel, 1883-1938) and the Black and white 20th century poets women are lovers, wives, mothers, and human beings. Recommended. G 6+.

509. Rogers, Eric. *Fasting: The Phenomenon Of Self-Denial.* Nelson Hall, 1976. $6.95. An account of the venerable and widespread practice of voluntary starvation. Famous historical incidents, current bio-medical research, and fasting-as-mental-illness are woven together in this provocative, interesting book.

510. Rudeen, Kenneth. *Roberto Clemente*. Il. Frank Mullins. Crowell, 1974. $3.95. A sensitive portrait of the Puerto Rican baseball star who died when his plane crashed during a good will mission. Enjoyable despite some nasty stories about racism among the Brooklyn Dodgers at the start of Clemente's career. Recommended for easy reading collections. G 2-4.

511. Samels, Gertrude. *The Story Of Ben-Gurion: Fighter Of Goliaths*. Rev. ed. Crowell, 1974. A Zionist view of the life of an Israeli leader. Excellent: *SLJ* 2/75. G 7+.

512. Seybolt, Peter. *Through Chinese Eyes*. Praeger, 1975. $7.50, $2.75. A two volume anthology of writings about the Chinese Revolution. In "Meng Hsiang-Ying Stands Up," a young woman speaks out against her tyrannical husband and mother-in-law. Starred: *Kirkus* 2/1/75. G 8+.

513. Sgroi, Suzanne, M.D. *V.D.: A Doctor's Answers*. Harcourt Brace, 1974. $6.50. All the facts about V.D., with an exhaustive list of treatment centers in the United States. Good: *Kirkus* 4/15/74; Poor: *SLJ* 9/74. G 7+.

514. Sharpe, Mitchell. *It Is I, Sea Gull: Valentina Tereshkove, First Woman In Space*. Crowell, 1975. $5.95. The private life of the scientist is emphasized. Kirkus deplored the ladies' magazine ending, but recommended the book for information about a woman's career in space science. Fair: *Kirkus* 2/1/75. G 4-7.

515. Sheppard, Sally. *Indians Of the Eastern Woodlands*. Watts, 1975. $3.90. The Algonquin and Iroquois Indians were matrilinear tribes, in which women played more important political roles than in most societies. Excellent: *CBRS* 5/75; Poor: *Kirkus* 2/15/75. G 5-7.

516. Silverstein, Shel. *Where The Sidewalk Ends*. Il. by author. Harper & Row, 1974. $7.95. A wonderful collection of songs, chants, nonsense rhymes and pictures from one of the writers of *Free To Be . . . You And Me*. A gold mine for story hours. All ages.

517. Snyder, Gerald. *The Right To Be Left Alone: Privacy In America*. Messner, 1975. $6.25. How technology can and has been used to pry, spy and ruin lives, when micro-computers, microphones and other devices fall into the hands of intelligence agencies and unscrupulous politi-cians. Good: *Kirkus* 3/15/75. G 6+.

518. Stein, Mark. *Good And Bad Feelings*. Il. Richard Cuffari. Morrow, 1976. $5.50. A simple, concise explanation of emotions and their effects on our behavior. Discusses the nature and possible roots of anger, fear, love and sorrow; introduces an important subject in terms with which chil-dren can identify. The book shows that people of both sexes experience good and bad feelings, and that no one can be good and happy all the time. G 3-5.

519. Sullivan, George. *Queen Of The Courts*. Dodd Mead, 1974. $4.95. Short biographies of six notable women tennis players who fought to improve the status of female sports. Good: *SLJ* 1/75. G 5-8.

520. Syme, Ronald. *Osceola, Seminole Leader*. Il. Ben Stahl. Morrow, 1976. $5.50. This biography of the rebel leader who fought for his people during the 19th century Semi-nole Wars "tells it like it was." Andrew Jackson's In-dian policies are described in brutal terms. (This was a personal blow to me, a graduate of Andrew Jackson High, Queens. I pictured our large class, 40% Black, 40% Jewish, singing: "As we gaily march on our way, we shall emulate his deeds each day.") Syme is especially horrified by the fact that the U.S. captured Osceola under a flag of truce. Is there ever honor in war? Interesting, easy to read, and a good supplement to school texts. G 2-5.

521. Thum, Marcella. *Exploring Black America: A History And Guide*. Atheneum, 1975. $10.95. This readable guide lists the museums and landmarks across the country which commemorate Black history. Excellent. G 6+.

522. Thurman, Judith. *Flashlight And Other Poems*. Il. Reina Rubel. Atheneum, 1976. $4.95. A collection of 25 brief poems, perfect for chldren ready to dip a toe into the vast ocean of poetry. The poems are bright and clear, and speak to childhood experiences. G 1+.

523. — ed. *I Became Alone: Five Woman Poets*. Il. James and Ruth McCrea. These are selected poems from the work of Sappho, Louise Labe, Ann Bradstreet, Juana Ines de la Cruz and Emily Dickinson. There is an informative introduction to each poet. The preface says, "Central to each one was her identity as a creator — an identity that puts her whole life in focus." A handsome book, recommended for learning or pleasure or both. G 6+.

524. Towne, Peter. *George Washington Carver*. Il. Eliza Moon. Crowell, 1975. $3.95. Carver was born a slave in Missouri: his master did not like slavery "but his wife wanted help with the housework." In this well-written and informative biography we learn about the agricultural scientist's quiet personality and monumental achievements, and about the controversy over his refusal to enter into civil rights activities. Recommended. G 2-4.

525. Vining, Elizabeth. *Mr. Whittier*. Viking, 1974. $7.95. John Greenleaf Whittier was a nineteenth century American poet, Abolitionist and feminist. Starred review: *SLJ* 1/75. Highly recommended. G 7+.

526. Walker, Greta. *Women Today: Ten Profiles*. Hawthorne, 1975. $6.95. Ten feminists talk about their careers, mostly in social service, and their lives; among them are Gloria Steinem, Lola Redford, and several minority women. The style is breezy, the interviews interesting but unmemorable. G 6+.

527. Warren, Ruth. *A Pictorial History Of Women In America*. Crown, 1975. $7.95. Highlights the achievements of American women — the "stars" rather than ordinary people. There are not enough of the excellent black and white photographs. An inadequate and far too optimistic discussion of women's current status. The format is handsome, and the price reasonable. G 6-12.

528. Whelan, Elizabeth. *Sex And Sensibility: A New Look At Being A Woman*. McGraw Hill, 1974. $6.95. This sex education book for teenaged girls really turned me off. "We do need men, and after all, most of them are pretty nice despite all those biological shortcomings!" This is really too cute. And the paragraph headings: "Have Fallopian Tubes Will Travel," or "The Vagina: A Connection to the

Outside World." This kind of thing is not necessary. Talking of sexual mores, the author promises to be Ms. Objectivity, but delivers the advice that "simple kissing is fine." I can't argue with her belief that premature sexual relationships can be risky. But I would not write a book promising to give only the facts, and then deliver all this heavy-handed advice. G 8+.

529. White, Anne Terry. *Eugene Debs: American Socialist.* Hill & Wang, 1974. $5.95. An objective, fictionalized biography of the man who led the American Socialist Party to its greatest success. Good: *SLJ* 2/75. G 6-12.

530. Williams, Selma R. *Demeter's Daughters: The Women Who Founded America, 1587-1787.* Atheneum, 1976. $9.95. A scholarly, very readable account of the lives and thoughts of many women who were part of Europe's adventure in the new world. Poems, anecdotes, journal entries, diaries and letters bring life to a solid history of our foremothers. A good source book for teachers. Recommended. G 9+.

531. Wise, William. *American Freedom And The Bill Of Rights.* Il. R. Rodegast. Parents, 1975. $4.59. An explanation of the Bill of Rights using historic instances and analogies from child/parent relationships. Good: *Kirkus* 3/15/75. G 2-4.

532. Wood, Nancy. *Many Winters: Prose And Poetry Of The Pueblos.* Doubleday, 1974. $6.95. An interpretation of the philosophy and daily life of the Pueblo Indians of New Mexico through poetry and brief prose selections. Excellent: *Booklist* 2/1/75. G 6+.

533. Zim, Jacob, ed. *My Shalom, My Peace.* McGraw Hill, 1975. $9.95. Ninety-five pages of poems and paintings about peace, by Jewish and Arab children. The book is handsomely produced; the paintings colorful and the poems sincere and touching. Not great literature but a wonderful way to introduce children to the talents and yearnings of young people in a miserable situation. G 3-7.

CHAPTER IX

ADULT BOOKS
FOR YOUNG ADULTS

534. Alcott, Louisa May. *Behind A Mask: The Unknown Thrillers Of Louisa May Alcott.* Madelein Stern, ed. Morrow, 1975. $8.95. Will the real Miss Alcott please stand up? These four melodramatic tales will leave you hungry for more bad, dangerous heroines to gladden your feminist heart.

535. Aldridge, Sarah. *Tottie: A Tale Of The Sixties.* Naiad. $4.50. Connie Norton, an attorney, is engaged to a boring, up-and-coming colleague. She falls in love with a childlike woman who is wanted by the police in connection with a bombing. I had never read a book about women lovers, and was delighted to find myself hoping they could stay together. I cared about the characters, believed in their love, and was not offended by their homosexuality because the author talked about their feelings, not their sexual activities. Recommended as an alternative to the prevalent images of lesbianism. G 11-12.

536. Angelou, Maya. *Gather Together In My Name.* Random House, 1974. $5.95. Beautifully written, moving autobiography of a Black woman. Excellent: *Kirkus* 4/15/74.

537. — *Oh Pray Wings Are Gonna Fit Me Well.* Random House, 1975. $5.95. Direct, forceful and succinct poetry about contemporary issues and lost love. Full of humor and truth, and without complex symbols or private meanings, these poems should be attractive to young students. Highly recommended. G 10+.

538. Beer, Patricia. *Reader, I Married Him: A Study Of The Women Characters Of Jane Austen, Charlotte Bronte, Elizabeth Gaskell, And George Eliot.* Barnes & Noble, 1975. $15.00. The purpose here is "To show how women and their situations were depicted in certain novels of the past." Carolyn Heilbrun recommends the book highly, but urges the author to raise her own consciousness (feminists are still "women's lib" to her): *NYT Book Review* 5/11/75.

539. Benetar, Judith. *Admission: Notes From A Woman Psychiatrist.* McKay, 1974. $7.95. An autobiographical account of internship in a N.Y. hospital. Excellent: *SLJ* 11/74.

540. Bernikow, Louise, ed. *The World Split Open: Four Centuries Of Women Poets In England And America, 1552-1950.* Vintage, 1975. $3.95. A long introduction to women poets and their place in literary history, followed by a feminist selection of poems. Excellent: *SLJ* 4/75 and *Ms* 7/75. Fair: a male critic irritated by the feminism, *NYT Book Review* 5/18/75.

541. Bird, Caroline. *Enterprising Women: Their Contribution To The American Economy, 1776-1976.* Norton, 1976. $8.95. Lives of many successful businesswomen. Excellent: *Kirkus* 1/15/76.

542. Burgess, Alan. *Daylight Must Come: The Story Of A Courageous Woman Doctor In The Congo.* Delacorte, 1975. $7.95. The fight of Dr. Helen Roseveare, a medical missionary, to open clinics in the northeastern Congo. Excellent: *SLJ* 11/74.

543. Butscher, Edward. *Slyvia Plath: Method And Madness.* Seabury, 1976. $15.95. Literary criticism is successfully combined with detailed biography of this American poet who committed suicide at thirty. Unfortunately, condescension pervades the book: Sylvia is called "a Bitch Goddess" or "a little girl." Her admiration for Dylan Thomas is dealt with in this way: "Perhaps she saw in him a male reflection of her secret bitch self, which was quite masculine in its consciousness of power." The notorious speech given by Adlai Stevenson at Sylvia's graduation from Smith in the fifties (praise for the educated "girls" because of the supportive role they could now play as wives and mothers) is called "reasonable, if somewhat innocent." I think the speech was both unreasonable and blatantly sexist. In short, a competent work which will alienate feminists and all enlightened people.

544. Carr, Virginia Spencer. *The Lonely Hunter: Biography Of Carson McCullers.* Doubleday, 1975. $12.50. A 600 page study of this gifted, eccentric writer. Excellent: *NYT Book Review* 8/24/75.

545. Cate, Curtis. *George Sand.* Houghton Mifflin, 1975. $15.00.
Well received, although not altogether sympathetic bi-
ography of the French novelist and humanist. Excellent:
NYT Book Review 8/24/75.

546. Clifton, Lucille. *Generations: A Memoir.* Random House,
1976. $5.95. Brief poignant prose poems tell the story of
the author's family: her great-grandmother who was
hanged, her half-white grandfather, and her adored
father Samuel, whose death appears to have inspired this
book, by a writer whose work spans age levels from pre-
school to adult, and who brings to life many generations of Black people before her. Recommended. G 8-
adult.

547. Coughlan, Robert. *Elizabeth And Catherine.* Putnam, 1975.
$10.00. Two extraordinary Russian monarchs. Good:
Kirkus 1/1/75.

548. Davis, Angela. *Angela Davis: An Autobiography.* Random
House, 1976. $8.95. Excellent: *SLJ* 2/75.

549. Ephron, Nora. *Crazy Salad: Some Things About Women.*
Knopf, 1975. $7.95. Timely essays about current events
and interesting people which cover the scene from "the
myth of liberation" in Israel to Bernice Gera, the first
woman umpire. The wit and wisdom in the last line of the
last essay about a man who underwent a sex change is
worth the price of the book. Highly recommended for
young adults.

550. Evans, Elizabeth. *Weathering The Storm: Women Of The
American Revolution.* Scribner's, 1975. $12.50. Il. prints.
Excerpts from the journals of a variety of 18th century
women. With bibliography and index.

551. Filene, Peter. *Him/Her/Self: Sex Roles In Modern America.*
Harcourt Brace, 1975. $10.00. A discussion of the de-
velopment of American middle-class sex roles from late
19th century to the present. Excellent: *NYT Book Review* 5/4/75.

552. Friedman, Richard, ed. *Sex Differences In Behavior*. Wiley, 1975. $25.00. A gathering of technical studies which support Eleanor Maccoby's findings that by the age of five children have developed rigid sex-role stereotypes, involving their self-images. Good: *NYT Book Review*. 4/13/75.

553. Godwin, Gail. *The Odd Woman*. Knopf, 1974. $8.95. An unmarried English professor makes some tough decisions about love, life and liberation. The book received well-deserved fantastic reviews from everyone. I enjoyed it immensely. For the mature young adult.

554. Gronoset, Dagfinn. *Anna*. Trans. from Norwegian by Ingrid B. Josephson. Knopf, 1974. $6.95. Non-fiction story of a farm woman's incredibly hard life and innate dignity. Excellent: *Kirkus* 2/1/75.

555. Hale, Nancy. *Mary Cassatt*. Doubleday, 1975. $10.00. Biography of the gifted artist who received the high (and dubious) compliment from Renoir: "She even carried her easel like a man." Fair: *NYT Book Review*. 8/31/75.

556. Hardwick, Elizabeth. *Between Myth And Morning*. Morrow, 1975. $3.95. The changes in women's roles and rights in our society.

557. Heidish, Marcy. *A Woman Called Moses: A Novel Based On The Life Of Harriet Tubman*. Houghton Mifflin, 1976. $8.95. The fictionalized story of the Black heroine of the Underground Railroad who led hundreds of her people to freedom. A stirring book.

558. Holt, John. *Escape From Childhood*. Dutton, 1974. $7.95. Children should be given adult rights and duties. Good: *Kirkus* 3/15/74.

559. Kaminski, Margaret, ed. *Moving To Antarctica: An Anthology Of Women's Writing*. Dustbooks, 1975. $3.95. A rich, varied collection of 36 poems, 7 short stories, 2 diary selections, 2 plays, 3 articles and one excerpt from a novel, all previously published in *Moving Out,* a feminist literary magazine, from March 1971 to Fall of 1975. Forty-eight women have contributed to this book, including Piercy, Rich and Alta, among others. A valuable, entertaining book. High school+.

560. Key, Mary Ritchie. *Male/Female Language*. Scarecrow, 1975. $7. A discussion by a social scientist of the differences, verbal and non-verbal between men and women, in various societies and historical periods. Good: *Spokeswoman* 8/15/75.

561. King, Billie Jean, with Kim Chapin. *Billie Jean*. Harper & Row, 1974. $6.95. How she fulfilled her desire to become "No. 1". Excellent: *SLJ* 11/74.

562. King, Billie Jean and J. Hyams. *Billie Jean King's Secrets Of Winning Tennis*. Il. photos. Holt Rinehart, 1974. $6.95. A technical guide, written in question and answer form. Recommended for young adults: *Booklist* 1/5/75; *SLJ* 1/75.

563. Kramer, Sydelle, ed. *The Balancing Act: A Career And A Baby*. Swallow, 1976. $4.95. Five professional women tell of the effect a new baby had on their lives, personal and professional. I found this book to be an enormous help during my own struggle to put motherhood and a career into comfortable perspective. Adult.

564. Le Guin, Ursula. *The Dispossessed: An Ambiguous Utopia*. Harper & Row, 1974. $7.95. Would you like to be a woman on the highly civilized planet of Urras where all social needs are met but personal ambition is not tolerated? Or would you prefer materialistic Anarres, where you can arrange jewels on small magnets planted in your skin? Excellent: *Spokeswoman* 3/15/75; *Horn Book* 6/75.

565. — *The Left Hand Of Darkness*. Ace, 1975. $1.50. Gethenians are sexless until a certain month of the year when they become male or female, through sheer luck. "One is respected and judged only as a human being. It is an appalling experience," says a visiting male from earth. Recommended: *Spokeswoman* 2/15/75.

566. Lewis, R.W.B. *Edith Wharton: A Biography*. Harper & Row. 1975. $15.00. Good: *NYT Book Review* 8/31/75. Adult.

567. Maccoby, Eleanor and Carole Jacklin. *Psychology Of Sex Differences*. Stanford, 1975. $18.95. The authors have concluded from relevant data that rigid sex roles are not

caused by innate differences between the sexes or by parental expectations of behavior, but by the self-image developed from the child's cultural background. Excellent: *NYT Book Review* 4/13/75.

568. MacKenzie, Midge. *Shoulder To Shoulder: A Documentary*. Knopf, 1975. $15; $8.95. A pictorial history of the English suffrage movement, dominated by the Pankhursts.

569. Maclaine, Shirley. *You Can Get There From Here*. Norton, 1975. $7.95. The story of the actress's trip to China as head of a delegation of middle-class American women. Good: *NYT Book Review* 3/16/75; *Kirkus* 2/15/75.

570. Medea, Andrea and Kathleen Thompson. *Against Rape*. Farrar Straus, 1974. $7.95, $2.25. From a feminist standpoint, statistics, reports and bibliographies are used in discussions of various aspects of rape. Good: *Horn Book* 8/74.

571. Meir, Golda. *My Life*. Putnam, 1975. $12.50. An engrossing autobiography of the former Israeli prime minister, beginning with her earliest memories of life in Russia.

572. Milne, Christopher. *The Enchanted Places: A Memoir Of the Real Christopher Robin And Winnie-the-Pooh*. Dutton. $6.95. A touching account of what it is like to be the son of someone famous and the model for an immortal storybook character. Mr. Milne (who was to have been a girl named Rosemary) is now a middle-aged bookshop owner, and a pleasant person too.

573. Moffat, Mary Jane and Charlotte Painter, eds. *Revelations: Diaries Of Women*. Random House, 1974. $10.00. Selections from the memoirs of more than thirty women, aged 7 to over 80, from the tenth century to the present. Fair: *SLJ* 11/74.

574. Murphy, Patrick. *Our Kindly Parent — The State: Juvenile Justice System And How It Works*. Viking, 1974. $8.95. Child welfare and juvenile justice system may do more harm than good. Good: *SLJ* 11/47.

575. O'Brien, Robert. *Z For Zachariah*. Atheneum, 1975. $6.95. Remember that old saying, "I wouldn't marry you if you were the last man on earth?" This is exactly Ann Burden's problem when, after a nuclear holocaust, she nurses a sick man back to physical health, only to discover that he is mentally ill and dangerous.

576. Orloff, Katherine. *Rock 'N Roll Woman*. Nash, 1974. $6.95. Twelve interviews with female rock stars by a music journalist. Good: *SLJ* 2/75.

577. Osen, Lynn M. *Women In Mathematics*. MIT, 1975. $4.95. The stories, with historical background, of eight female mathematicians from Hypatia(400 A.D.) to Emmy Noether (c. 1900). Bibliography. Good: *Booklist* 6/1/75. For young adults.

578. Polykoff, Shirley. *Does She . . . Or Doesn't She? And How She Did*. Doubleday, 1975. $6.95. The story of a genius in advertising: the woman who thought of the Clairol slogan and the ad-biz classic "that heavenly coffee". Don't expect feminism; settle for business sense and the voice of a bright, successful woman. Good: *NYT Book Review* 9/14/75.

579. Pomeroy, Sarah B. *Women In Classical Antiquity*. Shocken, 1975. $8.95. A scholarly account of the powerless status of the women of ancient Greece and Rome. Excellent: *NYT Book Review* 9/7/75.

580. Redinger, Ruby V. *George Eliot: The Emergent Self*. Knopf, 1975. $15.00. This book has received glowing praise for style and scholarship. Excellent: *NYT* 9/7/75.

581. Reed, Evelyn. *Woman's Evolution*. Pathfinder, 1975. $4.95. A look into history to discover how and why woman became an oppressed class. Excellent as feminine mythology: *Spokeswoman* 3/15/75.

582. Rowbotham, Sheila. *Hidden From History: Rediscovering Women In History From The 17th C. To The Present*. Pantheon, 1975. A humanistic approach to the history of women as a social force, and their recurrent problems. Recommended: *Spokeswoman* 1/15/75.

583. Russell, Diana E. *The Politics Of Rape: The Victim's Perspective*. Stein & Day, 1975. $10.00. The experiences of 22 rape victims: how to avoid rape, what to do if it is unavoidable, and an analysis of rape fantasies. Excellent: *SLJ* 2/75.

584. Sargent, Pamela, ed. *Women Of Wonder : Science Fiction Stories By Women, About Women*. Vintage, 1975. $1.95. Thirteen stories with a feminist cast. The introduction is called "Women in Science Fiction." Recommended: *Spokeswoman* 2/15/75; *SLJ* 5/75.

585. Schaeffer, Susan Fromberg. *Anya*. Macmillan, 1974. $8.95. The long, painful story of Anya, the last member of a wealthy Polish Jewish family, and her survival during World War II. Recommended: *SLJ* 5/75.

586. Schulman, L.M., ed. *A Woman's Place*. Macmillan, 1974. $5.95. A terrific collection of short stories by and about women. The one about the librarian is a chiller. A good choice for high school students and adults.

587. Slung, Michelle. *Crime On Her Mind: Fifteen Stories Of Female Sleuths From The Victorian Era To The Forties*. Pantheon, 1975. $10.00. These stories about independent, clever female detectives are entertaining, and some are still gripping mysteries. Recommended: *NYT* 6/1/75.

588. Spacks, Patricia Meyer. *The Female Imagination*. Knopf, 1975. $10.00. A discussion of well-known 19th century novels from a feminist perspective. Patricia Beer (See No. 538) reviewed the book in the *NYT Book Review*. I see now what Ms. Heilbrun means about Beer's consciousness. Recommended: *NYT Book Review* 5/11/75.

589. Strainchamps, Ethel. *Rooms With No Views: A Woman's Guide To The Man's World Of The Media*. Harper & Row, 1974. $5.95. An exposé of the anti-feminine communications world. Excellent: *SLJ* 3/75.

590. Strauss, Bert and Mary Stowe. *How To Get Things Changed: A Handbook For Tackling Community Problems*. Doubleday, 1974. $8.95. How to analyze issues, organize reform programs, and evaluate progress. Good: *SLJ* 2/75.

591. Terrell, John and Donna Terrell. *Indian Women Of The Western Morning: Their Life In Early America.* Dial, 1975. $8.95. Many roles were played by Indian women during the exploration of America by Europeans. Recommended: *Booklist* 2/1/75.

592. Tolchin, Susan and Martin Tolchin. *Clout: Womanpower and Politics.* Coward McCann, 1974. $10.00. The development of female political power from 1968 to 1974. Excellent: *SLJ* 4/75.

593. Tomlin, Claire. *The Life And Death Of Mary Wollstonecraft.* Harcourt Brace, 1974. $8.95. A biography of the 18th Century feminist whose "Vindication of the Rights of Women" many 20th Century legislators would do well to read. Excellent: *NYT Book Review* 1/5/75.

594. Washington, Mary Helen. *Black Eyed Susans: Classic Stories By and About Black Women.* Doubleday-Anchor, 1975. $2.95. By Gwendolyn Brooks, Toni Morrison, Alice Walker, and others less well known. Highly recommended: *Spokeswoman* 1/15/76.

595. Wilson, Dorothy. *Bright Eyes: The Story Of Susette La Flesche, An Omaha Indian.* McGraw Hill, 1974. $8.95. A biography of a woman who spent her life attempting to improve the lives of her people. Good: *Kirkus* 2/15/75; Fair: *SLJ* 11/74.

596. Zassenhaus, Hiltgunt. *Walls: Resisting The Third Reich - One Woman's Story.* Beacon, 1974. $7.95. The story of a German woman who fought Hitler from 1933, and saved more than 1200 lives. Good: *Horn Book* 8/74. For the mature reader.

CHAPTER X

NON-BOOK MATERIALS

1. Films and Film Packages

597. *Benjamin And The Tulip*. Weston Woods. 1975. $12.75. Filmstrip and cassette created from the clever non-sexist picture book *Benjamin And The Tulip* (Dial, 1973) by Rosemary Wells. Story is read by Nicole Frechette. The lively musical filmstrip version called excellent by *Horn Book* 2/76.

598. *Frog And Toad Are Friends*. Miller Brody, Inc. 1975. $16 each. Five filmstrips with recordings based on the tales from Lobel's 1971 Caldecott Honor Book. The two filmstrips I saw were "A Lost Button" and "A Swim," both very well done. Excellent narration by Bob McFadden. Arnold Lobel's characters are chiefly male, but they are sensitive and very "human," and so rate as non-sexist. Highly recommended for pre-school through grade three.

599. *Frog And Toad Together*. Miller Brody. 1975. $16 each. Another five films and recordings from Lobel's 1973 Newbery Honor Book. I saw "Cookies" and "The Garden" and found them most entertaining. Lynn Ahrens has written an original song, "It's More Fun". If your funds are limited, I suggest purchasing one or two from each set: the staff has done an equally fine job with both Lobel titles. G K+3. Teacher's notes with program.

600. *Identity: Female*. Dun Donnelly Publishing Corporation. $215. Dun Donnelly calls this "the first comprehensive women's studies program for young people aged 12 to 20." A multi-media curriculum package includes audio casettes, sound filmstrips, games, charts, news reprints, biographies and other materials on such subjects as family life, politics, work.

601. *The Impressionist Epoch: Based On The Exhibit Held At The Metropolitan Museum Of Art and the Louvre To Celebrate The 100th Anniversary Of Impressionism.* Miller Brody. 4 filmstrips; 4 records or cassettes; 24 p instruction booklet; colorful poster; mock newspaper handout. 68 minutes. $96 with records, $100 with casettes. Very well produced salute to Impressionism and its leading figures: Renoir, Manet, Degas, Cassatt, Sisley, and. others. Men and women narrate pleasantly against the lively musical background. A great deal of information about the paintings is presented in a way that is easy to understand without being too simple. An introductory art history program highly recommended for ages 12 and up.

602. *Learning The Library: A Skills And Concepts Series.* Written by Helen Rippier Wheeler. Produced by Norma Harris. Educational Activities, Inc. $49. This multi-media kit includes four filmstrips, four long playing records or cassettes, teacher handbooks, and visual material. Topics are: I. Let's Go to the Library; II. The Card Catalog; III. Decimal Classification; IV. Reference Tools. An interesting and lively presentation, with non-sexist narrative and a selection of titles, used for illustration, which is well-balanced for multi-cultural, non-sexist effect. Especially valuable for schools without professional librarians. G 2-6.

603. *Meet The Newbery Author: Isaac Bashevis Singer.* Miller Brody. Filmstrip & record, $28; Cas., $30. Mr. Singer is famous for his stories of life in the small Jewish ghettoes of Poland where he was born. Eli Wallach narrates, with occasional help from Mr. Singer. I recommend this entertaining introduction to the man and his work, for general audiences ages 10 and up, for Jewish schools and organizations, for senior citizens programs.

604. *Meet The Newbery Author: Virginia Hamilton.* Miller Brody. Filmstrip and record, $28. Cassett, $30. Ms. Hamilton is a gifted Black writer of whose many books the best known is perhaps *M.C. Higgins The Great.* Ms. Hamilton tells us about her life and her feelings for the farm near Yellow Springs, Ohio, where she grew up. She is a gifted narrator, too. Ages 10 and up.

605. *NEA Edupak On Sex Role Stereotyping.* (National Education Association: Academic Building, Saw Mill Road, West Haven, Conn. 06516. $66.) Three cassette tapes, two filmstrips, fact sheets, and leaflets which cover everything from definitions of sex role stereotyping to actions for change and consciousness-raising exercises. Items may be ordered individually.

606. *Noisy Nora.* Weston Woods, 1975. $12.75. Filmstrip and cassette created from the book *Noisy Nora* (Dial, 1973) by Rosemary Wells. Read and sung by Nicole Frechette. The lively, tuneful filmstrip version of a non-stereotyped and popular picture book was given an excellent review by *Horn Book* 2/76.

607. *Other Women, Other Work.* Churchill Films, 1973. Seven women who hold such nontraditional female jobs as truck driver and veterinarian talk about their places in a "man's world." Grade 12+. Recommended: *Booklegger* No. 9, 1976.

608. *People Who Work.* (*Beginning Concepts* Series. Nos. 3 & 4). Scholastic. Ten color/sound filmstrips which show men and women pursuing unusual untraditional careers. Elementary grades.

609. *Roll Over.* Herstory Films. 16mm. 10 mins. Color. Rental fee $23. Over one hundred women break into male-dominated job markets in this humorous satirical film. For high school and up. Recommended: *New Directions For Women.*

610. *Some Will Be Apples.* Odeon Films. 28 min. Color. Rental fee $35. Winner of the Merit Award at the Chicago International Film Festival. Suffragist and writer Zona Gale (1874-1939) describes life as an American woman in the days before suffrage. Recommended for high school and Women's Studies classes by *New Directions For Women.*

611. *Sugar And Spice.* Odeon Films. 32 min. Color. Rental fee $20. A film intended to tell parents and teachers of primary and pre-school children how to help in changing children's sex-role self-images. Recommended *New Directions For Women,* Winter 1975-6.

612. *We The People.* Miller Brady. 1 filmstrip, 6 paperbacks and 1 record. $37. With cassette $39. This package introduces the life and works of Elizabeth Yates, a writer of children's books; it contains also a novel about a young New Hampshire family the father of which joins the Revolutionary Army. The package is dull and amateurish. Intended for New Hampshire residents. Ages 9+.

Women And Film. See No. 770.

613. *Women And Health/Mental Health.* Microfilm. This is the Women's History Research Center collection of material on women's physical and mental health, on Black and Third World women; on nutrition, sexuality, abortion, aging, alternative health care centers, etc. For information write Women's History Research Center.

614. *Women Emerging.* Far West Labs, 1975. 27 min. Rental Price, $18. A group of young women students from many racial and economic backgrounds frankly discuss sex and race discrimination as it affects them, and the class barriors that separate them. A thought-provoking film.

615. *You Pack Your Own Chute.* Ramic Productions. 30 mins. Rental fee $100. Can be previewed. Dr. Eden Ryl, motivational expert, parachutes from an airplane 3,000 feet above the Pacific to prove that anyone can try to achieve anything.

2. Photographs

616. *Chicanas Prominentes.* ECA. $10. Introduction by Ernesto Galarza. Twenty-four portraits and bilingual texts. Five of the subjects are women.

617. *Community Helpers And Professional Women.* From *Free*, P.O. Box 185, Saxonville Station, Framingham, Massachusetts 01701. $2.75. Two sets of eight excellent 8x11 black and white photographs show women of different races doing untraditional jobs.

618. *I Am Woman: I Am Artist.* New Womb, 1973. $5.50. (33¢ in California). Fifty-three black and white drawings. and prints by seventeen San Francisco Bay area female artists. These drawings are 11x14 and come boxed. Interesting comments by the artists are included.

619. *Men In The Nurturing Role.* W.A.A. A set of eight black and white 8x10 photographs of men in the midst of their families, as well as in job situations. A poster is included of a grandfather and his small granddaughter.

620. *Picture Catalog Of The Sophia Smith Collection.* Smith College. Northampton, Mass. 01063. $6.00. Contains reduced photographs of prints available at various prices. There are photos of American Abolitionists, feminists, and entertainers, among others. A good source for schools.

621. *People At Work.* W.A.A. $6.00. Twenty-four black and white 8x10 photos of women and men working in various non-stereotyped jobs.

622. *A Portfolio Of Outstanding Contemporary American Indians.* E.C.A. $10. Twenty-four biographical sketches with black and white drawings by Robert Blanchard. 11x14 on heavy stock. Five women are included among the subjects.

Professional Women. See No. 617.

Sophia Smith Collection. See No. 620.

623. *Women At Work: A Collection Of 15 Photographs Of Non-Traditional Jobs.* Change For Children. $3.85.

624. *Women In Sports: A Collection Of 6 Photographs With Suggestions For Use.* C. Cade: 2103 Emerson, Berkeley, CA 94705. $3.35.

3. Records And Cassettes

From *Caedmon Records.* 505 8th Avenue, N.Y., NY 10018.

625. *Anne Sexton Reads Her Poetry.* $6.98 LP; $7.95 Cas.

626. *Great American Speeches.* Set of 2 records, $13.96 LP; $15.90 Cas. These selections vary in length from 1¼ mins. to 12 mins. They cover the personalities and issues involved in the struggle for women's rights in the 19th century. Eileen Heckart, Claudia McNeil and Mildred

Natwick read these speeches with dignified emotion and with pride. Highly recommended for home, school and library collections. Ages 12+.

627. *Gwendolyn Brooks Reading Her Poetry.* $6.98 LP; $7.95 Cas. This and No. 625 are highly recommended for young adult and adult collections.

628. *Hurray For Captain Jane! And Other Liberated Stories For Children.* $6.98 LP; $7.95 Cas. An excellent collection of role-free stories, read delightfully by Tammy Grimes. The ten tales include *Ira Sleeps Over* (Waber), *Noisy Nancy And Nick* (Gaeddert), *Martin's Father* (Eichler). Terrific for ages 4-10.

629. *The Love Game: A Shakespearean Entertainment.* With Arnold Moss and Kim Hunter. A marvelous mixture of narration, songs and scenes from ten Shakespearean comedies, all centered about the theme of love and courtship. I am sorry that Moss decided to end his entertainment with the scene from *The Taming Of The Shrew* in which Katherine glories in being a cushion for her husband's boot. Ten scenes of diverse and brilliant wooing seem to lead us to the preface of *Fascinating Womanhood*. Despite this, the recording is lively and amusing: beautifully acted and sung. Ages 14+.

630. *Pioneer Women: Selections From Their Journals.* 2 records. For price see No. 626. Highly recommended for high school students and adults are these four thirty-minute readings from the diaries of women who went West: Eleanor Plaistead (Dakota pioneer); Mary Walker (missionary), Martha Summerhayes (Army wife) and Elinor Steward (homesteader). Sandy Dennis and Eileen Heckart do the readings and hold our interest throughout them.

631. *Summer Of My German Soldier: A Dramatization Of The Book By Bette Green.* Young Adult Recordings. Record, $6.95; Cas. $7.95. The excellent novel dramatized here is about the doomed friendship of a Jewish teenaged girl who lives in Arkansas and a kind young German soldier who has escaped from a local POW camp during World War II. Although necessarily abridged, the drama presents the main theme of the book and its tone. The acting

and technical effects are adequate. The album cover gives a lot of interesting information about the author and the subject, and suggests ideas for rap sessions. Grades 5+.

632. *Young And Female.* Same price as 628. Readings from the autobiographies of 6 American women who flouted convention and attained success. Emily Hahn, Margaret Bourke-White and Shirley MacLaine are brought to life by Sandy Dennis, who gives each reading a personal and touching interpretation. Eileen Heckart reads from the work of Margaret Sanger and Dorothy Day in a voice that is clear and enthusiastic. We feel that hers is the foice of experience. Especially dramatic is the reading of Day's recollection of forcible feeding during her imprisonment for suffragist activities. Shirley Chisholm's description of her entrance into politics is read by Claudia McNeil with richness and depth. Lively and entertaining. Highly recommended for ages 12+.

From *Olivia Records*. P.O. Box 70237. Los Angeles, CA 90070. $5.95.

633. *The Changer And The Changed.* Chris Williamson. This songwriter, singer and feminist writes fine optimistic lyrics and has a lovely voice to sing them with. She sings about nature and the human soul on this soothing and uplifting album. Teenage and adult.

634. *I Know You Know.* Meg Christian. A musical autobiography. Meg writes and sings her music. My two favorites: "Song to My Mama", about her own lesbianism, and "Ode to a Gym Teacher", a funny love song. Teenage and adult.

635. *Mooncircles.* Kay Gardner. This album has beautiful music and haunting lyrics. I found it relaxing to listen to this while I typed. I loved especially the selection "Changing" about "the woman in the moon." Teenage and adult.

From *Redwood Records*, 565 Doolin Canyon, Ukiah, CA 95482.

636. *A Live Album: Holly Near.* $4.50. An entertaining album about all sorts of things: liberation, childhood, love and hope. The record is a delight: Holly's funny meaningful lyrics and Jeffrey Langley's great music should be in every library record collection used by people over 13. A fine gift for a young adult.

637. *Words And Music*. Holly Near and Jeff Langley. Herford Music, 1976. Distributed by Redwood. $2.50. A songbook containing words and music from Holly's two albums (Nos. 636 and 638). Black and white photographs are included in the book, along with a Guitar Chord Chart. This book is especially useful for people who want the music score, since the albums themselves contain copies of the lyrics.

638. *You Know All I Am*. Holly Near with Jeff Langley. $5.00. A fine selection of songs with interesting music and a good variety of lyrics. Holly sings about the assertive woman, who asks for what is fair in love and politics. Ages 15-adult.

Note: I have heard Holly Near in concert since reviewing her records, and I urge you to treat yourself to an exhilerating evening of her music if she and Jeff Langley ever come your way.

4. Toys And Games And Where To Get Them

639. *African People And Places*. Creative Playthings. $17. A set-up including the homes, the natural environment and the dress of the people. Also available are a set-up on Eskimos and one on American Indians. Ages 3-9.

640. *American Indian People And Places*. See No. 639.

641. *Children's Book And Music Center. Catalog 1977*. This mail order catalog consists of 176 pages: it has recommended books, games, and, especially, records for children. It lists also a huge selection of ethnic material as well as lots of educational aids. It appears to be a marvelous source for high quality material.

642. *Community Careers Flannel Board*. W.A.A. $5. 27 figures of women and men of various races, dressed in uniforms and other kinds of work clothes for a variety of non-sexist and non-racist jobs. Ages 3+.

643. *Eskimo People And Places*. See 639.

644. *Great Women Paper Dolls. A Coloring And Cut-Out Book.* Bellerophon Books. $2.50. Drawings, based on actual paintings and photographs, of women in costumes of all races and many historical periods. A *super* delight for kids from 5 to 105. (Susan B. Anthony is included, and Golda Meir and Amelia Earhart and MORE!)

645. *Learn Me, Inc.* A store with non-stereotyped toys and books. Write for a catalog to 642 grand Ave., St. Paul, Minn. 55105.

646. *Ms. Liberty.* Verse by M. Fischer. Il. by W. Wagstaff. Golden West Pubs. $1. (6% tax for California residents). A coloring book showing women of various races doing various possible jobs. Available from Graphic Communications, 1126 Hipoint St., Los Angeles, CA 90035.

647. *Our Community Helpers Play People.* W.A.A. $6. 12 men and women from various races are shown doing non-stereotyped jobs: the figures are cut from heavy cardboard, colored on both sides, and complete with stands. Very sturdy and attractive.

648. *Toys That Care: Non-Sexist Materials For All Children.* P.O. Box 81, Briarcliff Manor, N.Y., N.Y. 10510. $1. This interesting and worthwhile mail-order catalog has a variety of non-sexist, multi-ethnic toys, books, records, educational games and more.

649. *What Can We Be? A Coloring Book For Everyone.* Pamela Lechtman. AAUW Ventura Branch, 1975. Available from Elizabeth Schmidt, 379 Tulane Ave., Ventura, CA. $1.50. This coloring book crosses the sex and race line with paragraph-long descriptions of various possible careers. For instance, under "Sam the Secretary", we discover that "Ms. Jackson, Thomas's boss, is pleased with his work and plans to give him a raise soon." Included also are "Annette the Dentist" and "Bonnie the Truck Driver" and others. The drawings are a bit crude, but the message is crayon bright.

650. *Women In Revolt: The Fight For Emancipation.* Grossman Publications. $3.95. Replicas of letters, posters, games, newspaper articles and so on, which reveal facets of the British Woman Suffrage Movement and give a feeling for the times. High School.

PART THREE

Further Resources for Parents and Professionals

Fighting Sexism in the Schoolroom

Education is a major factor in the development of an individual. It influences attitudes, beliefs, and actions. Sex role stereotyping limits the personal development and expectations of a person. Studies have been done on the pervasiveness of sex role stereotyping in our educational systems and in educational materials, and many individuals and communities are acting on these studies to combat sexism in our schools.

Included in this bibliography are a few of these studies, as well as information on what can and is being done and how. Since teachers are the vehicles of education, their role cannot be ignored. They are included as a means for change in the classroom and as victims of sex discrimination themselves.

Joanne Leone, M.L.S.

1. Books & Bibliographies

651. *Afro-American Books For Children.* Martin Luther King Memorial Library, 1974. D.C. Public Library. Communications Dept., Rm. 422, 901 G St., Washington, D.C. 20001. 70¢ for postage and an 8½x11 envelope.

652. *American History And Related Biography And Fiction For The Junior High: An Annotated Bibliography.* Women's Rights Task Force on Education. 25¢ and a self-addressed stamped envelope.

653. *The Arbuthnot Anthology of Children's Literature.* Zena Sutherland, ed. 4th ed. 1976. Lothrop, $22. Scott Foresman. $14.95. This anthology of over one thousand pages is a basic source for the rich and varied body of children's literature. Part 1 contains over 500 poems; this 4th edition has new poems in "urban and ethnic voices". Part 2 has folktales, fables, myths, epics and modern fantastic stories from all over the world. In Part 3 are realistic stories, historical fiction, and biography and works of information, and Part 4 has reference aids, bibliographies annotated and critical, awards, an article on illustrations and suggestions for helping children appreciate literature. This is a valuable collection of works and excerpts for educators, students and parents. It is important, of course, to keep in mind that the choice of works and the critical evaluations of books and their authors reflect the personal opinions of the editor and do not constitute the final word on the subject, although the sheer size of this book is intimidating.

654. *Bibliography Of Materials On Sexism And Sex Role Stereo-typing In Children's Books.* Lollipop Power.

655. *Black Americana.* A bibliography of books by and about Black Americans. Contains titles of books both for adults and children. Detroit Public Library, Public Relations, 5201 Woodward, Detroit, MI 48202. Free with a self-addressed, stamped envelope.

656. *The Black Experience In Children's Books.* Revised ed. $2.50. Office of Branch Libraries, The New York Public Library, 8 E. 40th St., N.Y., N.Y. 10016. A wide range of fiction and non-fiction titles for all age levels.

657. *The Black World In Literature For Children: A Bibliography Of Print And Non-Print Materials.* 1975. Joyce M. Mills, ed. Atlanta University School of Library Science, Atlanta, Georgia 30314. $2. An annotated and evaluated list of 138 fiction and non-fiction titles and 63 non-print materials for children 3-13. The book seems geared to the parent or aide with little background in children's literature. The evaluations range from "highly recommended" to "not recommended". The bibliography is fairly well written.

658. "Books". Margaret Lichtenberg, ed. *Womensports,* Sept., 1974. A listing of stories about girls in sports.

659. *Careers and Contingencies.* S. Angrist and E. Almquist. Kenikat Press. $15. A study of the ways a group of college women planned their adult roles. Hard evidence for the impact of educators on women's choices.

660. *Children Are People: Annotated Bibliography.* J. Dhuyvetter. Il. by bulbul. $1. with 15% postage, 6% tax in California. P.O. Box 2428, Stanford, CA 94303. A worthwhile listing of multi-racial, non-sexist books for all age levels with an emphasis on small alternative presses.

661. *The Chinese In Children's Books.* New York Public Library, 1974. $2. Office of Branch Libraries, N.Y.P.L., 8 E. 40th St., N.Y., N.Y. 10016.

662. *A Community Of People: A Multi-Ethnic Bibliography.* $5. Educational Media Center. Portland Public Schools, 631 N.E. Clackamus St., Portland, Oregon 97208. An annotated listing of books and audio visual aids, organized by ethnic group.

663. *A Critical Handbook Of Children's Literature.* Rebecca Lukens. Scott Foresman, 1976. $4.50. A lucid, well-organized introduction to the analysis of children's literature. Although directed primarily to non-literary students, it can serve as a basic tool for parents and people beginning the study of library science. There are separate chapters on plot, character, setting, theme, point of view, style, etc. There are chapters on the evaluation of poetry and on non-fiction. A glossary of literary terms is included, along with an index. Reading exercises follow each chapter. The author makes no real mention of either racism or sexism in children's books. Although she believes that stereotyping people is unjust, she makes a distinction between real-life stereotyping and fictional stereotyping: "in literature . . . the stereotype, like the stock character who appears in many stories, is useful, since he or she quickly settles into a background position and performs there in an easily understood role." Ms. Lukens does not, unfortunately, give thought to the effect on one's self-image this kind of stereotyping can have, if one is or could become the stereotyped character. I disagree with her opinion that Theodore Taylor's *The Cay* "helps us discover that race doesn't matter." What *The Cay* helped me to discover was that paternalism and condescension were once mistaken for brotherhood. Ms. Lukens does however use "his/her" consistently, except for a slip on p. 200. On the whole this is readable and recommended.

664. *Free To Read: Non-Sexist Books For Children 3-8 Years Old.* Hunterdon County NOW. Box 217, Annandale, N.J. 08801. 25¢. Bulk orders available. An annotated bibliography of 100 role-free popular picture books. Good to hand out at PTA meetings, book fairs, etc.

665. *Guide To Non-Sexist Children's Books.* Judith Adell and Hilary Dole Klein, eds. Introduction by Alan Alda. $7.95; $3.95. Academy Press Ltd., 1976. An annotated list of over four hundred non-sexist books for pre-schoolers

through twelfth graders. Many of the titles have appeared in other bibliographies, although there are a fair
amount of new titles listed. This is a compact guide, with
some illustrations, which will be a help in building new
collections in homes and libraries.
NOTE: This book will be revised in 1978 by Enid Davis.
A new section will be added on multi-media materials.

666. *Human (And Anti-Human) Values In Children's Books: A
Content Rating Instrument For Educators And Concerned Parents.* CIBC Racism and Sexism Resource
Center, 1976. $14.95; $7.95. This is a controversial annotated listing of over 200 recently published children's
books. Each lengthy review is accompanied by a chart
with markings for elitism, materialism, ageism, sexism,
racism and three other -isms and their opposites. Literary
and artistic qualities are rated as well. The charts are fine
for consciousness-raising. However, as a professional
children's librarian and literary critic, I feel much more
comfortable with the descriptive reviews. This book provides a political analysis of children's literature; as a
literary selection tool it falls short.

667. *Images Of The Black In Children's Literature.* Dorothy
Broderick. Bowker, 1973. $13.25. An examination of over
100 books published between 1827 and 1967, this is a history of the image of Blacks in children's literature. It is
clearly and smoothly written and well-documented and
organized. and an introduction to racism in children's
books. The special plight of the Black woman is not dealt
with; the impression given by Broderick is that it is the
emasculated male who suffers most from stereotypic distortion in life and in literature. This book would have
been more valuable if the distortion by stereotype of the
Black female's personality had been explored. The book
should be read by all children's librarians.

668. *The Lesbian In Literature: A Bibliography.* Gene Damon
and others, eds. Naiad Press, 1975. $10. This biblio-
graphy lists a huge number of novels, short stories,
novellas, poems and plays with Lesbian themes and/or
characters, all written in English. The listing is alpha-
betical by author, there is no title index and only some
titles are annotated. Books are rated for literary quality.
Every title has been read by the three editors. No "trash"
has been included. This is a work of love and has involved
extensive reading.

669. *Little Miss Muffet Fights Back*. Feminists On Children's Media, 1974. Revised ed. Feminist Book Mart, 162-11 9th Ave., Whitestone, N.Y. 11357. $1.50. prepaid. A 62-page annotated list of non-sexist fiction and non-fiction for all reading levels.

670. *Little Miss Muffet Hang In There*. Minnesota Library Association, 5511 Twenty Seventh Avenue South, Minneapolis, Minn. 55417. 15¢ with a self-addressed stamped envelope.

671. *Living Black American Authors: A Biographical Dictionary*. Ann Shockley. Bowker, 1973. $12.95. A helpful reference tool. Recommended: *Bulletin Of the Center For Children's Books,* March 1975.

672. *A Mexican-American Bibliography*. Xerox, Book Catalogs Dept., 300 N. Zeeb Rd., Ann Arbor, Michigan. $5. A 38-page listing of materials for children from elementary to high school.

673. *Multicultural Bibliography*. Pre-School—Grade 2. Multicultural Resources. Box 2945, Stanford, CA 94305. $2. A listing of the holdings of the Resources Center which provides non-racist books, pamphlets etc. for all reading levels about Americans of Black, Latin, Asian and Indian origins.

674. *Multicultural Materials*. Adults Multicultural Resources. $2.50. See No. 673.

675. *The New Woman's Survival Sourcebook*. Susan Rennie and Kirsten Grimstad. Knopf, 1975. $5. A valuable source of information about companies which publish materials on feminism and notable women. Most of the companies listed are small and are run by women.

676. *Non-Sexist Curricular Materials For Elementary Schools*. The Feminist Press. $5. One hundred looseleaf pages of consciousness-raisng exercises for teacher and student. Includes sources for non-sexist teaching materials and bibliographies of non-sexist books.

677. *Non-Sexist Education For Young Children: A Practical Guide.* Barbara Sprung. Citation Press. $3.25. An excellent introductory guide for pre-school and early elementary educators, this grew out of the W.A.A.'s pilot study of sex-role stereotyping in four local pre-school centers. Included are chapters on: creating a non-sexist environment; getting parents involved; following or adapting programs; books, toys and audio-visual materials, and information on resources for further material. A 4-page "Check-list for a Non-Sexist Classroom" is particularly helpful. There is no index. This book is easy to read and digest. The rest is up to you.

678. *Non-Sexist Picture Books That Every Library Needs.* Children's Liberation Workshop, P.O. Box 207, Ancaster, Ontario, Canada.

679. *Notable American Women.* Edward T. James and others, eds. Harvard U. Press, 1974. 3 vols. $75; $25. Biographies of 1,300 remarkable American women who lived from 1607-1950. The biographies vary in length from one column to several pages, are signed, and include bibliographies. The third volume is indexed according to profession. Highly recommended as a reference tool for young adults and educators.

680. *Positive Images: A Guide To Non-Sexist Films For Young People 5-17.* Susan Wengraf, ed. Booklegger, $4. This book includes listings of distributors, rental and sales costs, a subject index, a bibliography, and illustrations from films, video tapes and slides.

681. *Recommended Non-Stereotyped Software And Educational Materials.* Software Committee for the Conference on Sexism in Education, Arizona State University, Nov., 1975. Available from: Dr. Arlene Metha, c/o Secondary Education, Arizona State University, Tempe, Arizona 85281. 50¢. Seven pages of recommended audio-visual resources on women's history, sex-role stereotyping, biography, etc. A handy tool.

682. *Sexism and Youth.* Diane Gersoni-Stavn. Bowker, 1974. $10. How sexism affects all aspects of a child's life and future. Reprints from notable magazine articles. Part 2: "Dear Old Sexist School Days."

683. *Sexism In Education.* Emma Willard Task Force on Education. $3.50. Contains articles on sexism, proposals for
change, non-sexist classroom materials, and an extensive
bibliography of resources.

684. *Sexism In School and Society.* N. Frazier and M. Sadker.
The Feminist Bookmart. $4.50. +50¢. See No. 672. This
book deals with women's experiences as students from
elementary school through college, and the possibility of
a brighter future once teachers begin to discourage rigid
sex roles.

685. *Sex-Role Stereotyping In Children's Books — Sources.* S.
Cheda. Seneca College, 1750 Finch Ave., E. Willowdale,
Ontario, Canada M2N 5T7. A bibliography of articles.

686. *She Said/He Said.* Nancy Henley and Barrie Thorne.
Know, Inc., 1976. $2.25. This critical and descriptive
bibliography was first printed as the bibliography for
Language and Sex: Difference And Dominance by Henley
and Thorne. It is an annotated bibliography of works
by specialists who have shown that there is a difference
between the way men and women use language and com-
munication like touching, smiling, etc. The feminist purpose of the book is to list work which points out the sexist
bias of English, and which attributes differences in com-
munication to the subjection of women rather than to inherent characteristics. This is fascinating reading which
should encourage the reader to delve further into the subject. Included is a special chapter on American
minorities, a list of relevant women's groups, and an index. Recommended for all educators.

687. *Tea And Muskets: A Bicentennial Booklist.* Boston Area
Women in Libraries. c/o Cyrisse Jaffe, 108 Pearson Rd.,
Somerville MA 02144. $2. with a self-addressed mailing
label. An attractive booklet which evaluates 51 works of
fiction for grades K-8, set in America from the first set-
tlers through 1812. The literature selected is non-stereo-
typic and of high quality. The reader might be discour-
aged to see that the first 11 books on the list are "Not
Recommended." In fact only 23 of the 51 are
recommended, and 3 of these are out of print; 14 are recommended "with reservation", and 29 are not recommended at all. The compilers of course can in no way be
blamed for this depressing situation. This book is a good
consciousness-raiser and should interest all librarians.

688. *Unlearning the Lie: Sexism In School.* Barbara G. Harrison. Morrow. $2.95. A parent describes how she raised the consciousness of self-satisfied teachers in her child's private, interracial school.

689. *We Can Change It! An Annotated List Of Non-Sexist, Non-Racist Books For Grades Pre-School-3.* Change for Children. $1.25. A good introduction to the changing attitudes, this book includes suggestions for using these titles in home and school activities.

690. *What Are Little Girls Made Of?* State of Vermont, Dept. of Libraries, Montpelier, Vt. 95602. Send self-addressed, stamped envelope. A non-sexist recommended list.

691. *What Can You Do About Sex Role Stereotyping In Texts?* Lucy Simpson, Textbook Comm., N.O.W., 744 Carroll St., Brooklyn, N.Y. 11215. 50¢+ self addressed, stamped envelope. An annotated bibliography of guidelines and aids.

692. *Who's Who And Where In Women's Studies.* Tamar Berkowitz and others, eds. Feminist Press, 1975. $12.50; $7.50. Recommended: *Spokeswoman* March 15, 1975.

693. *Women: Yesterday And Today.* M. Solovay, Libraran, Madison Jr. High, Main St., Madison, N.J. 07940. 50¢ Annotated list of materials emphasizing women's roles.

694. *Women's Films In Print: An Annotated Guide To 800 16mm Films By Women.* Bonnie Dawson, ed. Booklegger Press. $4. Includes a listing of 370 filmmakers, distributors, and a bibliography and subject list.

2. Articles

This is a checklist of periodical articles dealing with the subject of sexism in children's literature and other educational materials. A great many more such articles are undoubtedly to be found in such indices as *Education Index, Reader's Guide To Periodical Literature* and *Library Literature.*

For articles related specifically to sexism in fairy tales see: "Molly Whuppie Meets Cinderella", p. 18.

695. Beebe, Sandra. "Women in American Literature." *English Journal.* September, 1975. Pp. 32-35. Information to help in the creation of a high school women's studies course.

696. Bernstein, J. "Changing Roles for Females in Books for Young Children." *Reading Teacher.* March, 1974. Pp. 545-549. With bibliography.

697. Czaplinski, Suzanne. "Sexism in Award Winning Picture Books." Available from Know, Inc. $2. An analysis of books which have won the Caldecott, Lewis Carroll and *New York Times* awards.

698. De Filippo, Kathy. "Little Girls and Picture Books: Problem and Solution." *Reading Teacher.* April, 1976. Pp. 671-673.

699. "Eliminating Sexism in Schools and Educational Materials; a Roundup of National Developments." *Library Journal.* April 15, 1974. Pp. 1171-1172.

700. "Feminists on Children's Media. A Feminist Looks at Children's Books." *School Library Journal.* January, 1971. Pp. 19-24. (This can be obtained also from *Notes From the Third Year.* Box AA, Old Chelsea Station, N.Y., N.Y. 10011.) An evaluation of Newbery Award books from a feminist perspective.

701. Fisher, Elizabeth. "The Second Sex, Junior Division." *NYT Book Review.* May 24, 1970. Pp. 6+. Also printed in *Woman's Liberation: Blueprint For The Future.* Cookie Stambler, ed. Ace Books, 1971. Pp. 89-95. And from Know, Inc.

702. Gerhardt, Lillian N. "The Would-Be Censors of the Left." *School Library Journal.* November, 1976. P. 7. A strong attack on political reviews of any kind of children's books, this singles out the policies and publications of the Council of Interracial Books for Children, Inc.

703. Gersoni Stavn, Diane. "Feminist Criticism: An Overview." *School Library Journal.* January, 1974. Pp. 22+. A well-reasoned suggestion that feminists think carefully before attacking books for sexism.

704. — "The Skirts in Fiction About Boys: A Maxi Mess." *School Library Journal.* January, 1971. Pp. 62-72. A discussion of the picture of girls and women presented in books about boys.

705. Heilbrun, Carolyn. "All Pregnant Girls Have Boy Babies." *NYT Book Review.* November 8, 1970. Pp. 8+. An examination of the treatment of pregnant teenagers in novels for young adults.

706. Howe, Florence. "Sexual Stereotypes Start Early." *Saturday Review.* October 16, 1971. Pp. 76+. A discussion of the way school curricula, books and language implant sexism in young children.

707. Jones, B.C. "New Cache of Liberated Children's Literature in Some Old Standbys." *Wilson Library Bulletin.* September, 1974. Pp. 52-56. An anti-feminist approach to the issue of sexism in children's books.

708. Kelty, Jean M. "The Cult of Kill in Adolescent Fiction." *English Journal.* February, 1975. Pp. 55-61. A protest against the message that killing is a masculine birthright, which is to be found in some fiction for young adults.

709. Lanes, Selma. "On Feminism and Children's Books." *School Library Journal.* January, 1974. Pp. 23+. A discussion of the differences between propaganda and good literature. The author feels this difference is not always recognized by feminist critics.

710. Lukenbill, W.B. "Fathers in Adolescent Novels: Some Implications for Sex Role Interpretations." *Library Journal.* February 15, 1974. Pp. 536-540.

711. "Man! Memo from a Publisher; Excerpts from Guidelines for Equal Treatment of the Sexes in McGraw-Hill Publications." *NYT Magazine.* October 20, 1974. Pp. 38+. This excerpt is from McGraw-Hill's non-fiction for children policy statement.

712. Maryles, D. "Feminist Publishers Fight Back Against Sexism in Books." *PW.* May 13, 1974. P. 205.

713. Matthews, Dorothy. "An Adolescent's Glimpse into the Faces of Eve: A Study of the Image of Women in Selected Popular Junior Novels." *Illinois English Bulletin.* May, 1973. Pp. 1-14. (Available also from I.A.T.E., 100 English Bldg., Urbana, IL 61801.) An interesting feminist discussion of familiar books.

714. "Media Stereotypes of Women and One Modest Attempt at Erasing Them." *California Librarian*. April, 1976. Pp. 11-15.

715. Mischel, Harriet. "Sex of Author Changes Credibility . . ." *Psychology Today*. October, 1974. Pp. 32-33. A study demonstrating that male authorship is taken more seriously than female.

716. Mitchell, E. "The Learning of Sex Roles through Toys and Books: A Woman's View." *Young Children*. 1973. Pp. 226-231.

717. Nadesan, A. "Mother Goose Sexist?" *Elementary English*. March, 1974. Pp. 375-378.

718. Nilsen, Alleen. "Women in Children's Literature." *College English*. May, 1971. An excellent examination of sexism in the Caldecott Award books from 1951 to 1970.

719. Pogrebin, Letty. "Down with Sexist Upbringing." *Ms. Magazine*. Preview issue, Spring, 1972. Pp. 18+.

720. Reeder, Kik. "Pippi Longstocking — Feminist or Anti-feminist?" *Bulletin Of Council Of Interracial Books For Children*. 1974. A most interesting look at one of literature's most interesting heroines.

721. Sprung, Barbara. "An Overview of Non-Sexist Early Childhood Education; Current Trends, Programs and Resources." *Media Center*. October, 1975. Pp. 28-34.

722. Stewig, John and Margaret Higgs. "Girls Grow Up to be Mommies: A Study of Sexism in Children's Literature." *Library Journal*. January 15, 1973. Pp. 236-241. A close look at studies and analyses of sexism in literature for young children.

723. Thomas, Jane R. "Old Worlds and New: Anti-Feminism in *Watership Down*." *Horn Book*. August, 1974. Pp. 405-408. A discussion of female characters in Richard Adam's popular book.

724. Weitzman, Leonore and others. "Sex Role Socialization in Picture Books for Pre-School Children." *American Journal of Sociology.* May, 1972. Pp. 1125-1150. A reprint of this can be ordered from Warner Modular Publications, 11 Essex St., Andover, Mass. 01010. 60¢. An analysis of the presentation of sex roles in Newbery and Caldecott Award books.

3. Pamphlets and Reports

725. *Channeling Children: Sex Stereotyping On Prime T.V. Time.* Women on Words and Images, 1975. $2.50. Alas, we all knew television was a feminist parent's nightmare, but this well-researched pamphlet presents an in-depth analysis with diagrams and statistics, so that we know the bad dream is real. Recommended for parents, media students and people from age 9 up who want to stop and think about the anti-humanist medium of television.

726. *Community Workshops On Children's Books.* The Feminist Press. Handbook for setting up workshops with parents and teachers to examine sexism in children's books.

727. *Day Care For Your Children.* U.S. Gov't. Publ. 30¢. Superintendant of Documents, Washington, D.C. 20402. A guide to the selection of day care centers (if there are any) for particular needs.

728. *Dick and Jane As Victims: Sex Stereotyping In Children's Readers.* Women on Words and Images. $1.50. Detailed report with statistics on stereotypes found in the fifteen most widely read elementary readers.

729. *An Educator's Guide To The Correction Of Sex Bias In Education Or: Isn't It Time We Did Something For Title IX After They Went Through The Trouble Of Making It Law.* (Educational Service Area, Media Center, 301 N. 1st, Montevido, Minn. 56265. Write for price.) By L. MacDonald. An exploration of Title IX's application to classroom practices and textbooks. Lists resources.

730. *Fact Sheets On Institutional Sexism.* CIBC. $1. Graphs, tables and other statistics which illustrate the vast difference in career and earning possibilities for men and women and for minority men and women. While some of these statistics are six years old, most date from 1975-76. Especially useful for lectures, and for social studies classes.

731. *Female Studies V.* R.L. Siporin. (Know, Inc. no price.) Proceedings of the conference, "Women and Education: a Feminist Perspective." Seventeen essays.

732. *A Guide To Textbook Evaluation.* The Task Force for the Evaluation of Instructional Materials. Write for cost. Encourages parents, students, and teachers to get involved in the selection of educational materials. Suggests how to influence selections on the local level.

733. *Guidelines For Combatting Sexism In Language.* Free. Nat'l. Council of Teachers of English. 111 Kenyon R., Urbana, IL 61801.

734. *Guidelines For Improving the Image Of Women In Textbooks.* Research and Information Division, Scott Foresman. Free. How to free textbooks from sexist writing and illustrations.

735. *Guidelines For Women's Studies.* See No. 733. Same source.

736. *The Mother Who Works Outside The Home.* Sally Olds. Child Study Press, 1975. $1.50. Information on child care, career counseling, and the reorganization of home life, etc.

737. *Playgroups: Do It Ourselves Childcare.* Anita Yoskowitz and others. Child Care Switchboard/Single Parent's Resource Center. 75¢. 3896 24th Street, San Francisco, CA 94114. How to start a playgroup and keep it going. The emphasis is on resources available in San Francisco.

738. *Report On Sex Bias In Public Schools.* Rev. ed., 1972. NOW Chapter, 28 56th St., N.Y., N.Y. 10022. Write for price. A variety of articles and documents on sex bias in elementary and secondary education.

739. *Sex Bias In First Grade Reading Books, a Study.* Education Committee, NOW Midland Chapter, P.O. Box 1243, Midland, Mich. 48640. 50¢.

740. *Sex Bias In School Leadership.* J.P. Clement. Integrated Educational Association: Northwestern University, School of Education, 2003 Sheridan Road, Evanston, IL 60201. Attempts to document the pervasiveness of male dominance in educational leadership and to serve as a guide for Title IX implementation.

741. *Sex Role Stereotyping: Implications For the Human Services.* Minnesota Resource Center For Social Work, 731 21 Avenue South, Minneapolis, Minn. 55405. $3.00.

742. *Sexism In Schools — A Handbook For Action.* N. Rothschild. 14 Hickory St., Mahtomedi, Minn. 55115. $2.00. A how-to guide on learning how your school is run with strategies for action. Directed at the state of Minnesota but useful elsewhere.

743. *WEAL K-12 Education Kit.* Women's Equity Action League, 538 National Press Building, Washington, D.C. 20004. Write for price. Outlines major areas of discrimination in education, with emphasis on change you can create.

744. *You Won't Do: What Textbooks on U.S. Government Teach High School Girls.* Know, Inc. $2.25. A study of such texts and their message that "a woman's place is not in politics." Recommendations and resource list.

4. Serial Publications

745. *The Acorn Groweth.* Rita Kort, ed. 48 Sunset Ave., Venice, CA 94611. 3 issues a year. $1. An informative newsletter for people interested in non-sexist children's literature. It lists bibliographies, articles in magazines, various studies and guidelines, etc.

746. *Booklist.* American Library Association. 50 E. Huron St., Chicago, IL 60611. Reviews current adult, children's, and young adult books and media.

747. *Bulletin of the Center for Children's Books.* University of Chicago Press. 5801 Ellis Avenue, Chicago, IL 60637. A monthly review of new children's literature in a brief pamphlet form.

748. *Bulletin.* CIBC. 1841 Broadway, N.Y., NY 10023. $8. individuals, $15. institutions. 8 issues a year. Reviews non-racist, non-sexist children's books. It carries also extensive resource lists, bibliographies and long articles. A worth-while supplement to traditional publications of this kind.

749. *Children's Book Review Service.* 220 Berkeley Pl., Brooklyn, NY 11217. Reviews of current children's books, elementary through junior high. Sensitive to the problems of race and sex stereotyping.

750. *Edcentric: A Journal Of Educational Change.* P.O. Box 10085, Eugene, Oregon 97401. $6 for individual; $10 for institutions, six issues a year. This is a readable and thought-provoking periodical, with articles, book reviews and lists of resource materials, all dedicated to create social change through education. The June, 1976 issue is especially useful. It contains the "Educational Resource Guide": 32 pages of lists of alternative groups working for social reform, and available materials of interest.

751. *Emergency Librarian.* Barbara Clubb, ed. 697 Wellington Crescent, Winnipeg, Manitoba R3M OA7, Canada. $5, $8. An alternative feminist library journal with news, reviews and articles. No. 3 of Vol. 2 deals with material for children and young adults.

752. *ERIC/ECE Newsletter.* University of Illinois at Urbana, 805 W. Pennsylvania Ave., Urbana IL 61801. Quarterly. $2 a year. Lists of recommended activities, books, pamphlets, and various media resources for a non-sexist, non-racist education for young children. Articles and some publications can be ordered from *ERIC.* A good resource for the educator or parent of pre-school children.

753. *Horn Book Magazine.* 585 Boylston St., Boston, MA 02116. Issues contain articles on children's literature as well as many book reviews of titles for pre-school through junior high.

754. *Kirkus Review.* 200 Park Avenue So., N.Y., NY 10003. Highly critical pre-publicaton reviews of adult and juvenile books. Issued bi-monthly to libraries and bookstores.

755. *Melus.* Society of Multi-Ethnic Literature of the U.S. Affiliated with the Modern Language Association, Dr. Ernest Falbo, Dept. of Foreign Languages, N.Y. State U., Buffalo, NY 14222. $3 membership fee brings a one year subscription. Contains reports on the study of ethnic literature.

756. *Ms.* 370 Lexington Ave., N.Y., NY 10017. A monthly feminist magazine which often contains bibliographies of non-sexist children's books, as well as a regular section on new adult book reviews and a reprint of a new, non-sexist juvenile title.

757. *New Directions For Women.* Box 27, Dover, NJ 07801. An excellent quarterly newspaper with national appeal and containing a well developed book and media review section on adult materials.

758. *New York Times Book Review.* New York Times Co., Times Square, NY 10036.

759. *No More Teachers Dirty Looks.* Bay Area Radical Teachers Organization. 388 Sanchez, San Francisco, CA 94114. Quarterly. $3 individuals, $6 institutions. Articles, book reviews, resource lists and suggested curricula, all connected with ideas of radical change in our educational systems.

760. *PEER Perspective.* Free Newsletter. Project on Equal Rights Education Rights. 1029 Vermont Avenue N.W., Suite 800 Washington D.C. 20005. *PEER* monitors institutional compliance with Title IX and Affirmative Action.

761. *Resources Newsletter.* Richard Gardner, publ. Resources. Box 134, Harvard Square, Cambridge, MA 02138. $5. 12 issues a year. Lists of alternative journals, organizations, ideas, services, events and products. Good for the adult reference collection of any library.

762. *Research Action Notes.* An occasional newsletter. Suite 918, 1156 15th Street N.W., Washington, D.C. 20005. Information on laws, conferences and resources on reducing stereotyping of girls and boys.

763. *School Library Journal.* Bowker Co. 1180 Avenue of the Americas, N.Y., NY 10036. Articles concerning children's literature and library service and news, as well as many book reviews written by librarians all across the country of pre-school through junior high titles, make this the basic review guide of the profession.

764. *Sex Discrimination In Education Newsletter.* Dr. Sarah Ann Lincoln, ed. Psychology Dept., University of Michigan, Ann Arbor, MI 48109. Six issues a year. $10 institutions; $5 individuals. Published by the Feminist Research Project and partly funded by the University of Michigan. The first issue is a concise and detailed look at legislation, activities, organizations and publications dealing with discrimination in education. Highly recommended for educators and people working for change.

765. *Signs: Journal Of Women In Culture And Society.* University of Chicago Press, 11030 Langley Ave., Chicago, IL 60628. Quarterly. $9.60 students; $12 individuals; $16 institutions. International in scope and very scholarly in tone. Contains articles, book reviews by experts in many academic fields connected to women's studies. Recommended for college and research libraries, and especially for women's studies departments.

766. *Spokeswoman.* Karen Wellisch, ed. and publ. 53 W. Jackson, Chicago, IL 60604. 12 issues a year. $12 individuals; $20 institutions. An informative newsletter giving national news briefs on women's legislation and related matters and reviews of adult and young adult books and pamphlets. Good for public, high school and college libraries.

767. *WAGE.* Journal of the Ad Hoc Committee for Women and Girls In Education. 3409 S.W. Trenton St., Seattle, Wash. 98126. $5. 4 issues a year. This action group is concerned with the status of females in the public schools of the state of Washington.

768. *The Weewish Tree.* Jeanette Henry, ed. Indian Historian Press. 1451 Masonic Avenue, San Francisco, CA 94117. $6.50. 7 times a year. Written and illustrated by Native Americans of all ages. It contains poetry, stories and articles for various age and reading levels.

769. *Win News.* Women's International Network. Fran P. Hosken, ed. 187 Grant Street, Lexington, MA 02173. Quarterly. $15 individuals; $25 institutions. This letter is intended to "establish a world-wide open communications system by, for and about women of all backgrounds, beliefs, nationalities and age groups. To serve the general public, institutions and organizations by transmitting internatonally information about women and women's groups." The issue for November, 1975 contained an impressive amount of information about international health, politics, media, resources, etc. Recommended for high school and college libraries and women's studies courses.

770. *Women & Film.* P.O. Box 4501 Berkeley CA 94704. $4 individuals; $8 institutions. 3 issues a year. $1.50 each. The Summer 1975 issue was sent to me. It contained film and book reviews, full analyses of several films, some interviews and resource suggestions. The journal has a feminist orientation and is well-written. Recommended for libraries with patrons interested in all aspects of film.

771. *The Workbook.* Southwest Research and Information Ctr. P.O. Box 4524 Albuquerque, New Mexico, 87106. 12 issues a year. $7 students; $10 individuals; $20 institutions. "A fully indexed catalog of information about environmental, social and consumer problems. Aimed at helping people in small towns and cities across America to gain access to vital information that can help them to assert control over their lives." Lists new pamphlets, books, organizations, etc. on may subjects: health care, the economy, housing, women's problems, etc. A good addition to any library.

PART FOUR

INDEXES

AUTHOR INDEX

TITLE INDEX

TROUBLE WITH ALARIC, THE. No. 171.
TROUBLE WITH EXPLOSIVES. No. 309.
TRUDEL'S SEIGE. No. 235.
TUCK EVERLASTING. No. 243.
TURNABOUT. P. 33.
TURNING POINT, THE. No. 308.
TWO BEASTLY TALES ETC. P. 20.
TWO GOOD FRIENDS. No. 195.
TWO IS COMPANY. No. 196.
TWO PIANO TUNERS. P. 42.
TWO WORLDS OF BEATRIX POTTER, THE. No. 491.

ULTRA-VIOLET CATASTROPHE ETC. No. 109.
UNLEARNING THE LIE: SEXISM IN SCHOOL. No. 688.

V.D.: A DOCTOR'S ANSWERS. No. 513.
VERY LITTLE GIRL, THE. P. 19.

WALKED HOME TIRED, BILLY JENKINS. No. 156.
WALK TOGETHER CHILDREN: BLACK AMERICAN SPIRITUALS. No. 412.
WALKING THROUGH THE DARK. No. 342.
WALLS: RESISTING THE 3RD. REICH ETC. No. 596.
WALTER THE WOLF. No. 148.
WAR WITH THE SEMINOLES ETC. No. 471.
WAY IT WAS — 1876, THE. No. 462.
WEAL K-12 EDUCATION KIT. No. 743.
WE CAN CHANGE IT! ETC. No. 689.
WE, THE PEOPLE. No. 612.
WEATHER OR NOT. No. 430.
WEATHERING THE STORM: WOMEN OF THE AMERICAN REVOLUTION. No. 550.
WELL DONE. No. 123.
WE'LL HAVE A FRIEND FOR LUNCH. No. 48.

WHAT ARE LITTLE GIRLS MADE OF? No. 690.
WHAT BOYS WANT TO KNOW ABOUT GIRLS ETC. No. 465.
WHAT CAN SHE BE? AN ARCHITECT. No. 442.
WHAT CAN SHE BE? A FARMER. No. 443.
WHAT CAN SHE BE? A GEOLOGIST. No. 444.
WHAT CAN SHE BE? A MUSICIAN. No. 445.
WHAT CAN SHE BE? A POLICE OFFICER. No. 446.
WHAT CAN WE BE? A COLORING BK ETC. No. 649.
WHAT CAN YOU DO ABOUT SEX ROLE STEREOTYPING IN TEXTS? No. 690.
WHAT DO YOU DO WITH A KANGAROO? No. 121.
WHAT GIRLS WANT TO KNOW ABOUT BOYS. No. 465.
WHAT IF A LION EATS ME & I FALL INTO A MUD HOLE? No. 58.
WHAT I WANT TO BE WHEN I GROW UP. P. 42.
WHAT IS A MAN? P. 28.
WHAT SADIE SANG. No. 136.
WHATEVER HAPPENED TO THE BAXTER PLACE? No. 216.
WHAT'S THIS ABOUT PETE? No. 375.
WHEN IT FLOODED THE ELEMENTARY SCHOOL. No. 228.
WHEN LIGHT TURNS INTO NIGHT No. 43.
WHEN THE RATTLESNAKE SOUNDS. No. 419.
WHEN THE SKY IS LIKE LACE. No. 73.
WHEN THE WIND STOPS. No. 181.
WHERE IS MY FRIEND? ETC. No. 108.
WHERE THE LILIES BLOOM. P. 14.
WHERE THE SIDEWALK ENDS. No. 516.
WHERE THE WILD THINGS ARE. P. 31.
WHERE'S FLORRIE? No. 193.
WHIRLING RAINBOWS. No. 379.
WHIRLWIND IS A GHOST DANCING. No. 407.

SUBJECT INDEX: FICTION

ADOLESCENT PROBLEMS. 292. 309. 312. 313. 318. 321. 351. 356. 388. 392.

ADVENTURE. 134. 217. 221. 256. 270. 278. 286. 369.

AFRICAN LIFE & CULTURE. 1. 10. 304.

ALCOHOLISM. 318.

AMERICA: Civil War. 287. 307; Colonial Period. 233. 397; 19th Century. 218. 245. 246. 247. 249. 252. 255. 280. 285. 287. 297. 307. 323. 340. 345. 383. 395; 1930's & 1940's. 193. 256. 339. 342. 358. 392. 628. 632.

AMERICAN INDIAN LIFE & CULTURE. 13. 78. 281. 294. 296. 319. 323. 364. 373. 379. 389. 407. 532.

MARY ANN ANNING. 410.

SUSAN B. ANTHONY. 502.

APES & MONKEYS. 16. 62. 70. 97. 107. 207. 278.

ARTISTS. 162. 316. 327. 360.

ASTROLOGY. 356.

AUNTS. 133. 185. 257. 333. 348. 394.

BALLET. 74. 251.

BEARS & PANDAS. 61. 131. 154. 185. 186. 194. 195. 196.

BEAUTY CONTESTS. 349. 352.

BEDTIME. 66. 75. 99. 106. 130. 181. 182.

BIRDS. 151. 162. 213. 238.

BIRTH. 111. 317.

BIRTHDAYS. 84. 127.

BLACK EXPERIENCE. 2. 19. 29. 30. 31. 32. 42. 56. 119. 152. 155. 156. 187. 209. 266. 284. 290. 292. 295. 297. 327. 333. 334. 374. 390. 396. 412. 419. 546. 557. 594.

BLINDNESS. 334.

BOYS: Athletes. 142; Dancers. 74. 134. 251. 284; Non-Conformist. 28. 38. 63. 90. 148. 219. 226. 256. 289. 314. 333. 366. 375.

BROTHERS & SISTERS. 2. 18. 31. 32. 49. 56. 57. 154. 156. 166. 173. 209. 217. 244. 289. 302. 316. 321. 377.

CAMPING. 185. 301. 379.

CATS. 18. 26. 48. 71. 153. 176. 238. 239.

CHICANO & MEXICAN LIFE. See Latino Life & Culture.

CHILDHOOD FEARS & FRUS— TRATIONS. 58. 63. 80. 81. 98. 172. 223.

CHRISTMAS. 71. 85. 166. 212. 334.

CIRCUS. 161.

CITY LIFE. 64. 88. 89. 136. 155. 156. 158. 193. 203. 208. 219. 289. 341. 377.

COUNTRY & FARM LIFE. 43. 44. 109. 137. 151. 216. 252. 256. 264. 290. 354. 357. 358. 370.

CRAFTS. 13. 38.

CREATIVE ASPIRATIONS. 26. 27. 33. 57. 189. 327. 360.

EUGENE DEBS. 529.

DINOSAURS. 92.

DOGS. 102. 147. 171. 239. 289.

DIVORCE. 5. 91. 140. 225. 231. 291. 318. 332. 350. 351. 353. 356.

DREAMS & NIGHTMARES. 49. 75. 120. 372.

ECONOMICS OF BUSINESS. 184.

ELEPHANTS. 37. 108. 200.

ENGLAND: 1920's. 260. 335; 16th Century. 248. 631; World War II. 311.

FAIRY TALES. 41. 79. 159. 170. 230. 261. 299. 303. 338. 384.

FAMILY LIFE. 3. 45. 93. 152. 154. 167. 172. 173. 175. 222. 244. 264. 265. 269. 284. 292. 309. 317. 351. 386.

FANTASY. 15. 17. 34. 37. 40. 51. 55. 57. 59. 76. 82. 95. 113. 114. 115. 135. 141. 221. 229. 236. 237. 242. 243. 262. 328. 329. 330. 331. 344. 347. 367. 372. 382. 393. 394.

SUBJECT INDEX: NON-FICTION

PUBLISHERS, DISTRIBUTORS, AND ORGANIZATIONS

ALL OF US. Route 2, Box 128, Monmouth OR 97369

ATLANTA FILMS. (dist.) 340 East 34 St., New York NY 10016

BAY AREA RADICAL TEACHERS ORG. 388 Sanchez, San Francisco CA 94114

BELLEROPHON BOOKS. 153 Steuart St., San Francisco CA 94105

BOOKLEGGER. 555 29th St., San Francisco CA 94131

BOOKSTORE PRESS. Box 191, RFD 1, Freeport ME 04032

CANADIAN WOMEN'S EDUCATIONAL PRESS. 280 Bloor St. W.#305, Toronto, Ontario

CHANGE FOR CHILDREN. 2588 Mission St. #226, San Francisco CA 94110

CHILD STUDY PRESS. Child Study Association, 50 Madison Av., New York NY 10010

CHURCHILL FILMS. (dist.) 662 N. Robertson Blvd., Los Angeles CA

CORNELIA WHEADON TASK FORCE ON THE SOCIALI-ZATION OF WOMEN. 2214 Ridge Rd., Evanston IL 60201

CORONET INSTRUCTIONAL MEDIA. (dist.) 65 E. South Water, Chicago IL 60601

COUNCIL ON INTERRACIAL BOOKS FOR CHILDREN. 1841 Broadway#300, New York NY 10023

DAUGHTERS, INC. 22 Charles St. New York NY 10014

DRUM AND SPEAR. 1317 Fairmont St., Washington D.C. 20009

DUSTBOOKS. P.O. Box 1056, Paradise CA 95969

EDUCATIONAL ACTIVITIES, INC. P.O. Box 392, Freeport NY 11520

EDUCATIONAL CONSORTIUM OF AMERICA. P.O. Box 1057, Menlo Park CA 94025

EMMA WILLARD TASK FORCE ON EDUCATION. Box 14229 University Sta., Minneapolis MN 55414

FEMINIST BOOKMART 47-17 150 St., Flushing NY 11355

FEMINIST CONSULTANTS ON EDUCATION. P.O. Box 27556 Market Square Sta., Philadelphia PA 19118

FEMINIST PRESS. Box 334, Old Westbury NY 11568

HERSTORY FILMS. Box 315, Franklin Lakes NJ 07401

INDOCHINA RESOURCE CENTER. 1322 18th St. N.W., Washington D.C.

JOYFUL WORLD. 468 Belvedere St., San Francisco CA 94117

KENIKAT PRESS. 90 S. Bayles Av., Pt. Washington NY 11050

KIDS CAN PRESS. P.O. Box 5974, Postal Sta. A, Toronto, Ontario

KNOW, INC. Box 86031, Pittsburgh PA 15221

LOLLIPOP POWER. P.O. Box 1171, Chapel Hill NC 27514

NAIAD PRESS. 20 Rue Jacob Acres, Bates City MO 64011

NATIONAL EDUCATION ASSOCIATION. Academic Bldg., Saw Mill Road, W. Haven CT 06516

NEW SEED. P.O. Box 3016, Stanford CA 94305

NEW WOMB. P.O. Box 40596, San Francisco CA 94140

ODEON FILMS. 169 Broadway, New York NY 10019

OVER THE RAINBOW. Box 7072, Berkeley CA 94707

PEOPLE'S PRESS. 2680 21 Street, San Francisco CA 94110

RAMIC PRODUCTIONS. 58 West 58 St. New York NY 10019

SERIOUS BUSINESS COMPANY. (dist.) 1609 Jaynes St., Berkeley CA 94703

TASK FORCE FOR THE EVALUATION OF INSTRUCTIONAL MATERIALS. P.O. Box 4003, Stanford CA 94305

TIMES CHANGE PRESS. P.O. Box 98, Louisa VA 23093

THIRD WORLD PRESS. 7850 S. Ellis, Chicago IL 60619

WOMEN LIBRARY WORKERS. 555 29 St., San Francisco, CA

WOMEN ON WORDS AND IMAGES. P.O. Box 2163, Princeton NJ 08540

WOMEN'S ACTION ALLIANCE. 370 Lexington Av., New York NY 10017

WOMEN'S FILM CO-OP. (dist.) 250 Main St., Northhampton MA 01060

WOMEN'S HISTORY RESEARCH CENTER. 2325 Oak St., Berkeley CA 94708

WOMEN'S RIGHTS TASK FORCE ON EDUCATION. 549 Lenox Av., Westfield NJ 07090